ENHANCING ORGANIZATIONAL PERFORMANCE

Daniel Druckman, Jerome E. Singer, and Harold Van Cott, *Editors*

Committee on Techniques for the Enhancement
of Human Performance

Commission on Behavioral and Social Sciences and Education

National Research Council

NATIONAL ACADEMY PRESS
Washington, D.C. 1997

NATIONAL ACADEMY PRESS • 2101 Constitution Avenue, N.W. • Washington, D.C. 20418

NOTICE: The project that is the subject of this report was approved by the Governing Board of the National Research Council, whose members are drawn from the councils of the National Academy of Sciences, the National Academy of Engineering, and the Institute of Medicine. The members of the committee responsible for the report were chosen for their special competences and with regard for appropriate balance.

This report has been reviewed by a group other than the authors according to procedures approved by a Report Review Committee consisting of members of the National Academy of Sciences, the National Academy of Engineering, and the Institute of Medicine.

This project was supported by the Army Research Institute. Any opinions, findings, conclusions, or recommendations expressed in this publication are those of the author(s) and do not necessarily reflect the view of the organizations or agencies that provided support for the project.

Library of Congress Cataloging-in-Publication Data

Enhancing organizational performance / Daniel Druckman, Jerome E
    Singer, and Harold Van Cott, editors.
       p. cm.
    "Committee on Techniques for the Enhancement of Human Performance,
Commission on Behavioral and Social Sciences and Education, National
Research Council."
    Includes bibliographical references and index.
    ISBN 0-309-05397-8
    1. Organizational effectiveness. 2. Organizational change.
3. United Stgates. Army—Management. I. Druckman, Daniel, 1939- .
II. Singer, Jerome E. III. Van Cott, Harold P. IV. National
Research Council (U.S.). Committee on Techniques for the
Enhancement of Human Performance.
HD58.9.E54 1997
658.4'063—dc21   97-1782
                                                             CIP

Additional copies of this report are available from:

National Academy Press
2101 Constitution Avenue, N.W.
Box 285
Washington, D.C. 20418
800-624-6242 or 202-334-3313 (in the Washington Metropolitan Area)
http://www.nap.edu

Printed in the United States of America

Contents

Preface

In 1985, the Army Research Institute (ARI) asked the National Academy of Sciences to explore the utility and effectiveness of various techniques to enhance human performance. The Academy, through the National Research Council, established the Committee on Techniques for the Enhancement of Human Performance. The committee, composed primarily of psychologists, first examined and then evaluated commercial and proprietary techniques then being considered by the Army; later the committee broadened its inquiry to study a variety of related issues, including team learning, simulation training, and skills practice, among other topics.

This is the fourth report of the committee. Over the decade since it was established, the membership has evolved so that the fields of expertise covered are no longer almost exclusively in psychology, but include experts whose knowledge is suited to the particular tasks at hand, at the same time providing continuity from study to study.

This change in committee composition is relevant to this study, which examines the organizational context of individual and group performance. Accordingly, the membership draws less on the contributions of scientists in cognitive psychology, experimental social psychology, neuroscience, and motor performance and more on the scholarship of people engaged in organizational theory, industrial management, and business consulting. Our Army sponsor explicitly requested that we not produce a report directed exclusively toward military organization but rather to summarize the strengths and weaknesses of the best evidence for current organizational practices. The committee has stayed within those general guidelines, but to help ensure the relevance of our conclusions to the sponsor, several of our members are specialists in military leadership and organization.

The committee organized for its task by establishing a set of subcommittees, each directed toward a particular topic from the agenda to be addressed. The subcommittees worked well as units, not only executing their assignments in a timely fashion but also communicating their products to the others and responding well and promptly to suggestions for revisions and changes needed to produce the developing final report. Moreover, many members had skills and knowledge appropriate to more than one topic, making them important resource persons for other subcommittees.

Just as the committee's focus on organizations instead of individuals made its membership more diverse than that of previous phases, so, too, the nature of the evidence was different in emphasis than that surveyed in previous reports. The topics of the earlier reports were amenable to laboratory study and were supported by the kind of experimental data that permit the drawing of relatively clear and persuasive conclusions. In contrast, the organizational literature we examined dealt in large part with field studies and observational materials. Many aspects of management, leadership, and culture do not have a broad and extensive research database that would permit the drawing of definitive conclusions. In fact, for several interesting points, no data at all were available. Of necessity, the inferences and conclusions made here are the result of careful deliberation and the reasoned consensus of the members as they considered evidence that was not as strong or as firm as we would have liked. The members' mutual respect and collegial exchange of ideas and concerns made it easier to distinguish between firm and ambiguous conclusions.

No committee works alone; many people aided our efforts by giving generously of their time and knowledge. Appendix B contains a list of the organizations, places, and people visited and consulted by the committee, the subcommittees, individual members and staff. Several of those who aided us in the project are deserving of special mention. Edgar Johnson, director of the Army Research Institute, and Michael Drillings, chief of the Research and Advanced Concepts office at ARI, made contacts for us, helped to set up meetings, answered a variety of questions, and all in all were a model of what every committee would wish its sponsor to be. Mary E. Zellmer gave excellent service in reviewing the practitioner literature on organizational culture. William E. Siegel made a significant contribution to the work on interorganizational relations.

Most of our appreciation goes to the incomparable professional staff. Cindy Prince kept us on an even keel with superb meeting arrangements and the shepherding of the manuscript, parts of which kept arriving from different locations at different times from different people, and all of which was in constant revision. Thanks also to Mary DeLorey for her assistance in piecing together the various parts of the manuscript under time pressure and to Elsa Riemer for her assistance in preparing the final versions of the manuscript. Harold Van Cott served unstintingly as a consultant to the committee; his contributions and advice are reflected throughout the document.

A special debt of gratitude is extended to Christine McShane, editor par excellence of this report. She helped us to unify our styles, excise our infelicities of language, and give more shapely coherence to the whole report. In addition, she undertook the awesome task of producing a revised document that was responsive to our concerns about communicating the work to a wide audience of readers with diverse interests in the general topic. Whatever success we may have had in achieving this goal is due in large part to her effort.

Jerome E. Singer, Chair
Daniel Druckman, Study Director
Committee on Techniques for the
Enhancement of Human Performance

ENHANCING ORGANIZATIONAL PERFORMANCE

Summary

Organizations are among the most significant structures through which society functions. Through its business, civic, social, and religious organizations, society carries out much of its economic and social life. Understanding how organizations work, how they are designed, how they change through internal processes and can be changed from without, as well as how change can be guided, is of immediate interest both to those who work in organizations and those who study them.

In today's fast-paced, fast-changing, and increasingly competitive world, the effectiveness of business organizations has become the focus of considerable attention. When such organizations falter or fail, the consequences can be far-reaching, even devastating. Business organizations provide a rich, complex, but barely tapped lode of knowledge about organizational performance and the processes of change. Although research approaches in this field are still in their infancy and need to be further developed and validated, the field is fertile ground for greater understanding of organizations, organizational performance, and organizational change broadly conceived.

ENHANCING PERFORMANCE THROUGH CONSTRUCTIVE CHANGE

Organizations through the ages have been characterized by a tension between the forces of stability and the need for change. Much of the strength and utility of organizations comes from their inertia, helping to make them reliable in what they do and accountable for what they do. Indeed, some argue that their tendency to inertia can provide organizations with some short-term competitive advantage. From organization theory and much research, we know that organizations do not adapt readily or easily; many organizations that change do so in ways that are neither successful nor effective. Organizations must continually balance the forces of stability and the push for change.

Nevertheless, organization theory and managerial wisdom suggest that, to survive, organizations must be compatible with their environments, which include all the external social, economic, and political conditions that influence their actions. In the current environment of rapid technological and societal change, organizations must adapt quickly enough to maintain their legitimacy and the resources they need to stay viable. In the committee's judgment, the greatest opportunities for enhancing organizational performance today are likely to be found on the change side of the equation. The major focus of this book is therefore on considering organizations in the context of change.

THE CONTEXT OF CHANGE

Organizations today must function and attempt to flourish under conditions that are complex, rapidly changing, and in some respects unprecedented. The stakes are high and the risks are great. Of the 500 largest firms on the first such list published by *Fortune* magazine in 1956, only 29 remain. Voluntary mergers and joint ventures, hostile takeovers and poison-pill resistance to them, conglomerations and divestitures have created an organizational environment of prolonged turbulence.

These changes are manifestations of a deeper and more general transformation: the shift in the developed world from an industrial to an information economy. As recently as 1960, about half the workers in industrialized countries were involved in making things. By the year 2000, no developed country is likely to have more than one-eighth of its workforce performing such tasks. Only the earlier Industrial Revolution and the more gradual mechanization of agriculture were comparable in their magnitude of change and ramifying societal effects.

The driving force of these changes is technological and primarily involves information technology. This technology, which has been created within the lifetime of today's adults and which today's children take for granted, has developed at a remarkable pace. To illustrate: a musical greeting card that plays "Happy Birthday" has more computer power than existed in the entire world before 1950. A home video camera has more processing power than the original IBM 360 mainframe computer.

Our computer-transformed capacity to generate, store, analyze, and communicate information is changing the way we live, work, and think. New possibilities, new opportunities, and new demands arise at every level, from the individual to the transnational and the global.

THE COMMITTEE'S CHARGE

The request for this inquiry into the nature of organizations and organizational change came from the U.S. Army Research Institute. Like other organizations, the Army of the 21st century will face a world of new technologies, new and multiple missions, and new threats and opportunities. Under today's budgeting constraints, the challenges posed by these changes must be met with fewer personnel than have been available in the past. The Army must consider the possibility of utilizing new organizational designs, different ways of conceiving of leadership, changed value systems, and mission challenges that call for very different modes of preparation and training. The Army shares these concerns with other organizations in both the private and public sectors.

Accordingly, the Army Research Institute asked the National Research Council to form a committee to examine issues related to the improvement of individual and group performance in organizations. The committee was asked to perform the following tasks:

1. To assess the implications of organizational change and redesign for performance;
2. To evaluate new approaches to management designed to improve individual, team, and organizational performance;
3. To review and evaluate approaches to organizational leadership, including techniques for leader development, training, and motivation;
4. To develop a framework for evaluating approaches to intra- and interorganizational collaboration; and
5. To review and evaluate approaches to the management of conflicts within and between organizations, with special attention to implications for new Army missions.

The committee's charge is similar in approach to that which guided its previous work on individual and team performance: to summarize current knowledge in the field but not to focus specifically on the military. Elaborating its charge to the committee, the sponsor noted that the Army is cognizant of its own organizational features; of more use to it would be a summary and explication of the wider organizational literature in a way that is accessible to the informed but not specialized reader. The Army will judge for itself how much of the committee's work is applicable to its organizational processes and problems. This report therefore does not provide recommendations for organizational changes in the Army or other branches of the military, nor does it provide a research agenda for an agency that sponsors research on organizations. Only one topic, conflict management, is explicitly geared to current challenges faced by military organizations with changing missions. We do, however, include military examples in other chapters to illustrate key concepts.

CONTINUITY AND VARIATION IN THE STUDY OF PERFORMANCE

The committee's work over a 10-year period for the Army Research Institute resulted in three previous reports. The types of performance covered in those previous studies include individual performance, such as the execution of learned motor, cognitive, and social skills; performance as changed mental or emotional states; team performance and cohesion; joint decision making; and coordination. We continue to focus on these types of performance here. For example, many of the performance competencies discussed in the chapter on leadership are the result of developing basic cognitive and social skills. Similarly, the challenges of new military missions discussed in the chapter on conflict management require the use of interpersonal skills.

In this volume, we are concerned with the connections between individual or team skills and the way organizations perform. For example, in the chapter on organizational culture, we discuss how the relationship between culture and performance is mediated by the way culture influences thoughts and feelings, and we pinpoint some of the cultural levers that can be used to influence performance. In the chapter on conflict management, we discuss the relationship between individual training and mission effectiveness, noting that effective soldier performance does not necessarily translate into overall mission effectiveness.

Performance is also considered in the context of interorganizational relations. The concern here is with the way different organizations combine to create new entities or cooperate to meet new challenges. When entering into such alliances, organizations need to consider the extent to which each contributes value as it attempts to accomplish its objectives. The extent to which each organization's strategic objectives are accomplished can be assessed in terms of the value added by the alliance in accomplishing those objectives. This includes the efficiency of joint or integrated operations, the congruity or fit of the structures and cultures of the merged organizations, changes of impact on the sector in which the combined organizations function, longevity of the relationship, and—in the case of multilateral operations—mission success.

SCOPE OF THE STUDY

To provide a survey of current knowledge about aspects of organizations that may affect performance, this book draws on the nascent research that is available on organizational design, culture, leadership, interorganizational relations, and conflict management. It is not a primer on organizations, nor is it a typology for comparing different types of organizations. The topics covered are regarded as the ones most responsive to the charge and relevant to the issues currently confronting the Army. Other topics of organizational science not covered in this survey include organizational development (e.g., Burke, 1994), institutional theory (e.g., Powell and DiMaggio, 1991), organizational learning (e.g., Argyris, 1993), and organizational economics, including agency theory, game theory, and transaction cost analysis (e.g., Eisenhardt, 1989; Dietrich, 1994; Putterman, 1986).

Figure S-1 is a schematic presentation of some themes that are useful in thinking about the aspects of organizations that this book addresses: what an organization *needs*, what an organization *is*, and what an organization *does*. In Part I we begin by considering organizational design. We then look at three popular techniques for attempting to improve organizational performance: total quality management, downsizing, and reengineering. We go on to explore other important aspects of organizations: culture, leadership, and interorganizational relations. In Part II we focus explicitly on the Army and its changing missions, looking at ways to increase its capacity to deal with new challenges.

NATURE OF THE EVIDENCE

The diverse and fragmentary nature of the research evidence available to us has important implications for what we can say about organizational performance. Studies of factors that may influence organizational performance include laboratory simulations, field studies, comparative and organization-specific surveys, and descriptive accounts of organizational processes and interventions. The vast majority of this research is carried out in private-sector organizations, which often place restrictions on the use of proprietary data. Indeed, much of the available information comes from the practical experience of consultants and managers.

The different analytical approaches do not address the same issues or even employ the same standards of proof. Each type has its strengths and weaknesses, and each implies its own definition of what kinds of evidence are most relevant and useful. As is the case in other areas of behavioral research, looking at a single study or only a few studies does not yield results that are definitive. Consider, for example, studies on the effects of total quality management on organizational effectiveness. The studies ex-

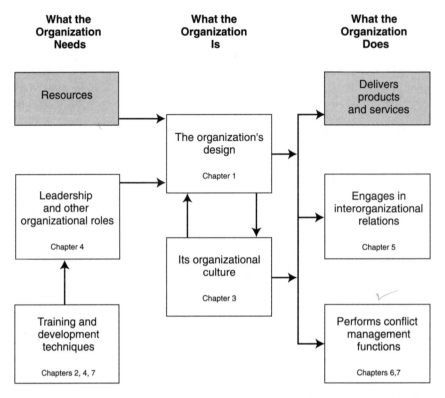

FIGURE S-1   Organizational functions, processes, and performance. Note: Shading indicates topics not considered by the committee.

amining this question suffer from a variety of flaws, including inadequate samples, problematic measures, and incomplete analyses or interpretations. This does not mean that the literature offers no insights. If the flaws differ across studies and the results of a number of studies converge, the convergent results can indicate the direction of effects.

For that reason, whenever possible, we have grounded our judgments in the accumulated results of multiple studies. In some areas, such as organizational culture, this was not possible; the committee's efforts to answer certain questions were hampered by the lack of adequate research. In other areas, such as leadership, we relied in part on technical reports that may not have benefited from such quality control mechanisms as peer review. In still other areas in which there is very little published research, such as on new organizational forms, the committee relied primarily on its collective informed judgment.

Another problem is the differing levels of analysis of studies on organizational performance. On some topics, we draw on studies of small groups for insights about organizational processes that have not been the subject of rigorous research. For example, findings from social-psychological studies on intergroup relations and negotiation contribute to an understanding of alliances and mergers. Similarly, experimental findings on the way people resolve conflicts in negotiating or mediating roles contribute to an understanding of the sorts of contact skills needed to meet the challenges of peacekeeping missions. When used in conjunction with nonexperimental analyses of the broad contexts within which organizations function, these studies help to elucidate the factors that may lead to effective collaborations or missions. On other topics also, the committee moves between micro- and macro-level analyses of organizational performance and, in so doing, learned about some of the difficulties involved in attempts to integrate the different kinds of studies conducted at these levels.

KEY CONCLUSIONS

The committee's key conclusions reflect broad themes that cut across the chapters in the book.

• **The Importance of Context.** Organizations function best when they are appropriately matched to their environments. For contemporary organizations, the environment is increasing in complexity and instability, both continuously and rapidly. The constant change in the environment is prompting complementary changes in organizations looking for an optimal match between their missions and their external conditions.

• **Changing Organizations.** Organizations are constantly changing, their boundaries are difficult to define and vary over time, some are expanding their missions and taking on new objectives, and others are cutting off functions and focusing on their central objectives. A shift in their missions is what leads to changes in almost all aspects of organizations.

There is no universal formula for producing effective organizational change; once a method of change has been selected, there is no widely accepted procedure for implementing it. And because of the complexity of the rapidly changing environment, it is not feasible to prescribe a standard strategy for change to better enable the organization to fit into its environment. A strategy that is beneficial for one organization may be inappropriate for another, even one with similar characteristics. Any strategy for change must be adapted to the particular set of conditions in place at the time.

• **Research Lags Practice.** Thirty years ago, organizational research was ahead of organizational practice. Research investigated new and potential practices and informed their development and implementation in the organization. The rapid growth in the complexity of the environment and the tempo of organizational change have altered the sequence of this relationship: research now lags practice. Given this and the fact that high-quality research takes time, organizations need a rational basis for developing strategies for change. When knowledge is lacking, organizational managers look for help wherever it can be found.

That explains the large and expanding market for popular approaches to organizational transformation. Although some of the current prescriptions may have utility, most of them will turn out to be passing fads. Yet these ideas should not be ignored; subjecting the most popular ideas to systematic evaluation provides a more rational basis for adopting or rejecting them.

• **Research Base Weak.** Despite the progress of pioneering researchers in certain areas, both the research base and organizational theory are in their infancy. Consequently, neither one is complete enough to derive strategies for change in a rational fashion. There is even a lack of descriptive taxonomies to provide a framework to carry out research. Much of the difficulty lies in the accessibility and complexity of the subject matter, not in any lack of effort on the part of organizational theorists and researchers.

The committee is therefore unable to draw conclusions, based on scientific evidence, on what does or does not work to enhance organizational performance in the areas studied. Although there are myriad innovations and claims, there is nothing we can point to with scientific support that invariably results in effectiveness. This negative conclusion includes the widely studied techniques of total quality management, downsizing, and reengineering. Negative findings, however, can embolden people to experiment and evaluate their experimentation.

• **Making Progress.** Research is more likely to address practical issues if it is guided by a conceptual framework that specifies relationships among the various influences on organizational performance, which are the subject of this book. Without such a foundation for research, results are likely to address only the narrow issues of whether one or another popular approach is more plausible. Developing theory and doing research on these relationships should take priority in any research agenda on organizational performance.

In carrying out research on interventions, such as total quality management, a primary challenge is the development of precise and bounded measures of effectiveness. Evaluations work best when the intervention is clearly defined and consistently applied and when the resulting outcomes are clear, cogent, and measurable. In this connection, it is significant to note that measures of satisfaction are not necessarily measures of effectiveness. Each component of an organization's effectiveness, like its overall effectiveness, can be assessed only in terms of its contexts.

PART I

Organizational Responses to Environmental Change

1

Organizational Change and Redesign

Organizational change is pervasive today, as organizations struggle to adapt or face decline in the volatile environments of a global economic and political world. The many potent forces in these environments—competition, technological innovations, professionalism, and demographics, to name a few—shape the process of organizational adaptation. As a result, organizations may shift focus, modify goals, restructure roles and responsibilities, and develop new forms. Adaptive efforts such as these may be said to fall under the general rubric of *redesign*.

In this chapter, we examine aspects of organizational environments that research and practice suggest are changing and are causing managers to redesign their organizations. We discuss the effects of increases in scientific knowledge, societal trends in professional roles, and changing technologies and demographic trends on organizations. We then examine several bases for organizational design and redesign: the work of organizational theorists, the practical experience of managers, and the precepts of doctrine. Finally, we consider new organizational forms as a response to environmental change.

ENVIRONMENTAL CONDITIONS DRIVING ORGANIZATIONAL CHANGE

The committee's reading of organization theory and managerial wisdom suggests that, for an organization to survive, it must be compatible with its environment, i.e., all external social, economic, and political conditions that can influence the organization's actions, nature, and survival.

When the environments change, the organization must eventually respond, and today this must occur at a rate and in ways never before seen or imagined. Organizations that are not able to adapt quickly enough to maintain their legitimacy or the resources they need to survive either cease to exist or become assimilated into other organizations.

Perhaps the most noteworthy change in the environment for business organizations has been the dramatic shift in the developed world from an industrial to an information economy. In 1991, for the first time ever, companies spent more money on computing and communications gear than on industrial, mining, farm, and construction equipment combined. In the 1960s, approximately half of the workers in industrialized countries were involved in making things; by the year 2000, it is estimated that no developed country will have more than one-eighth of its workforce in the traditional roles of making and moving goods (Drucker, 1993). But this is only the most obvious of the trends that are redefining the nature of contemporary organizations.

Population ecology, as its name implies, focuses on the changing nature of populations of organizations (Hannan and Freeman, 1977; Hannan and Carroll, 1992). Institutional theory focuses on the need for organizations to maintain legitimacy with societal norms and values, often embodied in governments, professions, and trade associations (Meyer and Rowan, 1977; Powell and DiMaggio, 1991; Scott, 1987, 1995; Zucker, 1977). Both of these perspectives are fruitful. They tend, however, to deemphasize the influences of management action and leadership in organizational change (but see Hannan and Freeman, 1984; Suchman, 1995). In this chapter, in contrast, we emphasize the role of managers as interpreters and even manipulators of their organization's environment. We emphasize in particular the idea that managers change and redesign their organizations primarily in order to adapt them to changes in the environment, but also to adjust them to changes in the managers' own aspirations and perceptions, or to unintended or unmanaged changes within the organization. Thus, whereas organizational environments and processes are often sources of change, we adopt the strategic choice point of view (Child, 1972), the idea that organizations vary in their choice of responses, the timing of their responses, and the means and effectiveness of executing their responses, and that these phenomena are managerially determined to a great extent.

Some of the most powerful forces identified by the business press and organizational literature that are motivating managers to redesign their organizations are the increase in scientific knowledge, changes in professional roles, the technology explosion, and the changing demographics of the American workforce.

Increase in Scientific Knowledge

There are strong reasons to believe that growth in the world's store of scientific knowledge is a long-term trend that can help to explain the changing nature of organizations. This environmental change is both long-term and antecedent. Consider, as an indicator of scientific knowledge, reports of scientific findings. From 1965 to 1980, the number of scientific articles published per day grew from 3,000 to 8,000, a 160 percent increase (Huppes, 1987:65). This increase is only a snapshot measure of the long-term trend in the generation of scientific knowledge. To get an idea of the longer trend, consider the accelerating increase in the number of scientific journals recorded by De Solla Price (1963). The first 2 scientific journals appeared in the mid-seventeenth century; by the middle of the eighteenth century there were 10 scientific journals, by 1800 about 100, by 1850 about 1,000. Recently, Goodstein (1995) stated that there are currently about 40,000.

These increases in scientific knowledge can be attributed to previous increases—knowledge feeding on itself—to increases in the size of the scientific community, and to increases in effective means of distributing scientific knowledge. Although exponential growth cannot continue forever, this general pattern of rapid growth is likely to continue into the intermediate future.

One reason to expect continued growth in scientific knowledge is that increased capability and application of advanced communications technologies will greatly increase the availability of whatever knowledge is produced. Even now, a weekday edition of *The New York Times* contains more information than the average person was likely to come across in a lifetime during the seventeenth century, and it is estimated that today the amount of information available to the average person doubles every five years (Wurman, 1989). In addition, reflecting on advances in information technologies during the last 50 years makes clear that (1) such technologies are still in their early stages of effectiveness or adoption and (2) other, better, technologies are in the making. Consequently, the availability of existing knowledge will increase as the technologies mature and become more widely used. Increased adoption of these knowledge-distributing technologies, in conjunction with the ongoing acceleration in the size of the knowledge base, will result in a knowledge environment that will be dramatically both more munificent and more burdensome than that confronting organizations today.

Increases in scientific knowledge have important practical impacts. For example, globalization, which may be the most important economic phenomenon of the 1980s and 1990s, is possible only because of advances in communication and transportation technologies. Advances in these technologies follow, in turn, from increases in scientific knowledge. Increases in scientific knowledge are therefore a root cause of change in organizational environments. This is much more true today than in earlier eras, when technological advances were more likely to result from localized insights and atheoretic experimentation rather than following from the worldwide accumulation and consolidation of scientific advances (Heilbroner, 1995; Mokyr, 1990).

Ultimately, we are interested in changes, even improvements, in organizational performance. The question is which features of an organization's environment, when they change, force changes in the organization itself, and hence alter its performance. The committee's reading of the literature suggests that there are three such features: environmental complexity, environmental turbulence, and environmental competitiveness.

Complexity arises not only from improvements in communication and transportation technologies but also from increases in both diversity and specialization, leading to interdependencies among organizations—that is, increased complexity of any single organization's environment and some loss of control by that organization. Environmental turbulence results from the fact that individual events happen more quickly—for example, the ever-shortening product life cycle. Environmental competitiveness arises from a number of factors, including new products competing with old ones, the removal of distance barriers that provided buffers from competition, and improved information technologies that enable producers of goods and services from far away to compete with local establishments for customers and clients. Organizations adapt to these changes by making decisions more frequently, more rapidly, and in more complex ways; by implementing decisions more rapidly; by requiring information acquisition to be continuous and more comprehensive; by reinforcing more selective information distribution; and by promoting more effective organizational learning (Huber, 1984; Huber et al., 1993).

Trends in Professional Roles

Changes in the concept of the professional and the development of professionalism have important implications for organizational forms and management structures. A profession is a calling requiring specialized knowledge and often long and intensive academic preparation. The concept further implies career and commitment to service, rather than casual employment and reliance on external incentives alone, and belief in collegial, rather than hierarchical, control of professional behavior. The concept of the professional was developed, beginning in the Middle Ages, to describe a special set of emergent occupations—freestanding, solo, private practice, and self-employed (Abbott, 1988).

Increasingly, however, the professions are being transformed from freestanding occupations to positions embedded in organizations, with important implications (Kornhauser, 1963; Abbott, 1988). This movement of professionals into organizations is neither uniform nor complete, nor is it likely to become so. As a result, members of the same profession now find themselves variously located in the societal structure of work—some in traditional solo practice; some in small groups or not-so-small professional organizations of their own construction, in which the professional service is the main organizational product; and some as staff specialists in organizations whose primary products or services are not those of its professionals. The first of these categories is familiar; the second is exemplified by the multilawyer legal firm and the medical group practice or health maintenance organization. Finally, the embedding of professional specialists in more conventional organizations is represented by the legal and medical departments of an automobile corporation.

Almost equally significant is the emergence of new professions, many of them created as part of a more general process of technological development. Computer-related expertise is among the most conspicuous examples of a new profession.

The movement of professionals into organizations involves an inherent tension between professionals and managers. Conventional organizations are basically hierarchical, and their governance is internal. Even managements that are enlightened about the advantages of delegation and employee participation in decision making operate on the assumption that authority is exercised through a sequence of supervisory levels, each of which can in principle overrule those below it. Moreover, this governance structure is almost wholly internal, although some intrusion from the outside world is discernible in corporate control. All organizations are required to conform to legal statutes; some must share power with labor unions; and corporate boards typically include some outside members. But the basic policies are internally determined, typically at or near the top of the organization, and overseeing their implementation is the responsibility of successive layers of management and supervision.

This is in marked contrast to the principles of individual autonomy and collegial control that are the hallmarks of the professions. As organizations have made increased the use of professionals, they have found it necessary to make significant changes. Professionals in organizations are not usually subject to the form and degree of supervisory control that is exercised over other nonsupervisory employees. As Freidson (1986) points out, managers do not specify directly the pace and method of professional work, although overall deadlines for project completion may be imposed or attempted. Most managers, unless they are themselves professionals in the same field as those they supervise, recognize their lack of expertise for imposing detailed controls over the work of professionals. But management allocates resources among competing claimants, and in this respect different professional groups are in competition with each other and with other functional subsystems of the organization.

Even organizations with high proportions of professionals require hierarchical decision authority to some extent, although they tend to be less centralized and are characterized by greater structural complexity (Hall, 1968; Trice and Beyer, 1993). Incompatibilities between the level of professionalism and the organization's design are associated with lower levels of organizational effectiveness (Huber et al., 1990).

Emerging Technologies

Changes in technology, broadly defined, have three important implications for organizational design. First, in the form of automation, the use of technology has had visible effects on the structure of organizations. Automation enables an organization to grow in terms of its output and impact (e.g., customer transactions per day in a bank, cans of peas produced per hour in a factory), while shrinking the number of personnel. Automation is often linked to a deskilling of the workforce, although new technology can also be associated with increases in the ratio of skilled to unskilled workers, as computer programmers, missile guidance technicians, and machine setup personnel are called on to maintain or interact with equipment that replaced bank tellers, cannoneers, and assembly line operators.

Often the "upskilling" of personnel reduces the number of persons coordinated by managers at the next hierarchical level, as the work tasks become more difficult to understand and to coordinate, even as the personnel themselves become more specialized and expert. Thus, although automation decreases the number of operating personnel, the number of vertical levels in the organization may not decrease accordingly, and this changes the shape of the organization.

Second, the use of computer-assisted communication and decision-aiding technologies tends to lead to changes in organizational design and decision processes (Quinn, 1992). Recent reviews (Brynjolfsson and Yang, 1996; Fulk and DeSanctis, 1995), theory-building efforts (Huber, 1990), and empirical works (Brynjolfsson et al., 1994; Leidner and Elam, 1995; Scott Morton, 1991) support the idea that the use of computer-assisted communication technologies (e.g., electronic mail, voice mail, visual image transmission devices, computer and video conferencing) and decision-aiding technologies (e.g., expert systems, decision support systems, spread sheets) affect organizational design and organizational decision processes, such as facilitating the elimination of layers of management and enabling the effective functioning of network organizations composed of other organizations. There is still considerable question, however, as to whether they create positive effects on performance, through their effects on organizational processes and structures (Harris, 1994).

Huber (1990) argues that they do. Synthesizing findings from several literatures, he concludes that, through their effects on organizational processes and structures, the technologies have positive effects on the acquisition and development of organizational intelligence and on decision-making processes. An example is provided by the air offensive against Iraq during the Persian Gulf War in 1991, during which information technology was used in allocation decisions—for example, decisions for allocating missions and weapon systems to Iraqi targets and for revising such allocations in light of communications (ranging from pilot observation to satellite data processed in the United States) about the effects of previous missions. Given that 30,000 missions were flown in less than two weeks (Schwarzkopf, 1992:240), it is difficult to imagine that the computer-aided decision support and communication system did not outperform what would have been possible in the past with decision makers who were not aided by modern information technology. Nevertheless, several studies, such as those by Loveman (1994) and Morrison and Berndt (1990), have found no effects or a negative effect on performance despite the fact that businesses around the world spend billions each year on information technology in the form of hardware, software, and support personnel.

Some explanation for the gap between expectations for the technology and its apparent performance may be found in the studies themselves, namely in measurement difficulties and sampling problems (Brynjolfsson, 1993). But a good part of the explanation may be simple cultural lag. Introduction of new technologies requires immediate capital investment and training costs. The benefits may be years in coming. The organizational learning required to know how to use the technology or to redesign work and managerial structures to take advantage of the technology is substantial.

The third area in which technology has had a strong impact on organizational change is that of the so-called high-risk technologies. Despite impressive improvements in safety technology in recent years, the number of accidents associated with new technologies has risen dramatically, along with the potential for enormous loss of life and property, environmental devastation, and economic costs. Examples are the Tenerife air disaster; the Three Mile Island and other nuclear accidents; the Bhopal, India, chemical accident; the Exxon Valdez oil tanker spill; and the Challenger launch explosion. Each of these disasters is associated with an organization's use of technology to achieve difficult, challenging goals that would be impossible to achieve manually.

Dependence on technology that brings with it potential risks is leading to the creation of a new type of organization—the high-reliability organization. The idea is to design organization specifically to manage the serious risks associated with the use of technologies that, if they fail, can have extremely serious consequences (Roberts, 1993). It is a complicated undertaking. A major characteristic of advanced and automated technologies is that their operators and managers are increasingly remote from the processes for which they are responsible. With older technologies, operators could see and touch what they controlled or produced. Mechanisms like gears and pistons were visible, and their action and means of control were obvious. Mental images of the way things worked and how they could go wrong were easily learned and readily shared. People, alone and in teams, were an integral part of the control loop that made these technologies run.

With the advent of remote sensing, computing, and automatic control, the role of the operator is shifting from that of direct sensor and controller to that of monitor and supervisor. Machine intelligence can either augment or displace human intelligence. All too often automation becomes the first line of defense. The human is moved to the periphery of the control loop but then is expected to intervene when safety systems fail.

Unfortunately, people are notoriously poor at monitoring and detecting low-probability events and are fallible in making decisions under stress. Inadequate engineering of the human-system interface sets people up to make errors in diagnosing and managing the systems that automatic systems have failed to control (Sagan, 1995). Thus, we are faced with a paradox: while human intelligence and decision making are being supplanted by automation, humans and human organizations nevertheless represent a last line of defense in the detection of faults and the management of emergencies when automatic safeguards fail. This is the challenge to be met by those who would posit or create the high-reliability organization.

The Changing U.S. Population

The final factor driving organizational change discussed in this chapter is shifts in the structure of the U.S. population. Increased life expectancy, increased racial and ethnic diversity—both in the U.S. population as a whole and in its labor force—and the increased labor force participation of women not only generate new demands on organizations but also offer new opportunities. How those challenges will be met and with what consequences for the performance of organizations, the competitiveness of industries, and the quality of life in the United States remains to be seen.

To say that the effects on organizational design of demographic diversity in organizations are well documented or synthesized would be a gross overstatement; there are some bodies of evidence concerning the effects on organizational processes, however. One is the body of literature indicating that demographic diversity contributes to higher-quality decisions in decision-making groups, provided it is not so great that it leads to a breakdown in group functioning (Cox, 1993; Griggs and Louw, 1995). Another is the idea that high levels of diversity are associated with lower levels of cooperation and proactive social behavior, an idea that follows from findings that demographic diversity is negatively related to interpersonal communications and positive relationships (Jackson et al., 1993) and that such communications and relationships, especially with supervisors, are positively related to cooperation and proactive social behavior (Wayne and Green, 1993). At present the field has little basis for a theory of how these phenomena affect organizational performance in a given situation (but see Cox et al., 1991; Golembiewski, 1995; O'Reilly et al., 1993).

What seems more certain is that an organization with demographically diverse stakeholders is better able to satisfy stakeholder demands if its decision makers, and members who interact with its stakeholders, include personnel whose demographic composition resembles that of the stakeholders (Cox and Blake, 1991).

We turn now to an examination of organizational design and redesign, which are influenced in important ways by these environmental conditions.

ORGANIZATIONAL DESIGN AND REDESIGN

An organization's design refers to its particular configuration of organizational characteristics. These characteristics include structural dimensions, such as size, number of vertical levels, and degree of specialization among organizational units or personnel. Other organizational features, such as culture, primary operating processes, and even strategy, are also included in the concept of organizational design. Because many more organizations are changed each year than are founded, much of organizational design is actually redesign. Redesign is usually an intensively managed endeavor, as illustrated by the well-known redesigns at General Electric and Xerox. Both of these redesigns involved comprehensive changes in strategy, technology, staffing, and culture.

Because there are an immense number and great variety of characteristics on which organizations can differ, a great number of organizational designs are possible. The actual number of significantly different designs found in any population of organizations, however, tends to be much smaller than the theoretical possibilities. This is because many combinations of organizational characteristics or features are not workable or result in inferior performance and are selected out of the population. It is also because, once organizational forms are established and appear to be effective, many will tend to quickly copy them. In contrast, other designs result in smooth and effective organizational functioning, that is, in high levels of organizational performance. Eventually, these latter patterns or clustering of organizational characteristics become more frequently observed.

Organizational scholars and practicing managers have given names to the more common organizational forms. Based on the work of Mintzberg (1993), Table 1-1 outlines four "pure forms" of organizational design. Hybrid combinations of two or more pure forms also occur; the matrix structure, for example, often combines the functional form and the team-based form. Other organizational forms are combinations of somewhat independent organizations; Table 1-2 outlines four such "supraorganizational" forms.

Although the forms described in the two tables and the more common hybrids can be observed, the actual designs of almost all organizations depart from these pure forms. Whether by accident or intention, the evolved composite of a series of design decisions causes actual designs to be idiosyncratic. This fact raises an interesting question: What are the sources of managerial knowledge or belief that cause design decisions to be what they are? The remainder of this chapter addresses this question. We begin by discussing systematically derived theory as a basis for organizational design.

Organization Theory as a Basis for Design and Redesign

Shortly after the beginning of the twentieth century, behavioral scientists began conducting empirical studies of the determinants of human and organizational performance, such as the famous Hawthorne studies at Western Electric (Roethlisberger and Dickson, 1939). Especially after World War II, psychological and sociological studies of behavior and performance within organizations became more theory driven, more methodologically sophisticated, and more numerous. These studies have resulted in descriptive theories about the organizational-level factors and features that determine organizational performance. The best-known of these is called contingency theory; with its extension, configuration theory, it is the basis for most recommendations for organizational design made today by organizational scientists and many management consultants (Burke and Litwin, 1992; Lawrence, 1993; Burton and Obel, 1995; Galbraith, 1977).

Contingency Theory and Configuration Theory

Early work in organizational science focused on the need for an appropriate alignment (i.e., fit or match) between an organization's structure and its environment. This idea was called *contingency theory*—the appropriate structure is contingent on the environment. For example, organizations with low levels of centralization and formalization are more effective in turbulent environments, whereas organizations with high levels of centralization and formalization are more effective in placid environments. As organizational scientists continued investigating relationships between pairs

TABLE 1-1 Four Most Common Organizational Designs

Characteristic	Simple Structure	Functional Form/ Machine Bureaucracy	Professional Bureaucracy	Adhocracy/ Team-Based
Primary control mechanism	Direct supervision	Formalization of standards	Professional standards	Mutual adjustment
Specialization of jobs	Little specialization	Much vertical and horizontal specialization	Much horizontal specialization	Much horizontal specialization
Flexibility to adapt to environmental change	High	Moderately high if top management is sensitized to need for change, low otherwise	Low	High
Most favorable environment	Simple, fast-changing	Simple or complex	Simple or complex, stable	Simple, fast-changing
Examples	Start-up firm, small unit patrols in enemy-held terrain	Large hotel, military procurement organization	University, military research organization	Performing arts theater, product design team

TABLE 1-2 Three Most Common Supraorganizational Designs

Characteristics	Multidivisional	Prime Contractor/ Subcontractor	Network or Virtual Organization
Component organizations	Headquarters and subordinate divisions	Prime contractor and independent subcontractors	Broker and partner
Primary control mechanism	Comparison of divisional performance, allocation of budgeted resources	Adherence to contractual agreements, parties have options not to continue relationship after each contract cycle	Adherence to contractual agreements, need to maintain reputation for cooperative behavior
Horizontal interunit competitiveness	High	High within specialties, low otherwise	Low
Most favorable environment	Stable	Stable	Fast-changing
Examples	Automobile company, Army corps	Aerospace firm military base	Multifirm alliance for major construction project, military joint-service operation/exercise

of other variables (e.g., Woodward's 1957 study of the relationship between manufacturing technology and organizational structure), it became clear that performance is related to the match between particular pairings of organizational features, such as strategy, structure, technology, culture, human resources, leadership, and environment. One of the more practical prescriptive contingency theories is organizational information-processing theory (Huber, 1982; Tushman and Nadler, 1978). In its prescriptive form (see Galbraith, 1977), this theory offers guidelines for designing organizations such that organizational processes and structures are congruent with the nature of the information-processing load imposed by the organization's environment. For more general references to prescriptive guidelines following from contingency theory, see Burton and Obel (1995) and Lawrence (1993).

More recently, perhaps as an extension of systems thinking (Katz and Kahn, 1978), the importance for performance of a simultaneous fit among *all* organizational characteristics as well as with the organization's environments has become clear (Miller, 1981, 1987; Van de Ven and Drazin, 1985). This idea is the basis for *configuration theory*. Miles and Snow (1978), for example, articulate the necessity of simultaneous congruence across an organization's strategy, production processes, and administrative structure. In recent years, configuration theory has been advanced both conceptually (Burke and Litwin, 1992; Doty and Glick, 1994; Meyer et al., 1993) and methodologically (Doty et al., 1993; Drazin and Van de Ven, 1985). Although not necessarily labeled as such, configuration theory is becoming dominant in theory-based organizational design (see Burke, 1994; Miles and Snow, 1994; Mintzberg, 1993).

Theories of Organizational Change

While numerous organization theories deal with organizational change—including population ecology and institutional theory (mentioned earlier), which emphasize why change is so difficult to accomplish—we examine here two theories about organizational redesign that more clearly depend on managerial action. One of these we term the *evolution and revolution* theory of organizational change. It addresses the rather qualitative difference between evolutionary change, in which incremental adjustments to an organization's characteristics are made over long periods of time in order to align these characteristics with each other and with the organization's environment, and revolutionary change, in which all features are changed radically and simultaneously, generally to realign the organization with its environment. This theory, the organizational science version of Gould and Eldredge's (1977) "punctuated equilibrium" theory, seems to have considerable potential for the field of organizational redesign.

The evolution and revolution perspective on organizational change is still in its youth and perhaps should be recognized only as a theory in the making. Early researchers in the area (Miller and Friesen, 1980; Tushman and Romanelli, 1985) continue to extend and influence its development (Miller, 1987; Tushman et al., 1986), but findings by other researchers unaffiliated with these early pioneers also confirm and elaborate the central thrust of the work (Amburgey et al., 1993; Gersick, 1994). This perspective and body of work seems likely to gain influence in organizational redesign for three reasons: (1) its thrust is relevant to today's changing organizational environments, (2) few executives have the opportunity to acquire the breadth or length of experience necessary to learn its lessons on their own, and (3) early indications are that some of its prescriptive guidelines will not be intuitively obvious.

Another theory of organizational change is *life-cycle* theory (Greiner, 1972; Kimberly et al., 1980). It describes how different features of an organization change more or less in harmony as organizations mature. For example, as organizations mature, they become more internally specialized and consequently need more coordination processes, personnel, and units.

Life-cycle theory seems to have received acceptance largely on the basis of case studies (Kimberly et al., 1980), although some larger sample studies have supported the concept of stages that reflect congruent characteristics (Miller and Friesen, 1984; Quinn and Cameron, 1983) but not the idea that the sequence of stages is fixed. It seems plausible that combining two ideas—that there are phases within an organization's life cycle and that there should be congruence among the organization's features within each phase—can lead to prescriptive organizational redesign guidelines for improving performance.

We close this section on theories of organizational change by mentioning two related bodies of literature. One is the large literature on organizational development (Burke, 1994; French and Bell, 1990), which focuses primarily on organizational change for improving the quality of working life in organizations; for a review of this literature, see Faucheux et al. (1982) and Beer and Walton (1987). The other is the relatively newer and smaller body of literature on organizational learning (see Cohen and Sproull, 1996). Reviews by Huber (1991) and Levitt and March (1988) indicate that research on organizational learning has not yet become systematic. The potential for development of prescriptive guidelines seems high; an early attempt at this is the best-seller by Senge (1990).

Experience as a Basis for Organizational Design

Individual managers can learn from their experience in an organization about the appropriateness of its design by seeing and hearing about defects in the design. In addition to learning about organizational designs and their efficacy by comparing different organizations, managers may learn by observing the defects of changed designs in their own organization. Sometimes individual organizations change to mimic certain features, such as designs, of other organizations that are considered to be leaders (Tolbert and Zucker, 1983). Changes enable managers to observe before-and-after pairings of design and performance and, hence, to learn. Of course, a variety of factors limits the validity of such learned relationships. Some of these are difficulties associated with all human learning, including cognitive and motivational biases (Bazerman, 1986; Mayer, 1992). Others have to do with the problems of verticality in organizational information flows (Huber, 1982), such as inadvertent distortions at multiple nodes in a communication network and deliberate distortions by those who seek to gain from such distortions. A manager who observed a large number of design changes might be less prone to learning incorrectly by making comparisons or averaging across instances, but few managers experience a large number of organizational changes that are comparable.

Some of the difficulties associated with firsthand observation of a very limited number of pairings of organizational design and performance are overcome by managers through vicarious learning. Managers talk with other managers in other companies, they talk with consultants who themselves have had many opportunities to observe design-performance pairings, and they read the business press reports of organizational design and performance pairings in individual companies. Although there is little research on managerial learning through these media, we speculate that managers do learn about alternative ways of organizing this way. We also speculate that due to the absence of useful frameworks about organizational designs and of specific and comparable performance data, what managers learn this way is fairly superficial and of only modest validity. Some support for these speculations is the research of Burns and Wholey (1993), who found that hospitals adopted matrix structures of organization more to follow a current fashion rather than because the structural form fitted their situation.

Perhaps the most obvious way for a manager to extend his or her own experience is to consult an expert, a person who has seen more design alternatives and has been in a position to evaluate them. Individual consultants and consulting firms vary greatly in the extent to which they accumulate and codify their experience, however. Authors and consultants are overlapping categories; many authors are also consultants, and their experience in that role informs their books. And in some cases, their ideas about organizational design are also shaped by specific theoretical models and research.

This combination is well exemplified by the best-seller on organizational design and practice, *In Search of Excellence,* by Peters and Waterman (1982). Both authors were members of a large consulting firm, McKinsey and Company, and both were experienced consultants. They worked within a schema, the McKinsey 7-S framework, which is more a listing of classes of factors to take into account than a theory of organization. The framework consists of seven factors that in combination are assumed to determine organizational effectiveness. All seven are drawn as interconnected and all are identified by words beginning with the letter S, hence the copyrighted 7-S label: structure, systems, style, staff, skills, strategy, and shared values. These at least serve to remind consultants of things to look for as they advise managements.

Peters and Waterman went beyond such a priori guides, however, in their search for excellent companies. With funding from McKinsey and from client firms, they set up a research project. They chose 75 "highly regarded companies" and, for the 62 based in the United States, they did a retrospective performance review for the preceding 20 years and conducted structured interviews with some members of management. Six measures of growth and financial performance and a judgmental measure of innovativeness were thus added to the initial rating of "high regard." The use of all these criteria produced a set of companies considered exemplars of excellence: Bechtel, Boeing, Caterpillar Tractor, Dana, Delta Airlines, Digital Equipment, Emerson Electric, Fluor, Hewlett-Packard, IBM, Johnson and Johnson, McDonald's, Proctor and Gamble, and 3M.

Peters and Waterman warned their readers about the limitations of their work: "We don't pretend to account for the perfidy of the market or the whims of investors. . . . Second, we are asked how we know that the companies we have defined as culturally innovative will stay that way. The answer is we don't" (1982:24-25). Their premonition was justified, as a third of the "excellent" companies performed poorly shortly after publication of their book (*Business Week,* 1984:76–88).

Doctrine as a Basis for Design

Doctrine-driven design is an approach that applies codified, normative principles to organizational design. These principles are derived from the experiences, beliefs, values, and ideologies of an organization's key leaders and are often influenced by societal values. In the long run (indeed, sometimes across generations of managers), the beliefs, values, and ideologies that become formalized into design doctrine are the result of multitudes of experiences, and the revision of doctrine in the light of experience is often a very slow process. It is important to note that the beliefs and values of an organization's leaders are often determined in great part by the larger society, and also to note that society exerts some degree of influence over the doctrines of all organizations in its midst. Both of these insights are provided by institutional theory, mentioned earlier.

Clarifying the Meaning of Doctrine

The dictionary defines doctrine as a body of working principles laid down by authority, generally held to be true, and often used as the fundamental basis for instruction and training. In this section we explore the characteristics of doctrine-based organizational design in the context of military doctrine, calling attention to the fact that manifestations of doctrine are found in other organizational domains as well: government, hospitals, fire and emergency departments, power utilities, religious groups, and radical political groups.

Because doctrine-based design is generated, promulgated, and reinforced by authority, it tends to resist criticism, lag relevant events, and eventually become ineffective. Corporate doctrines can resist evidence that demonstrates their obsolescence. An example of the failure of doctrine-based organizational design is the American automotive industry of the 1970s, which persisted in adhering to an outmoded doctrine despite massive loss of market share to foreign manufacturers who had developed radically different doctrines based on such values as quality and reliability. In contrast, doctrine that is constantly reviewed and updated in response to current conditions can be a sound basis for organizational design.

Army Doctrine in the Unit Design Process[1]

The U.S. Army uses doctrine in the design of its units and forces to a great extent, in a way that is important, explicit, and almost beyond question. We note that this use of doctrine in organizational design is atypical in its intensity; most organizations are influenced by doctrine in their design efforts much less intentionally and systematically.

To perform different functions, Army units must be adequately equipped and staffed with appropriate numbers of trained personnel and types of equipment. Decisions on appropriate mixes of these elements are made within the context of a broad force-structuring process initiated by the joint chiefs of staff and the secretary of defense. Design is a top-down process, and unit design provides the building blocks for this activity.[2] The principal output of unit design is a set of requirements for each unit. These requirements are translated into tables of organization and equipment. The Army reviews and revises its current unit designs in response to changes in its doctrine, concepts, and new technology, as well as global trends and threats. The goal of a unit designer is to design effective units with the fewest possible resources.

The unit design process is part science and part art. Some capabilities required by a unit, such as the number of refueling vehicles needed to achieve specific levels of mobility, can be derived quantitatively. Others, such as the reconnaissance assets needed to carry out a mission, depend on assumptions and judgments based on experience, values, and ideology. Planning how best to organize to fight a war is an extraordinarily complex process. Hundreds of interactive considerations and contingencies must be taken into account. Here we summarize the part of this process that must go on just to organize a unit (U.S. Army, 1995).

Step 1: Identify unit design issues. In this step, all of the external conditions that are likely to affect or alter the design of a unit are identified and described. External conditions include threats (e.g., enemy missiles), revised objectives (e.g., contain versus destroy), new alliances among possible enemies, and changes in economic or political conditions that could lead to conflict. Internal conditions include new or revised missions, changing funding, technology advances, lessons learned from training and combat, and new or revised doctrine. The product of this step is a requirement to change a unit design in order to bring it up to date and tailor it to internal and external conditions.

Step 2: Develop unit design concepts. In this step, a set of design concepts is constructed given the issues, needs, and constraints that were spelled out in Step 1. The concepts identify the required capabilities for employing forces on the battlefield. They define needs but not particular means for meeting the needs. Once they have been formulated, unit design concepts drive changes in training, doctrine, leader development, and materiel requirements.

Given a requirement to design a unit, knowledge of its required capabilities, and the doctrine that will govern the performance of its mission, the unit designer draws on a knowledge base about what makes an organization effective. This knowledge base contains a number of important design principles. Design principles act as a filter to evaluate unit design alternatives. Army doctrine often suggests which principles are most relevant to a particular unit being designed. The similarity of many of these principles to those derived from organizational theory, and particularly to contingency theory, is striking.

Step 3: Analyze and test unit designs. In this step, design alternatives are examined and compared in effectiveness and efficiency. The methods used to assess effectiveness include training exercises, computer simulations, and war games. The assessment of efficiency typically centers on cost and resource analysis.

Step 4: Develop tables of organization and equipment. A table of organization and equipment lists the personnel and equipment required for organizations during wartime. A "good" table reflects a balanced structure of the minimum essential personnel and equipment for a unit to accomplish its mission under conditions of sustained combat.

Step 5: Implement and evaluate the table of organization. The implementation and evaluation of tables of organization requires the integration of each unit design with other units in the force, with other services, and with allies. Ultimately, the success of the unit design process is measured by the ability of units in the field to carry out required mission tasks. Lessons learned and data collected from actual operations (e.g., Just Cause, Desert Shield/Storm) and training exercises provide feedback for the unit design process and for the revision of tables of organization. The modeling and simulation tools used in Step 3 are also applicable to this step.[3]

Assessment of the Bases for Organizational Design

The major sources of guidance for organizational design are research and theory, experience, and doctrine. Each of these has its own characteristics strengths and weaknesses, which are briefly outlined below.

Experience

A manager's experience can often be a poor basis for organizational design, for two reasons. One is that in some important respects the environment in which managers work is not conducive to learning. Learning is most efficient when feedback is fast and unambiguous. The outcome data from many managerial decisions, particularly changes in organizational design, are generally months or years in coming. By that time, many events, some unknown to the manager, have transpired that confound the relationship between the design decision and the outcome, thus introducing ambiguity. Furthermore, outcome data are often selectively perceived or interpreted by the managers themselves or are distorted by upward-communicating subordinates, thus rendering the feedback ambiguous, biased, or both.

The second reason is that the organizational circumstances that influenced the efficacy of a particular design in the past are not likely to be the same as those for which a new design or a redesign is contemplated. In a fast-changing world, past experiences are generally not representative of current situations. If managers have a fairly complete and accurate mental map of which contingencies influenced the effectiveness of the designs previously encountered and how the contingencies and design features interacted, account could be taken of the differences in circumstances, but this is hardly ever the case.

The experiences of management consultants may not suffer so greatly from this extrapolation problem. As we noted earlier, consultants are often knowledgeable about the organizational theories that might relate contingencies, the design features, and performance, and they may incorporate these theories into their mental models. In addition, their wider variety of experiences gives them more opportunity to identify the relationships among these variables.

Prescriptive Organizational Theory

Although, to our knowledge, there are no systematic studies of the sources of ideas used by executives when they design or redesign organizations, it is generally agreed that, on the whole, theories from organizational science have had only modest impact on organizational design (Bettis, 1991; Daft and Lewin, 1990; but see Guillen, 1994), for at least three reasons. One is that organizational theories are often not very accurate when applied to a specific case (Miner, 1983; Daft and Lewin, 1990). This fact follows from the methodological problems inherent in the study of complex human systems, such as the multiplicity of performance measures and the multiplicity of causal forces. It also follows from the fact that scientists attempt to create theories that are very general and that apply to many situations. As a consequence, more broadly generalizable theoretical advances are more rewarded by the scientific community and are sought more vigorously by scientists. However, all else being equal, a general theory is less accurate about a particular situation than is a theory derived only from studies of organizations in that situation—and managers are interested in their particular situations.

Related to this issue is the matter of studying typical versus atypical organizations. The potent argument for studying atypical organizations is that by definition they have unique properties that may render general theories invalid. Some in the organizational science community are calling for more studies of atypical organizations in which mistakes can have disastrous consequences, such as atomic energy plants, toxic chemical factories, airlines and air traffic control systems, and space satellite launching organizations (Roberts, 1993).

A second reason that organizational theory has had only modest impact on organizational designs is that the large body of empirical studies on which it draws includes many studies carried out under conditions that no longer exist. For example, managers are involved in command, control, and communication—functions that have been transformed by computer-enhanced communications technology. Yet, as noted by Huber (1990), organizational theories concerning these functions have generally not accounted for the massive changes in the availability, effectiveness, and usability of technologies for command, control, and communication. Similarly, other environmental forces, such as the increasing diversity of the workforce, impinge on organizations much more strongly than in previous eras.

A third reason is that some executives with broad firsthand experience, or with long histories of learning from other executives, seem to know the essence of a theory before organizational scientists articulate it. Although scientists often identify subtleties that executives may not have had the opportunity to grasp, such subtleties are often so situation-specific that they do not apply to the circumstances in which executives find themselves.

In spite of these concerns, there are important conditions under which prescriptive organizational theory can be of considerable use to organizational designers (see Donaldson, 1985, 1995). One of these is when trial-and-error learning is prohibitively expensive and applicable personal experience is unlikely to be available. For example, research shows that organizations tend to remain relatively unchanged, even as their environments shift, leading eventually to the need for radical and swift redesign (Hannan and Freeman, 1984). Unfortunately, swift redesign leaves no time for experiential learning, so redesign decisions need to be right the first time. Without the products of systematic empirical studies, many executives would have little basis for making informed choices.

The value of organizational theory as a basis for organizational design is understood best in relation to the alternatives. As we noted, in a fast-changing world, personal experience applicable to any current choice situation is unlikely to be available. Also, because the feedback from executive action is both slow and subject to cognitive and motivational biases, it is very difficult for accurate learning to occur. Thus, although the aggregate personal interpretations of experience by a team of executives are likely to be superior to any single executive's interpretation, they are unlikely to be superior to the systematically evolved theory that comes from the careful integration of the results of scores of scientific studies.

Doctrine

Doctrine consists of design principles derived from the experiences, beliefs, values, and ideologies of an organization's key leaders. Because doctrine follows from the careful review and integration, by many experts, of many experiences, idiosyncratic confounding variables and noise are reduced in their impact, and contingencies are often recognized and accounted for. Thus, with respect to experience, doctrine does not suffer from some of the problems involved in using the experience of individual managers.

It is also true that beliefs, values, and ideologies are generally extremely slow to change and often very resistant to revision in light of new data. As a consequence, the use of doctrine can lead to periods of poor organizational performance when conditions are changing rapidly.

Doctrine as a basis for organizational design has an advantage over the more general organizational theory, in that it is specific to a particular type of organization. It does not suffer from the low levels of accuracy that sometimes occur when highly generalized, cross-industry theories are used to predict the relationship between design and performance in specific situations. In this respect, it avoids the criticism that Starbuck (1993) would direct at prescriptive organization theory—that it does not account for the properties that make organizations distinctive.

Experience, organization theory, and doctrine each serve as a basis for the design of organizations. Because they draw on past events, they tend to perpetuate previous designs (albeit designs that led to satisfactory performance); they tend not to lead to new organizational forms. New forms or designs are appearing, however, and we turn now to a discussion of them.

NEW ORGANIZATIONAL FORMS

As organizational environments undergo accelerating change, it is no surprise to discover distinctively new forms of organizations emerging as managers attempt to create organizations better suited to these changes. In this section we examine several "new" organizational forms: the adhocracy or the team-based organization, the network or virtual organization, the horizontal organization, and the matrix organization (the oldest of the new forms). The first three of these new forms have so far received little empirical examination. Indeed, a reason to mention them here is to make them more conspicuous as objects and opportunities for study by organizational scientists. A second reason to note them is that, individually and collectively, they may portend the future set of organizational forms from which managers choose and which organizational scientists study for their survivability. As such, these forms can be regarded as archetypes or as new general models or templates for constructing organizations (Hinings and Greenwood, 1989).

Team-Based Organizations

In today's fast-changing organizational environments, competitive pressures and stakeholder demands have compelled many organizations to redesign large portions of their operations as team-based structures. In such structures, specialists from different domains work together to complete projects. Although sometimes a team is self-managed, generally a team leader is appointed by higher-level management. When a team's task consists of projects rather than ongoing activities, the team typically disbands after a project is completed and its members move on to other projects.

Organizations in which the temporary team structure is dominant are

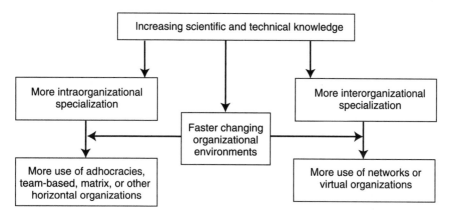

FIGURE 1-1 Drivers for new organizational forms.

called *adhocracies*. The adhocracy form of organization has developed in order to deal simultaneously with the coordination problems associated with intraorganizational specialization and the requirement for quick responses associated with fast-changing environments (see Figure 1-1). Not all team-based organizations are adhocracies. The term refers specifically to organizations in which the teams are temporary structures, as in the production of theatrical performances in which producers, directors, technicians, and actors come together to form a temporary company that produces a play. The teams then disband when the production has been completed and the members join other teams to produce a different play. In contrast are permanent multispecialist teams, such as professional sports teams and surgical teams in hospitals.

Adhocracies and other project-based team structures are currently in fashion and seem to be appropriate design solutions in certain situations (see Katzenbach and Smith, 1993; Mohrman et al., 1995). Widely accepted solutions have not yet been developed to the problems of team rewards, including compensation, and the maintenance of technical expertise for experts whose team assignments do not provide opportunities for technical learning.

Network or Virtual Organizations

The increases in knowledge specialization that lead to an adhocracy's intraorganizational specialization also lead to interorganizational specialization, as organizations seek to exploit niches with their own distinctive products and services. The network form has developed in order to deal simultaneously with higher levels of interorganizational specialization and the greater need for fast adaptation that follows from more instability and turbulence in organizational environments (see Figure 1-1). When organizations specialize, they often are forced to limit the range of their competencies and team with other organizations with different specializations to satisfy customer needs. Such interorganizational teaming results in what is called a *network organization*[4] or a *virtual organization* (see Powell, 1990, for an overview of research on networks). Network organizations are generally formed by a "broker" who selects the member organizations and coordinates their network-related strategic activities. In some instances, only strategic planning and financial accounting are performed by the broker; all other functions, such as design, manufacturing, and advertising, are carried out by other organizations in the network.

In essence, a network organization is an integrated set of alliances. In network organizations, membership is not permanent, although if the network has a continuing market, good performance by member organizations usually leads to continuing membership. Member organizations are generally members of other network organizations. The instability of organizational environments can cause one network member to become mismatched, either as the network changes focus or as the member organization finds new opportunities outside the particular network. (For an example of creating and managing network structures, see the Eccles and Crane, 1988, study of investment bankers.)

The network organization is an extension of the concept of a vertically integrated organization that contains all necessary functional units within itself. As other organizations specialize in certain functions and become more practiced, capable, and efficient in performing them, vertically integrated organizations can eliminate their corresponding functional units and instead subcontract these functions to the external specialist organizations to form a network organization; they can then focus on their functional "core competence" (Quinn, 1992). Theories of transaction costs are a basis for prescriptions about the types of activities that organizations should conduct within their firms and those they should contract out—the "make or buy" decision (Williamson and Masters, 1995). This sequence of events can certainly occur, although a more common scenario is that of an entrepreneur or an entrepreneurial organization that sees an opportunity to engage in a large endeavor without creating a large vertically integrated or multifunctional organization, creating instead alliances with other organizations (Harrison, 1994).

Network organizations are an increasingly common supraorganizational form. As noted by Kanter (1989), they pose problems of interorganizational coordination and the development of trust; these problems and others are examined in Miles and Snow (1992) and Kanter (1994).

Horizontal Organizations

One of the most common and important tasks of the middle manager is coordination, yet, during the past decade or two, layers of middle management have been eliminated. One substitution for the deletion of the middle manager coordination function is to require and authorize first-line managers and operations-level personnel to coordinate work and work flow across functions. The term *horizontal organization* refers to the organizational form in which coordination is done by direct and prescribed interaction between persons of different units. This form of organization is employed in hospitals, when a patient is processed through a series of departments without the use of coordination by superordinate authority. The horizontal form was created in response to a demand for faster decision making and decision implementation and greater efficiencies. It goes beyond the capabilities of what has been called the "informal organization" in that it increases reliability by formalizing accountability and procedures.

Matrix Organizations

A *matrix organization* exists whenever there are overlapping sources of formal authority. This organizational form originated in the electronics and space industries shortly after World War II. Its adoption was fashionable for several decades, and it is still popular today.

Early in the evolution of the matrix form, problems in coordinating functional specialists caused organizations to create coordinating roles on behalf of the functional department managers. At this early stage, functional managers generally delegated no authority to the coordinator. That form has been termed a *functional matrix* (Larson and Gobeli, 1987). Increasing pressures for both shorter project completion times and less proprietary resource allocations from departments led to project managers acquiring more authority and attaining more influence. This organizational form is called a *project matrix*. The extension to a team-based organization, in which functional departments have no authority over team members during a project's life, followed.

The matrix form is a stable form in some organizations, such as the hospital industry, in which a unit manager has coordination responsibility as well as a high level of responsibility for the performance of medical wards, but functional specialists also have some level of responsibility to their function supervisor, as does a nurse to the head nurse. In other organizations, it seems to be serving as a transition form between the functional form and the team-based form. For an interesting analysis of the adoption and abandonment of matrix management in the hospital industry, see Burns and Wholey (1993).

Other Organizational Forms

Several additional organizational forms, not yet included in any generally accepted taxonomy and without widely accepted names, have emerged over the years in response to particular situations. Toffler (1990) describes several of them, including the following:

- Pulsating organization. This organizational form expands and contracts rhythmically. Examples are the U.S. Bureau of the Census, which expands when a census is taken; retail firms that expand and contract around holidays; and pickup crews used in film and TV production.
- Two-faced organizations. This organizational form is designed to operate in two modes, depending on circumstances. Examples include fire, rescue, ambulance, military, and antiterrorist organizations. These organizations have a shadow management for normal operations and special units or teams for crisis management. The values and cultures of the two modes differ.
- The skunkworks. This form denotes a team that is given a loosely specified problem or goal and allowed to operate outside company rules (Kidder, 1981). Official channels and rules can be ignored. This design form may be greatly creative, but success depends heavily on team member competence.

Quinn (1992) discusses decentralized organizations (as "intimately flat" organizations), extremely dispersed organizations (as "spider's web" organizations), "inverted" organizations when all nonboundary-spanning units serve the units that interface with the customers and clients, and other new and not yet common organizational designs. As organizational environments become more differentiated, we can expect more new organizational forms, but as these environments continue to change, we can expect a sizable proportion of the new forms to pass away, as the niches for which they are well matched disappear.

CONCLUSIONS

Organizational Change

1. Increases in scientific knowledge, professionalism, the performance of technologies, and demographic diversity are key features of organizational environments.

2. Many major changes in organizations are prompted by changes in organizational environments, often changes that threaten organizational performance or legitimacy. Top management interprets these changes, often as

threats or opportunities, and determines or at least influences how the organization changes in response to these changes.

3. Increases in scientific knowledge have led and continue to lead rather directly to changes in the organizational structures and processes that deal with organizational learning, decision making, and adaptation.

4. Increases in scientific knowledge, professionalism, and the performance of technology are having significant impacts on organizational design and performance.

5. Environmental changes that are having subtle but nevertheless significant changes in organizations are changes in the demography of society and the workplace. Increases in demographic diversity within an organization can lead to improved decision making through the introduction of a wide variety of knowledge, to a reduction in cooperation and prosocial behavior, and to improved interaction with resource controllers in the organization's environment.

Organizational Design

1. The strongest driving force for organizational redesign is the necessity to adapt to a changing organizational environment.

2. The most widely employed theory concerning adaptation of organizations to their environments and the internal alignment of organizational features is that of contingency or configuration theory. This perspective corrects the tendency of early organizational theorists to assume that certain universal prescriptions would be optimal for all organizations and all environments.

3. The major sources of guidance for organizational redesign are research and theory, pragmatic experience and, in special cases, the existence of doctrine or overarching principles regarding "the way things are done here." Doctrine as a guide for organizational decisions has been developed most fully in the military, although doctrinal elements are apparent in many organizations. Each of these three bases for organizational redesign—theory and research, experience, and doctrine—has its own characteristic strengths and weaknesses.

4. Although many organizational designs are conceivable, relatively few are encountered with any frequency. Four basic types are commonly recognized: simple hierarchies, machine bureaucracies, professional bureaucracies, and team-based adhocracies. Both hybrids, which result from a combination of two or more basic types, and supraorganizations develop as organizations attempt to address more complex tasks and environments.

5. The history of individual organizations often shows a pattern of evolution and revolution. Organizations tend to alternate between relatively

long periods of incremental adjustment and resistance to environmental change and occasional brief periods of major redesign.

6.   Some organizational changes, incremental for the most part, seem to be age related.   As organizations grow older, they develop greater internal specialization of roles and more coordination processes and structures.

NOTES

[1]Many of the missions and roles central to the U.S. Army and other forces during the cold war are adjusting to new realities and their requirements.   Although the United States will be prepared, as it was in the Persian Gulf War, to respond to conventional military threats, it is still struggling with new and unfamiliar missions such as peace-keeping and humanitarian relief.   Our examination focused on the redesign of force structures and unit organizations for responding to traditional hostile threats.   Although we have considered peacekeeping issues elsewhere in this report, our focus is on the process rather than the design of peacekeeping units.

[2]The process of force development is far more complex than can or need be reported here in order to understand the basic doctrine-driven design approach used in unit design.   Army force structuring and force development are accomplished in response to a National Military Strategy Document, which is updated every two years.   Information on the process may be found in U.S. Army (1995).

[3]The Army's use of mathematical modeling and computer simulation to determine the organizational design characteristics most likely to lead to high levels of performance prompts us to note that organizational and management scientists frequently use least square statistical analysis and occasionally data development analysis to determine the relationships between organizational design characteristics and organizational performance for particular groups of highly similar organizations.

[4]Organizations and teams can be networked internally and externally with the aid of electronic networks.   However, the electronic network is not a requirement for networking to occur.

2

Techniques for
Making Organizations Effective

Three approaches to organizational change—total quality management, downsizing, and reengineering—are currently being used by many organizations attempting to change their designs, cultures, missions, and external relations. One attribute these techniques have in common is that they are being applied in many types of organizations across industry lines. This chapter reviews each of these approaches and their relationships to organizational effectiveness.

TOTAL QUALITY MANAGEMENT

Total quality management (TQM) is not yet a precisely defined construct. It encompasses many management practices and prescriptions that have been part of the organizational literature for several decades. The multiple dimensions of quality make it difficult to draw precise conclusions about its relationship to organizational effectiveness. Although there is much anecdotal evidence that TQM increases the effectiveness of modern organizations, a surprising dearth of systematic empirical research exists.

Quality as a Construct

One difficulty with studying quality is that its definition is neither precise nor consensual. Quality, like terms such as effectiveness, satisfaction, empowerment, and leadership, is a construct rather than a concept, and no objective referents exist. Its definition is constructed in the minds of the definers, so no single definition is correct for every circumstance.

Quality is used to refer to an ultimate outcome as well as a predictor of an ultimate outcome. Prior to the late 1980s, the scholarly literature usually treated quality as an indicator of organizational effectiveness (Campbell, 1977; Conrad and Blackburn, 1985). In this first sense, quality referred to the rate of errors or defects in goods-producing organizations (Crosby, 1979), to institutional reputation in higher education organizations (Webster, 1981), to the presence of ambience and legitimacy in arts organizations (Tschirhart, 1993), and to reduced morbidity and mortality rates in health care organizations (Scott et al., 1978). In every case, quality was always used as a qualifier in describing some product or service—high-quality products, high-quality education, high-quality art, high-quality health care. It was only one aspect of what organizations were interested in accomplishing.

In recent years, the focus on quality has changed. More and more, quality has begun to take on the appearance of the summum bonum of organizational performance. Managers and other organization members have become converted to the pursuit of quality as the single most important organizational objective (Deming, 1986), and scholars have scrambled to catch up by substituting quality as the dependent variable of choice.

Attempts to Define Quality

Many scholarly attempts have been made to define quality in a meaningful way (Table 2-1). Garvin (1988) has identified four "eras" of quality development in the United States: (1) an inspection era, in which quality was associated with mistakes and errors detected in products or services after they were produced; (2) a statistical control era, in which defects were reduced by controlling the processes that produced the products; (3) a quality assurance era, in which techniques and philosophies encompassed total quality control and top management took responsibility for ensuring quality throughout the organization; and (4) a strategic management era, in which quality was defined from the customer's point of view and the organization's strategy became centered on quality.

Another perspective on quality development is the shift from a one-best-way approach to quality, to a contingency approach to quality, to a multiple-constituencies approach. For example, the first two eras, inspection and statistical control, represent a uniform approach, implying that it is good under every circumstance for every organization. This approach is best characterized by Shewhart's (1931) classic *Economic Control of Quality of Manufactured Product*, in which he outlined universal techniques as well as a philosophy that emphasized the one correct way to define and achieve quality. Deming (1986), the best-known disciple of Shewhart, perpetuated this view of quality to some extent. His famous 14 points were an effort to create organizational forms that prevented errors but did not

TABLE 2-1   Major Definitions of Quality

Approach	Definition	Example
Transcendent	"Quality is neither mind nor matter, but a third entity independent of the two . . . even though Quality cannot be defined, you know what it is" (Pirsig, 1974)	Innate excellence Timeless beauty Universal appeal
Product-based	"Quality refers to the amounts of the unpriced attributes contained in each unit of the priced attribute" (Leffler, 1982)	Durability Extra desired attributes Wanted features
User-based	"Quality is fitness for use" (Juran, 1989) "Quality consists of the capacity to satisfy wants" (Edwards, 1968)	Satisfies customers Meets needs Fulfills expectations
Manufacturing-based	"Quality means conformance to requirements" (Crosby, 1979)	Reliability Adherence to specifications Variation within tolerance limits
Value-based	"Quality means best for certain conditions . . . (a) the actual use and (b) the selling price" (Fiegenbaum, 1961)	Performance at an acceptable price Value for the money spent Affordable excellence
System-based	"[Quality is] a system of means to economically produce goods or services which satisfy customers' requirements" (Japanese Industrial Standards Committee, 1981)	Utilizing accepted quality procedures Quality processes Integrated approach
Philosophical	"[Quality] means that the organization's culture is defined by and supports the constant attainment of Mind-set customer satisfaction through an integrated system of tools, techniques, and training" (Sashkin and Kiser, 1993)	Management philosophy Lifestyle

Source: Cameron and Whetten (1996).

discard or correct them after they had been made. The next quality era—quality assurance—sees quality as a relatively specialized function, not everyone's responsibility, and something one "inspected for" after the product was finished rather than something one "built in" to the product. Juran (1951) and Fiegenbaum (1961), for example, identify different approaches to and different meanings of quality. Quality definitions could differ among functions (e.g., manufacturing, purchasing, sales) as well as among activities (e.g., new product design, inventory control, assembly) (Fiegenbaum, 1961). The fourth era—strategic quality management—parallels the multiple-constituency approach to organizational effectiveness in emphasizing differences in the definition of quality depending on which constituency's perspective is adopted.

Juran (1989) invented a distinction to differentiate a "big Q" approach to quality from a "little q" approach. Big Q is associated with the strategy, culture, and overall functioning of the organization. Little q is associated with quality as an attribute of a product or a process; it refers to specific tools, techniques, and activities. Only recently has quality taken on the big Q connotation. The phrase *total quality management* is generally taken to refer to big Q quality (Sashkin and Kiser, 1993).

Dimensions of Quality

Writers who attempt to characterize quality as an attribute of products and services (little q) include Garvin (1988), Juran (1989), Teboul (1991), Fornel and Johnson (1993), Zeithaml (1988), and Maynes (1976). The dimensions they identify include such attributes as reliability, durability, serviceability (Garvin, 1988), safety, prestige (Teboul, 1991), freedom from deficiencies, meeting customer needs (Juran, 1989), quality in terms of value, and customer satisfaction (Fornel and Johnson, 1993).

In characterizing quality as a more comprehensive set of characteristics (big Q), the list of possible attributes is even longer (see Malcolm Baldrige National Quality Award, 1995; Deming, 1986; Juran, 1992):

Continuous improvement in all activities and in all people,
Customer satisfaction for internal and external customers,
Efficient deployment of resources,
Employee, supplier, and customer development and recognition,
Environmental well-being,
Exemplary, visionary, and aggressive leadership,
Fast response time,
Full participation of employees, suppliers, and customers,
Life-long relationships with customers,
Long-range perspectives,

Partnerships upstream, downstream, and across functions,
Prevention of error by designing in quality,
Process mapping and process improvement,
Providing customer value,
Quantitative measurement and management-by-fact,
Root-cause analysis,
Shared values, vision, and culture,
Standard quality tools,
Top management sponsorship and involvement, and
Waste reduction and cost containment.

Again, various writers have come up with different sets of dimensions they associate with TQM—big Q (Hackman and Wageman, 1995; Greene, 1993). In 1988 the U.S. Department of Commerce established the Malcolm Baldrige National Quality Award and developed a framework for quality that is claimed to be comprehensive in terms of the dimensions it incorporates. These dimensions are hypothesized to have a particular relationship to one another, as illustrated in Figure 2-1. The leadership dimension is classified as a driver of quality. Four dimensions—information gathering and analysis, quality planning, quality assurance, and human resource management—are all classified as process dimensions. Two dimensions are assumed to be desirable outcomes, namely, customer satisfaction and quality results. Empirical research on these hypothesized relationships is very scarce. In one of the few studies of the Malcolm Baldrige award, Winn (1995) found partial support for the model in a study of higher education organizations. He determined that the leadership dimension (the driver) had direct impact on the process dimensions but indirect impact on the outcome dimensions. The effect of the driver on outcomes was through the process dimensions, not exactly as the figure illustrates.

This award program (and its counterparts, the more recent European Quality Award and the older Japanese Deming Prize) have probably had as significant an effect on organizational practices as any planned change effort other than automation. Almost no organization in the industrialized world can be found that has not adopted some kind of change in order to improve its quality, partially due to the impact of these national awards on business functioning. Until recently the Malcolm Baldrige award has been limited to large businesses, small businesses, and service firms (two awards can be given in each category each year); the award program is now being expanded to include educational and health care organizations as well.

Quality and Effectiveness

Although a great deal of writing and storytelling has made a case for

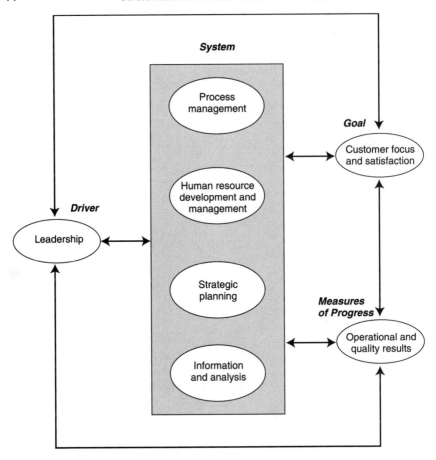

FIGURE 2-1   The Malcolm Baldrige National Quality Award framework.

the importance of quality in ensuring organizational success, firm conclusions must be tempered by the fact that relatively little empirical work has
been done to assess the relationships between TQM and organizational effectiveness. In a broad review of the literature up to 1995 in higher education, for example, Peterson and Cameron (1995) found that only 3 percent
of the published articles were empirical studies of TQM, 59 percent were
commentaries or editorials about TQM's merits or attributes, and 36 percent
were case study descriptions of TQM's application in a single organization
or setting. It seems that much more is known about the attributes and
dimensions of TQM than on its impact on organizational effectiveness.

    Some empirical research has been conducted on the relationships be-
tween various aspects of TQM and organizational effectiveness, but it is

both sparse and limited mainly to such correlated indicators of performance as productivity, customer satisfaction, and error rates. Moreover, there is no agreed-on definition of effectiveness. All investigations are correlational in their approach, and causation has not been carefully examined. Whereas these findings provide limited support for a relationship between quality and effectiveness, the popular press is becoming more and more critical of TQM based on the rate at which quality improvement programs are being abandoned—a fact that gives one pause. It is clear that many questions are yet to be addressed.

Negative Results

Some recent surveys have reported nonsupportive results in exploring the relationship between TQM and organizational effectiveness. For example, a survey by McKinsey and Company of U.S. and European firms found that 67 percent of the TQM programs that were more than two years old died for lack of results. Although quality processes and practices were pursued, an inadequate level of payoff occurred in these firms to maintain support for change efforts associated with quality. A Rath and Strong survey of *Fortune* 500 companies also found that only 20 percent reported having achieved their quality objectives; over 40 percent indicated that their quality initiatives were a complete flop. Ernst and Young's study of 584 companies in four industries (autos, banks, computers, and health care) in the United States, Japan, Germany, and Canada found that most firms had not enjoyed success as a result of their TQM practices. Most firms labeled TQM a failure and were actually cutting back their budgets for it. The American Quality Foundation's survey of companies found that most had adopted a "shotgun" approach to quality improvement, as evidenced by more than 945 different quality tactics, tools, and techniques employed, and such unsystematic actions led to failure. Criticism of quality programs has thus begun to escalate, especially in the popular press, and some writers have even described it as an outdated management fad of the 1980s (Jacob, 1993).

Positive Results

Despite this criticism, however, the relationship between quality and several desirable outcomes is relatively well accepted in the popular mind, even though organizational effectiveness per se has been understudied. A frequent criticism of quality as an approach to enhance organizational effectiveness is that quality processes are overemphasized to the exclusion of an analysis of outcomes and effects (e.g., Bowles, 1992; Crosby, 1992; Hammond, 1992; Crawford-Mason, 1992; McKoewn, 1992). This led the U.S. General

Accounting Office (1991) to conduct a study of organizations that had implemented quality processes to a significant extent. The intent was to investigate the relationships between quality processes and desirable outcomes. The 20 firms investigated all were finalists in the Malcolm Baldrige competition in 1988 and 1989. Each reported outcome data from the present back to the time they initially embarked on a path to win the award by implementing quality processes. Table 2-2 summarizes the annual percentage improvement in four categories of desired outcomes often associated with prescribed quality processes.

The major conclusion of the study was that firms that implemented the quality process advocated by the Malcolm Baldrige program experienced continuous improvement in performance indicators and exceeded the industry averages in each of the four outcome categories—employee-related indicators, customer-related indicators, operational results, and financial results.

TABLE 2-2   Results of a General Accounting Office Study of the Relationships Between Quality Processes and Desired Outcomes

Outcome Category Improvement	Reported Annual Percentage
Employee related indicators:	
Employee satisfaction	1.4
Attendance	0.1
Turnover (decrease)	6.0
Safety and health	1.8
Suggestions	16.6
Operating indicators:	
Reliability	11.3
On-time delivery	4.7
Order-processing time	12.0
Errors or defects	10.3
Product lead time	5.8
Inventory turnover	7.2
Costs of quality	9.0
Customer satisfaction indicators:	
Overall customer satisfaction	2.5
Customer complaints (decrease)	11.6
Customer retention	1.0
Financial performance indicators:	
Market share	13.7
Sales per employee	8.6
Return on assets	1.3
Return of sales	0.4

Of course, no causal or even statistical associations were made in this study, so whether successful firms tended to implement quality processes or whether firms that implemented these processes tended to become more successful is not known.

Other studies have focused on the relationships between particular quality dimensions and organizational outcomes.

Customer Satisfaction

Customer satisfaction has been addressed in quite an extensive literature in the field of marketing (Churchill and Surprenant, 1982; Oliver and DeSarbo, 1988; Anderson and Sullivan, 1993). Although empirical evidence is limited, increases in customer satisfaction are generally believed to shift the demand curve upward, reduce marketing costs, increase marketing costs for competitors (satisfied customers are more difficult for competitors to take away), lower transaction costs, reduce customer turnover, increase cross-selling (more products, larger accounts), lower employee turnover, enhance reputation, and reduce failure costs.

Competitiveness

Some claim that quality has a positive association with increased demand (Abbott, 1955) and with inelastic demand (Porter, 1980). Porter claimed that organizations differentiate themselves from their competitors mainly by providing more durable or reliable products, adding desirable features, providing high levels of customer service, and having an extensive dealer network—all aspects of TQM. The Profit Impact of Market Strategies (PIMS) analyses confirm this competitive advantage by showing perceived product quality to be the most powerful predictor of corporate financial success when compared with market share, productivity, low-cost production, diversified product mix, and other common predictors of performance (e.g., Buzzell and Wiersma, 1981).

Productivity

Although a number of quality gurus have been writing extensively since the early 1970s that "quality is free" because high quality eliminates the costs associated with lost customers, rework, excess time, indirect engineering, modified specifications, data collection and analysis, field service, reinspection, and waste (Crosby, 1979; Deming, 1982; Schonenberger, 1982; Imai, 1986; Ferdows and DeMeyer, 1990; Cole, 1993), empirical evidence remains sparse. Ittner (1992) found that nonconformance costs go down simultaneously with reductions in conformance costs, thus enhancing productivity. Various marketing studies (e.g., the PIMS studies— Buzzell and Wiersma, 1981; Philips et al., 1983; Fornell and Johnson, 1993) and field studies in manufacturing (e.g., Garvin, 1988; Ittner, 1992; Khurana, 1994) found evidence that quality processes are associated with higher productivity, which in turn translates into higher firm value (Singhal and Hendricks, 1993). Reynolds (1988) surveyed 69 firms and found that quality circles lead to improved productivity, cost-effectiveness, and employee morale. Ansari (1984) surveyed 150 firms and found that just-in-time practices led to productivity improvements. Griffin (1988) found in 73 firms that productivity initially improved as a result of quality circles but then fell back to previous levels. Krafcik (1989) found that certain "lean production" techniques (all associated with TQM) led to higher productivity. Flynn et al. (1993) studied U.S. and Japanese firms and found seven critical dimensions of quality management to be associated with superior product quality.

Quality Culture and Effectiveness

As we've said, few studies have investigated directly the relationship between organizational effectiveness and quality. One of the few investigations was conducted by Cameron and his colleagues (Cameron et al., 1991; Cameron, 1992, 1995) in which they studied the relationships between quality culture and organizational effectiveness among automotive, electronics, and educational organizations. Quality culture is a particular organizational orientation toward quality—that is, a set of values, principles, and definitions related to quality. A quality culture represents a way of working, a way of thinking, a personal commitment, and a lifestyle that is shared by members of an organization.

This research was guided by investigation of a model of four quality cultures that have developed in recent decades: (1) status quo, (2) error detection, (3) error prevention, and (4) perpetual creative quality. Table 2-3 summarizes the attributes of each of these orientations to quality. Cameron and his colleagues found that organizations that had developed an advanced quality culture (i.e., error prevention and perpetual creative quality) were more successful in their downsizing activities (a finding that we return to later) and had higher levels of organizational effectiveness than organizations with a less advanced quality culture. Organizations with a less advanced quality culture (status quo and error detection) are less successful in downsizing activities and have lower levels of organizational effectiveness.

Khurana's (1994) study of the worldwide picture tube manufacturing industry also confirmed this linkage between dimensions of quality culture and organizational effectiveness. He found that organizations with strong quality cultures performed better than those without them.

TABLE 2-3 A Model of Quality Cultures in Three Stages

Error Detection
Regarding Products
 Avoid mistakes
 Reduce waste, rework, repair
 Detect problems
 Focus on outputs
Regarding Customers
 Avoid annoying customers
 Respond to complaints efficiently and accurately
 Assess satisfaction after the fact
 Focus on needs and requirements
Error Prevention
Regarding Products
 Expect zero defects
 Prevent errors and mistakes
 Hold everyone accountable
 Focus on processes and root causes
Regarding Customers
 Satisfy customers and exceed expectations
 Eliminate problems in advance
 Involve customers in design
 Focus on preferences or nice-to-have attributes
Perpetual Creative Quality
Regarding Products
 Constant improvement and escalating standards
 Concentrate on things gone right
 Emphasize breakthroughs
 Focus on improvement in suppliers, customers, and processes
Regarding Customers
 Expect lifelong loyalty
 Surprise and delight customers
 Anticipate expectations
 Create new preferences

Source: Cameron (1992).

Unanswered Questions

With the dearth of empirical research on quality and the absence of theory regarding how, why, and even whether TQM affects organizational performance, there is little clear understanding about the relationships between quality and organizational effectiveness. Serious questions remain regarding TQM as a strategy for change. Among these questions are:

1. *What is TQM?* Is TQM a change strategy, a culture, a package of management principles, a set of organizational values, a definition of an organization, a constituency's evaluation, or some combination of these

alternatives? When writers use the term, what are they referring to? Is it the ultimate dependent variable or a fad that is likely to fade over time?

2. *What are the key dimensions of TQM?* In light of the variety of models and definitions available, are some dimensions more crucial than others in defining quality? How would one determine a necessary and sufficient list of dimensions? On what basis would one select the core dimensions of TQM?

3. *What are the relationships among the dimensions of TQM?* Assuming that one can identify its core dimensions, what are the relationships among those dimensions? Do they have a temporal ordering, as some models suggest (e.g., should leadership involvement precede the development of certain organizational processes as implied in the Malcolm Baldrige program)? Do some dimensions subsume others?

4. *Are TQM principles universal or are they contingent on other factors?* Thus far, most TQM literature has adopted an ideal type approach. Are there situations in which TQM won't work? What aspects of TQM are situationally dependent? Is a theory of TQM possible?

5. *What is new?* If TQM is in large part a restatement of traditional social science principles, as argued by Kahn (1994), is there anything new here? Have we learned anything by talking about quality as a construct? Why not go back to basic principles of empowerment, System 4 thinking, teamwork, and so on?

6. *What isn't TQM?* Almost every good management practice and prescription has been included in someone's definition of TQM. What does TQM exclude? What are the conceptual boundaries of the construct? Without an understanding of what it is and what it is not, no good theory or stream of research can be developed.

7. *What is the role of timing in TQM?* How much time does it take to implement TQM? Is it a short-term change strategy, a long-term change strategy, both, or neither? What aspects should be addressed first—and last?

8. *What is the relationship between TQM and organizational effectiveness?* With the multidimensional nature of organizational effectiveness and the apparent multidimensional nature of TQM, how are the two constructs related? In what ways are they the same, predictors of one another, substitutes for one another, or independent of one another?

9. *How is TQM measured?* What are the key indicators of successful implementation or successful accomplishment of TQM? Whose perspective is the most legitimate in assessing it (e.g., customers, those involved in the operations of the organization, those leading the organization)? Do different constituencies use different measurement criteria?

10. *What are the policy implications of TQM?* Is it an organizationally specific approach, or could national policies be formulated to elevate output

and customer service levels for an entire nation? What aspects of TQM are or are not legislatable? Does it represent a particular set of values, making it impossible to superimpose on a diverse and eclectic set of industries and organizations?

DOWNSIZING

The second pervasive approach for achieving improvement in organizational effectiveness is downsizing. Like TQM, the term *downsizing* has been used in a variety of ways to describe a variety of activities. In the literature, writers have used the term in referring to phenomena as diverse as personnel layoffs, industry consolidations, mergers and acquisitions, organizational redesign, hiring freezes, and process consolidation.

Although its definition is neither precise nor consensual, organizational downsizing can be thought of as a set of activities, undertaken on the part of the management of an organization, designed to improve organizational efficiency, productivity, or competitiveness—or all three—by reducing the size of the organization. A precise definition seems to matter much more to scholars than to managers, who use an array of terms, such as *compressing, consolidating, contracting, demassing, dismantling, downshifting, rationalizing, reallocating, reassigning, rebalancing, redesigning, resizing, retrenching, redeploying, rightsizing, streamlining, slimming down,* and even *leaning up*.

Key Attributes

Four attributes help to define and separate downsizing from related concepts: (1) downsizing is first and foremost an intentional set of activities (of course, it is clear in the psychological literature that attributing intent is fraught with difficulty; however, intent in this case differentiates actions implemented knowingly and with forethought from those that occur unwittingly, even unknowingly, by management); (2) although downsizing usually involves reductions in personnel, it is not limited solely to them; (3) downsizing is focused on improving the efficiency of the organization; and (4) downsizing affects work processes, for better or worse.

Downsizing is not the same as decline. Organizations can downsize without declining, as when downsizing is used proactively to enhance competitiveness (see Tomasko, 1987; D'Aunno and Sutton, 1987), and they can decline without downsizing. Downsizing may be a response to decline, a reaction to certain missteps or environmental constraints or, in proactive and creative instances, it can be an anticipatory action to improve organizational performance. One should be careful not to confuse cause and effect.

Downsizing is not synonymous with personnel layoffs, as some authors have implied (for example, see Gilmore and Hirschorn, 1983; Brockner,

1988). Whereas layoffs refer to a single tactical, reactive operation used to implement a downsizing strategy, downsizing may be both strategic and proactive, referring to an array of additional options for reducing the workforce other than layoffs.

Because the opposite of downsizing is growth, some writers have assumed that downsizing is synonymous with growth-in-reverse—that is, dynamics that are the opposite of organizational expansion. The stages in growth-in-reverse may involve more centralization, less specialization, and less boundary spanning (see Behn, 1980; Gilmore and Hirschorn, 1983; Krantz, 1985). However, neither the stages nor these organizational outcomes are necessarily associated with downsizing. The intentional nature of downsizing means that an organization may get smaller in order to decentralize, to specialize, or to become more externally connected through boundary-spanning activities—the same outcomes that are associated with growth. In diversified corporations, a form of downsizing that was pervasive in the 1980s consisted of selling off their separate divisions in order to increase efficiency and profits.

In summary, downsizing should be investigated separately from other related concepts that are associated in the literature with the dynamics of decline, ineffectiveness, layoffs, and shrinkage in organizations. Like TQM, its unique dynamics remain underdeveloped theoretically at least in part because of the lack of empirical investigations of the relationship of downsizing to organizational effectiveness.

Downsizing and Effectiveness

Ironically, downsizing remains among the most pervasive strategies for organizational change in the 1990s, despite the dearth of evidence of its success. From the research produced thus far, downsizing as a strategy for improvement has proven to be, by and large, a failure. It is true that downsizing announcements have usually led to positive reactions on Wall Street, because of the possibility of cost savings, reduced expenses, and increased competitiveness. But the pattern of evidence described below is one of negative results far outweighing positive ones.

Organizational Results

A survey of corporate executives in six industrialized countries found that less than half had achieved their cost-cutting goals, and even fewer met operating objectives, such as improved productivity (Swoboda, 1995). Another survey found that 74 percent of senior managers in downsized companies said that morale, trust, and productivity suffered after downsizing, and half of the 1,468 firms in another survey indicated that productivity deteriorated after downsizing (Henkoff, 1990; Bennett, 1991). A majority of organizations that downsized in a fourth survey failed to achieve desired results, only 9 percent reporting an improvement in quality.

In a review of the scholarly literature on the effects of layoffs, turnover, and job rotation policies, Cole (1993) identified a variety of organizational problems associated with job loss resulting from downsizing: loss of personal relationships between employees and customers; destruction of employee and customer trust and loyalty; disruption of smooth, predictable routines in the firm; increases in formalization (rules), standardization, and rigidity; loss of cross-unit and cross-level knowledge resulting from longevity and from interpersonal interactions over time; loss of knowledge of how to respond to nonroutine challenges faced by the firm; less documentation and therefore less sharing of information about changes; loss of employee productivity; and loss of a common organizational culture.

Another set of negative outcomes was uncovered in a study of more than 200 organizations (Cameron et al., 1987, 1993; Cameron, 1995). Effects of downsizing included: increased centralization of decision making (less participation); the adoption of a short-term, crisis mentality; loss of innovativeness; increased resistance to change; decreasing employee morale, commitment, and loyalty; the escalation of politicized special interest groups and political infighting; risk aversion and conservatism in decision making; loss of trust among customers and employees; increasing interpersonal conflict; restricted communication flows and less information sharing; lack of teamwork; and loss of accessible, forward-thinking, aggressive leaders.

McKinley (1992) found that downsizing actually increased costs, bureaucracy, and redundancy, particularly when it was accomplished through layoffs. Other studies have reported net decreases in return on equity, net sales, and return on assets with downsizing, suggesting that it did not help reverse a performance decline in organizations that were facing one, and it may have actually caused such a decline to occur (McKinley et al., 1994). In other words, downsizing often appears to have a negative effect on organizational costs, even though reducing those costs is the single most common reason for implementing it.

Individual Results

The effects of downsizing on individuals have been no less disconcerting. A review of the research on individual outcomes by Kozlowski et al. (1993) has shown that, in a variety of types of organizations and with a variety of types of employees, downsizing has produced negative rather than positive results. In these studies, downsizing is used interchangeably with job loss. For example, financial loss, decreased job stability, and deterioration in working conditions have been found to be associated with downsizing (Leana and Ivancevich, 1987; Podgursky and Swain, 1987; Buss and Redburn, 1987; Burke, 1986). Personal well-being is negatively affected in terms of physical symptoms of strain (e.g., headaches, stomach problems, elevated blood pressure, increases in drinking and smoking) (Burke, 1984; Kessler et al., 1987; Kasl and Cobb, 1979, 1980; Linn et al., 1985) as well as negative psychological symptoms (e.g., anxiety, depression, insomnia, feelings of helplessness, cognitive difficulties) (Dooley and Catalano, 1988; Fineman, 1983; Iversen and Sabroe, 1988; Liem and Liem, 1988; Hamilton et al., 1990; Kinicki, 1989; Shamir, 1986; Bolton and Oatley, 1987; Feather, 1989; Haworth et al., 1990).

An adverse impact has also been found on individual attitudes such as loss of self-esteem, loss of self-mastery, dissatisfaction with self, pessimism, powerlessness, and rigidity (Stokes and Cochrane, 1984; Pearlin et al., 1981; Rowley and Feather, 1987; Burke, 1984; Noble, 1987; Pliner, 1990). Marriage and family deterioration have been noted among individuals affected by downsizing, notably with decreases in family cohesion, increases in conflict, decline in spouse's psychological well-being, increases in arguments, deteriorating family climate, and a seven-fold increase in divorce and separation (Liem and Liem, 1988; Wilhelm and Ridley, 1988). Even among those whose jobs are preserved during a downsizing, researchers have found adverse effects. Reduced trust and loyalty to the organization (Buch and Aldrich, 1991), role conflict, role ambiguity, role overload, and a decrease in positive feedback (Tombaugh and White, 1990), decreased morale (Sutton et al., 1985), and feelings of guilt (Brockner, 1988) are all negative outcomes of downsizing among individuals who remain in the organization.

Reasons for Negative Results

According to Kozlowski et al. (1993), the fact that negative outcomes seem to appear in the literature more frequently than positive ones is due to poor implementation and an absence of supporting interventions, such as outplacement, counseling, and training. Their review of the literature found that when firms provided support in the form of buyout packages, outplacement services, counseling, retraining, and other similar benefits to employees affected by downsizing, the impact was positive for selected individual outcomes. A recent National Research Council report (Broderick, 1996) focuses on the results that organizations want from investments in outplacement services and the activities and practices most likely to achieve them.

For example, Greenhalgh (1983), Leana and Feldman (1989), and Schweiger and DeNisi (1991) found that communicating openly about downsizing strategies, procedures, and rationale was associated with reduced stress, increased commitment, and improved productivity. Providing adequate outplacement service, training, compensation, relocation assistance, clerical support, and extended benefits also were found to have positive relationships to employee loyalty, commitment, and productivity (Feldman and Leana, 1995). Brockner et al. (1987) found that, when individuals were adequately informed, adequately compensated, treated fairly, and perceived that others were treated fairly, the negative effects of downsizing on survivors (guilt, loss of loyalty, distrust) did not occur.

Davy et al. (1991) found that perceived fairness in downsizing implementation was positively related to increased job satisfaction and organizational commitment, which, in turn, led to higher levels of effectiveness. In other words, at the individual level of analysis, the means by which downsizing was implemented—i.e., the supportive activities that supplement downsizing—explains why downsizing is sometimes positive and sometimes negative in its effects. Poorly implemented or unsupported downsizing is negatively associated with desirable outcomes, whereas supportive implementation is associated with positive outcomes.

This is the same conclusion reached by Cameron et al. (1991, 1993) in their studies of the effects of downsizing at the organizational level of analysis. They also argued that the way downsizing is implemented is more important that the fact that downsizing is implemented in affecting various dimensions of organizational effectiveness.

In sum, although downsizing is ubiquitous in the business world today, many more negative than positive associations have been reported between downsizing and organizational effectiveness. This negative association, however, seems to be due more to the manner in which downsizing is implemented than by the fact that organizations have engaged in it.

Unanswered Questions

Although case studies abound, and popular accounts of downsizing among companies are frequent, empirical research on the effects of downsizing on organization-level performance is still rare in the organizational studies literature. Much more research has been accomplished on the individual level of analysis than on the organizational level. Studies of the impacts of job loss, plant closings, and unemployment on individual attitudes, health, and behavior, in particular, have appeared quite frequently in the literature (see Price, 1990; Kozlowski et al., 1993). Systematic investigations of linkages between downsizing and organizational effectiveness, however, are hard to find. Much of the organizational literature is either purely descriptive or prescriptive in nature, and many questions about what is really going on when downsizing occurs remain unanswered:

1. *What is and what is not downsizing?* Because many different kinds

of actions can be undertaken to reduce expenses, improve efficiency, and eliminate waste, what are the conceptual boundaries of downsizing? To build theories of downsizing, it is critical that the definitional boundaries of the construct be clear.

2. *Does a hierarchy of downsizing strategies exist?* Downsizing is approached in different ways by different organizations, in that some take a long time to plan and implement downsizing and others announce and implement downsizing very quickly. When conducting downsizing, is there a temporal priority to particular strategies? Are some strategies or some actions more crucial than others? What are the prerequisites?

3. *What aspects of downsizing are the most powerful predictors of organizational effectiveness?* Do certain features of downsizing (e.g., time frame, communication patterns, involvement, scope) impact organizational effectiveness more than others? Are different dimensions of organizational effectiveness (e.g., financial performance, morale and cohesiveness, productivity, quality) influenced differently by downsizing?

4. *What aspects of organizations change after downsizing?* Because the psychological contract between the organization and its employees is often broken when downsizing occurs, does a different set of constraints and requirements arise in organizations after downsizing? Are effective organizations managed differently after downsizing compared with those that have not downsized? What are the crucial dynamics in downsized organizations that influence performance?

5. *What is the role of environmental conditions on the effectiveness of downsizing?* Downsizing can be proactive or reactive. In general, reactive downsizing occurs as a result of the organization's facing threatening financial conditions. Does downsizing have a different relationship to organizational effectiveness when the external environment is severely constrained? What features of the organization's external conditions are most important in determining an effective implementation strategy? How does proactive downsizing differ from reactive downsizing?

6. *What kinds of organizational changes must accompany downsizing to ensure that it enhances organizational effectiveness?* Other than simply cutting the head count, eliminating positions or hierarchical levels, and trying to become more cost-conscious, are other organizational changes required for downsizing to positively affect organizational performance? Does the act of downsizing require that special attention be paid to other aspects of the organization?

7. *What is the relationship between downsizing and long-term effectiveness?* Some discussion has occurred about the impact of downsizing on short-term and long-term costs. Trade-offs have been proposed, such that cutting the budget in the short run may help create long-term costs (e.g., replacing workers). How long does it take for downsizing to have an im-

pact on organizational effectiveness? Can short-term and long-term costs be reduced simultaneously? What is the role of time frame in drawing conclusions about the relationship between downsizing and effectiveness?

8. *What policy implications associated with organizational downsizing are most important?* For example, what impact does downsizing have on the overall gross domestic product in a nation? What is the implication of the elimination of several million jobs in a decade? Does downsizing help stimulate entrepreneurship and new business formation in the macro economy, or does it slow down innovation and create pockets of cynicism and deep discouragement?

REENGINEERING

The third strategy for enhancing organizational effectiveness we consider is reengineering. Reengineering as a strategy for change is more recently developed than either TQM or downsizing, and much less research has been conducted on its association with organizational effectiveness. In fact, the term *reengineering* was not used before 1990 and did not generally appear in the popular media until about 1993.

"Business process redesign," an activity similar to reengineering, has been discussed in the literature relating to applications of information technology (Davenport and Short, 1990), but little attention was paid to reengineering by organizational scholars. The redesign of work processes and work layout, also related to reengineering, has also been studied in industrial engineering since Frederick W. Taylor (1911), and work design has received attention from industrial psychologists for several decades (Hackman and Lawler, 1971).

Reengineering as applied to modern organizations, however, is somewhat different from those earlier movements (Teng et al., 1994). The initiators of the modern reengineering movement, Hammer and Champy (1993:32), defined reengineering as "the fundamental rethinking and radical redesign of business processes to achieve dramatic improvements in critical, contemporary measures of performance, such as cost, quality, service, and speed."

Reeingineering is not incremental change or small alteration. It is an activity that emphasizes reinventing, or radically changing, the processes in the organization that are directly connected to producing an output. For example, reengineering is illustrated by a project at IBM in which the number of steps required to receive a customer's order and produce a sales agreement was reduced from a seven-day, six-step process to a four-hour, two-step process. It is illustrated by a project at Ford Motor Company in which the number of accounts payable employees was reduced from 500 to 125 by reconfiguring the way the people do their work. Taco Bell redesigned the food preparation process and restaurant layout so that the ratio of kitchen area to customer eating area was reversed from 70 percent kitchen space to 70 percent customer space, thereby cutting costs and speeding up service.

Key Attributes

Much of the writing about reengineering has occurred in the information technology literature because reengineering often involves the application of computers or information technology to formerly manual or nonautomated work processes. Reengineering is not the same as automation, however, since it is possible to automate a process without changing or redesigning it. Automation provides a more efficient way to do something; reengineering involves rethinking how the process unfolds.

Reengineering is also not the same as restructuring. At the organizational level of analysis, restructuring involves changing the number of layers, the hierarchical arrangements of units, or the reporting relationships of functions. Traditionally, organizational structures have been built around either products or functions (and sometimes geography). Reengineering focuses instead on the work processes or work flows, regardless of the hierarchical level, the functional unit, or the product involved. Restructuring asks how various components should be arranged, whether the components should be present in the first place and, if so, then how they should be arranged to enhance a process flow.

Reengineering often involves the redesign of work, but it is not the same phenomenon that the traditional work design literature addresses. Writers on work design focus on the attributes of tasks and the structure of work. For example, Hackman and Oldham (1980) identified core task or job dimensions that must be present in order for work to be motivating. Designing work so as to include those attributes was found to lead to desirable organizational outcomes (e.g., low absenteeism and turnover, high productivity). Reengineering focuses on the flows or interrelationships among tasks more than on the design of the specific tasks themselves, as well as the interrelationships among a stream of connected tasks. Work design addresses the attributes of each individual task.

Although downsizing and reengineering are sometimes used synonymously or interchangeably, they are fundamentally distinct. Most reengineering projects have resulted in identifying excess capacity or resources that are subsequently eliminated through downsizing. Eliminating steps and the need for workers, as in the IBM and Ford examples above, led the organizations to downsize. Moreover, one of the main downsizing strategies is labeled organizational redesign, and it sometimes involves some reengineering activity. However, most downsizing activity is designed fundamentally to reduce what exists in the organization, whereas reengineering activity is designed fundamentally to reconfigure what exists by starting over.

In general, reengineering is designed to dramatically change an organization's trajectory. Most organizations engage in reengineering either because they are threatened with decline or extinction or because they have the foresight and slack resources to try something entirely different from what they have been doing before. That is the intent of reengineering: begin again and design new processes from scratch. Practically speaking, reengineering relies heavily on the application of information technology to formerly slow, cumbersome processes, and it is especially intended to focus on the desired results of a process rather than the functional or unit needs (Dixon et al., 1994).

Reengineering and Effectiveness

Very little systematic research has been published on reengineering and almost none on its relationship to organizational effectiveness. By far the bulk of writing on reengineering consists of case study descriptions of projects or prescriptive articles describing how to do it. Hammer and Champy (1993), for example, described the successful reengineering activities of several firms, such as Hallmark, which now designs cards in a new way; Capital Holding's DRG business, which changed from a mass market to a customer-focused business; and Bell Atlantic, which reengineered its long-distance carrier access services. These case study descriptions are typical of the success stories that are easily found in the popular press. Reengineering is usually claimed to have produced dramatic improvements in various performance indicators in these descriptions.

Dixon et al. (1994) conducted one of the few investigations of multiple reengineering projects and the factors associated with their success. They surveyed 23 reengineering cases to identify the attributes associated with successful reengineering efforts. They found that successful reengineering was characterized by a clear vision of the future and specific goals for change, the use of information technology, top management involvement and commitment, clear milestones and measurements, and the training of participants in process analysis and teamwork. These authors did not systematically assess the impact of reengineering on organizational effectiveness, but instead merely implied that each was a successful project. They discovered that the single characteristic differentiating reengineering from other kinds of efforts at organizational change was a modification of organizational direction (p. 97):

> In every case, reengineering projects involved "changing direction." Major improvement was sought, but, more important, the direction of the goal had changed. For example, flexibility replaced cost reduction, time-to-

market superseded product performance, or cost reduction replaced process performance as the objective considered to be most important. In other words, the set of organizational priorities had changed.

The fact that reengineering implies an alteration of direction helps explain why its success in organizations may not be predicted to be very high. Most organizations have a great deal of inertia—for reasons ranging from the expectations of the external environment, the reward system, and the organizational memory to individuals' fear of the unknown, lack of ideas for new alternatives, and distrust among organization members. A complete change of organizational direction is likely to create a great deal of resistance, not to mention stumbles along the way. Continuous improvement (Imai, 1986) or small wins (Weick, 1984) that come from ongoing incremental change are more likely to meet with success, even in the face of crisis or revolutionary change (Weick, 1993). This may explain why, other than a few highly successful and highly touted reengineering projects, the success rate of reengineering projects would not seem to be high (for examples, see Hammer, 1990; Davenport and Short, 1990; Hall et al., 1993).

This prediction is supported by a recent survey of reengineering projects conducted by the consulting firm that initiated reengineering as a change process (CSC Index, 1994). That study polled 497 companies in the United States and another 1,245 companies in Europe and found that 69 percent of firms in the United States and 75 percent of firms in Europe have engaged in at least one reengineering project. They reported that 85 percent of those firms found little or no gain from their effort. Less than half achieved any change in market share, one of the primary goals. The authors conclude that reengineering is not enough to achieve desirable change. It must be integrated with other efforts at change specified by the corporation's overall strategy.

Unanswered Questions

The lack of empirical results on reengineering thus far suggests that it may turn out to be just a management fad. Management fads follow a predictable pattern in which a new term is introduced for an apparently new activity. Promises of dramatic improvement in organizational effectiveness are made in the business press on the basis of a few visible case studies. The activity is widely applied by organizations hoping for the same dramatic success. Dramatic improvements are not forthcoming, and easy solutions to organizational problems do not occur. By the time systematic research can be produced in which the conceptual boundaries are specified (what it is and is not), the dimensions of the term are identified, relationships to effectiveness are investigated, and contingencies are identified relating to when it is and is not associated with desirable performance factors, a new term is introduced and the first one is seen as outdated. Before it is clear if and under what circumstances the concept is useful, it is abandoned. Reengineering may be well along in that process. Without systematic empirical research, it risks being cast aside as one more management fad.

Numerous questions are unanswered regarding reengineering as a strategy for improving organizational effectiveness:

1. *What are the key dimensions of reengineering?* What is and what is not reengineering? How does it differ in practice and in theory from other major types of change efforts, such as transformational change or restructuring? What are the key activities that must be included in any reengineering effort?

2. *What is the relationship between reengineering and TQM?* Since TQM advocates a focus on process, constant improvement, increasing efficiency and speed, is reengineering merely one technique in a broader array of approaches to change called TQM? What is similar and what is different about what TQM advocates and what reengineering advocates? Do research findings on TQM apply to reengineering?

3. *Is reengineering merely a disguised, more palatable form of downsizing?* Since an important outcome of reengineering is shedding waste, redundancy, and obstacles that increase cost and time, is it simply one of the alternative approaches to be used in the organizational redesign strategy in downsizing? Is there ever a time when effective downsizing does not include some form of reengineering (i.e., systemic downsizing strategies)? Do research findings on downsizing apply to reengineering?

4. *Under what conditions is reengineering appropriate?* What are the attributes or preconditions in the organization that make it ready to successfully reengineer a process? What are the environmental constraints that must be accounted for in successful reengineering?

5. *What is the role of information technology in reengineering?* Can reengineering occur without the application of information technology? Is dramatic improvement in process speed and efficiency tied inextricably to the application of information technology? Does the research on automation and technology application apply to reengineering?

6. *What is the relationship between reengineering and various dimensions of organizational effectiveness?* Is reengineering applicable only to outcomes such as speed and cost? What other latent outcomes are associated with reengineering? What is the impact, for example, on the human resource system, customer satisfaction, and organizational culture?

7. *What is the relationship between reengineering and time?* For example, is reengineering sustainable? Is it a one-time event that reaches a conclusion? How long does it take to reengineer a complex process so that

it functions smoothly in a new way? What are the short-term and the long-term impacts?

8. *Are there certain stages that must be followed to successfully reengineer?* Does a predictable life cycle exist in reengineering projects? Do certain aspects of reengineering take temporal precedence over others?

9. *What must be measured to ascertain the success of reengineering?* Aside from measures of outcomes such as profitability, response time, and productivity, do new measures of process need to be developed? How could one tell if the process of reengineering was unfolding successfully and on schedule? How do process measures relate to outcome or input measures?

10. *What are the policy implications of reengineering?* Is it possible to generalize the reengineering process across industries and sectors? For example, could policies be established that prescribe reengineering as a process for cost containment? Is reengineering antithetical to policy making since reengineering, by definition, strives to eliminate buffers and entrenched procedures in organizations, whereas policy making is often focused on reinforcing buffers and entrenched procedures?

CONCLUSIONS

Three approaches to change have emerged in the past two decades as the most frequently applied strategies for trying to improve organizational effectiveness. This chapter has focused on trying to define each underlying construct and identify the relevant attributes of each. Indeed, in order to begin to build a theoretical and empirical research base, it must be clear what each of the three change approaches includes and excludes. For each technique, we have reviewed key studies of its relationship to organizational effectiveness.

We have focused primarily on the relationship between these three approaches and their individual and organizational consequences and effects. The macro-economic, sociopolitical, and international policy implications of the three strategies have not been addressed. For example, issues such as the impact of corporate downsizing on national unemployment trends, the relationship between the adoption of TQM and national competitiveness in the semiconductor industry, and the implications of reengineering for federal deficit reduction have been ignored. Such topics are beyond the scope of this book.

We make the following observations about the effectiveness of each of these three approaches:

1. *All three approaches to change have a number of elements in common.* Six such elements seem to link TQM, downsizing, and reengineering

together: (a) Each of these three approaches seeks to change core parts of the organization; each aims at transformational change. (b) Each approach entails a focus on teamwork and involvement. (c) Each focuses on the improvement and rationalization of processes. (d) Each advocates the involvement and support of top managers as key elements in success. (e) Each advocates that it become a way of life in the organization—continuous quality improvement, continuous downsizing and cost containment, and continuous reengineering. (f) Each approach also relies on a clear vision of the future, a tool to lead to a new, better, more effective condition rather than to merely avoid a negative or uncomfortable situation. Each should be opportunity-driven rather than crisis-driven.

2. *Each approach to change is also designed to accomplish something different.* At the organizational level of analysis, writers argue that downsizing helps the organization become smaller (fewer resources utilized) and more efficient (doing things right). Reengineering is seen to help the organization become better (improves old processes) and more effective (doing the right things). TQM writers argue for helping the organization achieve perfection (zero defects) and a high degree of excellence (surprising and delighting customers).

The three strategies range from an emphasis on smaller (downsizing) to an emphasis on better (reengineering) to an emphasis on being perfect (TQM). Similarly, moving from efficiency (downsizing) to effectiveness (reengineering) to excellence (TQM) also can be seen as a hierarchical progression.

3. *None of these three change approaches appears to have a consistently positive relationship with organizational effectiveness, although there is some limited evidence that positive results can be achieved under some circumstances.* On one hand, an abundance of anecdotal evidence has been published in the popular press touting dramatic successes, and a large majority of organizations have engaged in each of these three change efforts. On the other hand, the empirical evidence to indicate the effectiveness of any of these approaches to change is limited. Also, recent survey data suggest that a large number of the organizations that implement these approaches have not achieved the hoped-for advantages. In each case, the way in which the approach was implemented is more important than the fact that it was implemented.

4. *The reasons for wide-scale failure of these approaches remain unclear.* Although there is limited evidence that each of these three approaches has positive associations with effectiveness, so many negative effects have been reported that it is possible that dynamics other than poor implementation are also operating. Without systematic investigations, it is not clear what leads to a failure to achieve improvement or (in the case of downsizing) what leads to actual deterioration in organizational performance. Although

the principles and processes of TQM, downsizing, and reengineering are reminiscent merely of commonly prescribed "good" management practice, a majority of organizations that embark on these change efforts do not accomplish their objectives.

One can speculate that lack of success may occur because each of these approaches to change strikes at a very deeply rooted, core part of the organization. Certain aspects of organizations are difficult to change; indeed, their very inertia may contribute in some ways to their effectiveness. In the case of reengineering, an attempt to radically change the processes and direction of the organization may create enough discomfort and resistance that most efforts to switch directions fail. In the case of downsizing, the fear, distrust, uncertainty, and potential for personal harm may mitigate against *any* organizational downsizing strategy. In the case of TQM, changing the culture of an organization so that it is based on a new set of principles, regardless of how desirable they may be, may represent an affront to fundamental elements in an organization and therefore may be resisted. It is not yet clear why the failure rate is so high when organizations implement these three approaches to change, yet it is not hard to see that the fundamental change that each aspires to achieve is not easily attained.

5. *Key questions remain unaddressed by research regarding each of these approaches to organizational change.* Among the most important questions are those relating to definitions and dimensions, contingency conditions, time frame, implementation strategy, measurement criteria, and policy implications.

It is evident that three highly popular and widely applied approaches to organizational change have captured managers' attention. Each promises dramatic improvements, increased effectiveness, and a change in the way of life in organizations. Each risks the threat of being relegated to the management fad ragbag, however, because none has been rigorously studied in systematic, empirical ways, especially regarding its impact on organizational effectiveness. Spotty evidence of impact on effectiveness exists, but evidence also exists that each is useless if not harmful. These conditions combine to produce an area that is ripe for important scholarly research.

3

Organizational Culture

We begin our discussion of organizational culture with a case study from the aerospace industry (Snyder, 1988):

Plant 10 of Lockheed-California's L-1011 program was considered an albatross by Lockheed's top management. In 1979, when Dan Daniels was named vice president of manufacturing and given direct responsibility for the plant, he faced a myriad of performance problems in Plant 10, including production behind schedule, production costs significantly over budget, quality problems, a climate of fear that suppressed information needed to correct problems, and open hostility between departments. Fortunately, from his experiences over the years, Daniels had developed a strong managerial philosophy that was very different from the autocratic and demeaning style of management for which Plant 10 had been known.

From his first week there, Daniels embarked on actions of cultural significance. He began by sending a memo to all employees expressing his philosophy. Realizing they would read more into what he did than what he said, he then promoted his philosophy by walking around and talking to people throughout the plant. At first they were reluctant to talk, but Daniels was persistent and open. He worked with people to solve problems and urged his managers to do the same. He made it clear to his managers that employees were to be treated considerately and fired one punitive manager who was unable or unwilling to change his style. Another manger who would not provide accurate information was replaced. To build team spirit, managers were issued special blue flight jackets that they wore with pride.

In these and other ways, Daniels consistently put his philosophy into action. By 1981, two years later, the entire plant was on schedule and under budget. Morale had also greatly improved. Daniels had succeeded in drastically changing the plant's culture and, in the process, had achieved impressive gains in performance.

Organizations have always had cultures, and some managers have probably always been astute enough to figure out how to manage them, as this case illustrates. Systematic research on the cultures of work organizations and how they might be managed to enhance performance and productivity, however, was not pursued with any frequency until the 1980s. A number of popular management books published at that time called attention to cultural issues in the management of organizations (Ouchi, 1981; Pascale and Athos, 1981; Peters and Waterman, 1982; Deal and Kennedy, 1982). The general theme of these books was that managers can shape the cultures of the organizations they manage in ways that enhance performance and productivity. Each organization, it was suggested, could develop a distinctive culture with the enlightened guidance of management. The appearance of these volumes and the competitive threat posed by Japanese organizations that was evident at that time awakened substantial interest in the cultures of work organizations within the management community. Another example (Wilmer et al., 1994) comes from the automobile industry:

> In 1984, when GM and Toyota formed the NUMMI joint venture, they undertook a dramatic cultural transformation of what had been one of the worst GM plants in the U.S. Union-management conflict had raged for 20 years resulting in strikes, absenteeism, and low productivity and quality. The original intent was simply to adopt and learn Toyota's highly successful production system. But because the Japanese production system depended on positive relations between management and labor, many Japanese management principles and practices were also adopted and gradually modified to fit the American work force. These changes gave rise to a new culture that fostered trust, mutual respect, and the recognition of the interdependencies between management and labor and between different parts of the plant. Employees and management ate together in a communal cafeteria; there were no reserved parking places; offices were open. Work charts, attendance boards, and defect records hung on the wall in work team areas. Consensual decision making became the norm. By the late 1980s, the Japanese had scaled back their presence at the plant, but the original U.S. management team remained almost intact. NUMMI continued to be both efficient and to have high quality, producing the same number of cars as GM did in the same plant in the past with much higher quality and half the work force. In May of 1994 its Geo Prizm won the highest quality score ever attained by a U.S.-made vehicle.

From these and other cases, it became clear that cultural factors play an important role in organizational performance, but there was a dearth of systematic knowledge on which to base interventions into organizational cultures. Academic researchers found the popular treatments of culture too simplistic to match the known complexities of organizational life. Before the popular books appeared, research on organizational cultures was sparse. After their appearance, the research literature grew rapidly, but researchers have thus far failed to reach consensus on either theoretical or methodological issues. The field of organizational culture research is still at a very early stage of development.

Because every definition of culture involves sets of ideas that cannot be directly observed, and because these ideas and related behaviors are theorized to be interconnected and likely to form unique patterns within any given organization over time, empirical study of them is extremely difficult. Established quantitative methods using questionnaires, archival data, and laboratory observations have severe limitations, primarily because they require researchers to decide in advance what a culture is like in order to measure it, and they usually fail to capture the continuity and all of the context in which the studied phenomena occur. Qualitative methods adapted from anthropology, sociology, and other fields require intensive observations over substantial time periods and thus limit how many organizations can be studied by any group of researchers.

As a result, theoretical discussions and debates about organizational cultures far outnumber empirical studies, and empirical results do not cumulate well. Any discussion of what is known about organizational cultures must depend heavily on theory to fill in the gaps and connect empirical results from one study to another. In this chapter, we distinguish empirical results from theory and conventional wisdom by the use of such terms as "___ *found* . . ." and "*as* ___ *showed* . . . ."

Because of the paucity and scattered nature of the empirical findings on organizational cultures, we do not know for certain exactly how the cultures of the Lockheed L-1011 program and of NUMMI affected employee performance. The current state of knowledge, however, is sufficient to be able to specify likely pathways through which cultures affect individual and collective work performance and to identify levers that can be used by managers and others to enhance such performance. But first we address what culture is, what it does for people, how it arises, and where it is found.

CULTURE AS A CONSTRUCT

Although the research literature contains many different conceptualizations of culture, researchers agree reasonably well on what culture is, what it does, and how it arises. Most basic is that culture is a collective phenomenon. People who belong to the same culture think and behave similarly in key respects. Most researchers agree that organizational cultures have both ideational and observable aspects (Kopelman et al., 1990:283). In terms of the two examples given above, the new management principles people subscribed to and what they actually did differently together constituted the changed cultures of the Lockheed plant and of NUMMI. Two influential treatments of culture present these two elements of culture—ideas and actions—in somewhat different terms.

Schein (1992) portrays culture as existing at three levels of awareness. The most apparent are artifacts, which are visible organizational structures and processes. Somewhat less evident are espoused values, which are the strategies, goals, and philosophies expressed by managers and other members of the organizational culture. Least evident are what he calls the basic underlying assumptions, which are unconscious and taken-for-granted beliefs, perceptions, thoughts, and feelings. He sees the latter as the "ultimate source of values and action" (1992:17). Other writers have applied the metaphor of layers to Schein's basic conceptualization, portraying culture as consisting of successive encompassing layers, like those of an onion (Ott, 1989; Rousseau, 1990; Hunt, 1991). The outer layer is composed of the observable aspects of culture, whereas the two inner layers are ideational.

Trice and Beyer (1993) describe these two aspects of cultures as substance and forms. The substance of cultures consists of shared, emotionally charged belief systems that they call ideologies. By ideologies they mean "shared, interrelated sets of beliefs about how things work; values that indicate what's worth having or doing; and norms that tell people how they should behave" (p. 33). Although they agree with Schein and others that cultural substance is often taken for granted and tacit, they suggest that certain circumstances or informed efforts can bring cultural substance to awareness. They define cultural forms as the observable entities, including actions, through which members of a culture express, affirm, and communicate the substance of their culture to one another. Team meetings, the communal cafeteria, posted defect records, and consensual decision making are examples of cultural forms that symbolically communicated and affirmed new beliefs and values at the NUMMI plant.

What cultures do for human societies is manage collective uncertainties and create social order, continuity, collective identity, and commitment (Trice and Beyer, 1993). On the down side, they also encourage ethnocentrism, we-versus-them thinking (Druckman, 1994). Of course, cultures are neither monolithic nor simple, but rather have underlying dualities. Some of their consequences are practical, others are expressive; some are obvious, others are hidden; some are positive for the cultural entity; others are negative. To illustrate just the latter duality, the cultures of organizations may enhance performance in relatively stable times but prove to be an impediment to needed change when environments become unstable.

Another important conceptual issue concerns the origins of culture. Schein sees culture as the result of a complex learning process that occurs among groups of people. Their shared learning addresses two major problems: (1) survival, growth, and adaptation in the environment and (2) internal integration that permits a group to function and adapt (Schein, 1992). Because human beings have the capacity to abstract and be self-conscious, this learning can occur at both a behavioral and an abstract internal level. Culture formation then occurs as people strive toward stability, consistency, and meaning.

An early analysis of ways of studying culture pointed out that it can be viewed either as a property of organizations—something the organization *has*—or as something the organization *is* (Smircich, 1983). Most popular treatments of culture describe it as just another variable that characterizes the organization—in effect, as something that the organization has. Scholarly treatments of culture, however, vary considerably. Studies that use quantitative methods usually treat culture as a variable that can be measured much like other properties of organizations (Denison, 1990; Schneider, 1990; Hofstede et al., 1990). Studies that use qualitative methods, particularly those in the ethnographic tradition, are more likely to treat cultures as something the organization is (Rohlen, 1974; Barley, 1983, 1986; Van Maanen, 1973, 1975; Trice and Sonnenstuhl, 1988; Kunda, 1991; Browning et al., 1995). Many of these studies seek to describe cultures and their contexts in rich detail and from their members' point of view and to develop grounded theory—that is, theories derived from a rigorous analysis of qualitative data systematically generated from observations, interviews, and relevant documents. Such theory helps to explain what was observed in the setting and contributes to general theory by abstracting those elements and relationships from the situation that appear to have the most explanatory power for possible future study in other settings.

Despite differences in approach, most organizational researchers agree on six aspects of organizational culture:

1. Cultures are a property of groups of people and not individuals.
2. Cultures engage the emotions as well as the intellect.
3. Cultures are based on shared experiences and thus on the histories of groups of people; to develop a culture takes time.
4. Cultures are infused with symbols and symbolism.
5. Cultures continually change because circumstances force people to change.
6. Cultures are inherently fuzzy in that they incorporate contradictions, paradoxes, ambiguities, and confusion.

The multiplicity of cultures to which organization members belong greatly complicates the analysis of how cultures affect work performance. Although the presence of multiple cultures in organizations is generally recognized, most empirical studies and theories of organizational culture have tended to focus on one level of culture at a time. Researchers have focused on national cultures (Williams, 1970; Hofstede, 1980; Bellah et al., 1985), industry-wide cultures (Abrahamson and Fombrun, 1994; Browning et al., 1995), occupational cultures (Van Maanen, 1973, 1975; Barley, 1983, 1986; Trice and Sonnenstuhl, 1988; Trice, 1993), managerial cultures in general (Bendix, 1956; Sutton et al., 1956; Chatov, 1973), organizational cultures (Rohlen, 1974; Biggart, 1977; Denison, 1990; Kunda, 1991; Martin et al., 1985), and work group cultures (Roy, 1960; Zald and Berger, 1978; Brown, 1983). The most likely reason for this limitation of focus is methodological. Studying even one level of culture well is difficult and time-consuming. Studies sometimes incorporate some treatment of adjoining levels of culture, either by design or because they emerge as important during the course of the study, but these inclusions are neither systematic nor similar enough to make the separate effects of different levels of culture evident.

Because this chapter focuses primarily on the organizational level of analysis, the term *culture* is used to refer to the cultures of whole organizations and the term *subcultures* is used to refer to any other cultures existing at lower levels of analysis within organizations. Although few studies have tried to look at more than one type of culture at a time, all of the cultures to which organization members belong have the potential to affect their work performance. The limits of empirical evidence to date make us dependent on theory to suggest which levels of culture might matter most for the performance of employees and organizations and to specify how cultures affect that performance. Before discussing the little that is known about culture and performance, we examine some of the problems involved in evaluating effects.

DIFFICULTIES IN EVALUATING EFFECTS

Documenting an empirical link between organizational culture and effectiveness is fraught with difficulty (Siehl and Martin, 1990). For example, determining the relationship between culture and performance requires researchers to control for and thus measure other factors likely to affect performance. A later section on theoretical linkages between culture and performance specifies some of these, but it does not exhaust the possibilities. One reason identifying such mediating factors is difficult is because it is not clear what is *not* affected by culture. Also, unless studies of culture are longitudinal and long term, the direction of causality associating culture and effectiveness is ambiguous because performance may have significant effects on culture as well as vice versa. Separating out these reciprocal effects is extremely difficult.

Similarly, measuring performance itself is difficult because effectiveness is multidimensional (Cameron, 1978). Any comprehensive assessment of the relationships between culture and effectiveness must therefore take account of multiple relationships. The measurement of firm performance with financial measures is the most common approach, yet it has provoked endless controversy about reliability and validity. Also, theoretical links are needed to identify which aspects of culture are associated with which aspects of effectiveness. In addition, most effectiveness measures are fraught with well-documented methodological weaknesses (e.g., Cameron and Whetten, 1983). Coupling the ambiguity associated with culture measurement to the multidimensional complexity associated with effectiveness measurement makes the research task difficult indeed. Finally, research on effectiveness needs to control for contextual factors that could affect performance, like industry competitiveness, employee demographics, technological sophistication, and worker experience. We discuss three of the major issues associated with the characteristics of culture that make it especially difficult to assess— definitional issues, measurement issues, and dimensional issues.

Definition

First, some ambiguity surrounds the definition of culture itself. Multiple cultures may be present within an organization that may affect performance—for example, a national culture, a functional culture, a gender-based culture, a work group culture, and a company culture. With a few exceptions (e.g., Hofstede, 1980; Barley, 1983; Trice and Beyer, 1993; Van Maanen, 1973), empirical researchers have failed to identify the specific level of culture studied. Without such specificity, it is difficult to determine what measures of effectiveness are appropriate. Similarly, because of the different disciplinary perspectives on culture research (e.g., organizations *have* cultures versus organizations *are* cultures), there is no consensus about whether any influence cultures have on organizational performance can be assessed. The former approach—that cultures are properties of organizations—assumes that researchers and managers can identify differences among organizational cultures, can empirically measure cultures and performance separately, and thus can assess the impacts of cultures on performance. The latter perspective—that organizations are cultures—assumes that cultures are unique and underlie everything that happens in organizations. They are inseparable from other organizational phenomena, including effectiveness.

In this book, we try to take a middle ground. Culture is treated as a property of organizations, so that it makes sense to try to assess its effects on people's performance in organizations. At the same time, culture is treated as a pervasive force, so that most actions and beliefs can be seen as having cultural as well as practical significance.

Measurement

A second set of issues relates to the measurement of organizational culture or the most appropriate methods for obtaining data on organizational culture. Three strategies have been used: (1) a holistic approach, in which the investigator becomes immersed in the culture and engages in in-depth participant observation; (2) metaphorical or language approaches, in which the investigator uses language patterns in documents, reports, stories, and conversations in order to uncover cultural patterns, just as detectives use fingerprints, voiceprints, and word prints to detect a person's identity; and (3) quantitative approaches, in which the investigator uses questionnaires or interviews to measure particular dimensions of cultures, with numerical scales or codes.

Heated debates are common among culture researchers about the best ways to measure culture. A central issue is whether a quantitative approach to culture assessment is valid, or whether an in-depth, qualitative or holistic approach is the only way to detect and describe culture. The basic issue is: When assessing culture via questionnaires, interviews, documents, is one really measuring superficial characteristics of an organization—namely organizational climate—rather than in-depth cultural values? Because culture is based on underlying values and assumptions, often unrecognized and unchallenged in organizations, one perspective argues that only by utilizing in-depth qualitative procedures in which artifacts, stories and myths, and interpretation systems are studied over long periods of time in an in-depth way can cultural attributes be identified (Schein, 1992; Trice and Beyer, 1993; Siehl and Martin, 1990). Alternatively, assessing perceptions or practices of organization members is likely to capture climate and structure rather than the underlying culture. In addition, questionnaires, it is argued, measure the dimensions of culture determined in advance by the researcher, thus potentially missing or distorting the actual dimensions of cultures existing a priori in the organization itself. "One can understand something in depth only if one has experienced it" is an underlying philosophy represented by this approach.

The opposing point of view argues that breadth and comparability are sacrificed by employing a qualitative approach. The investigation of multiple organizational cultures becomes impossible when immersion in each one is mandatory. To conduct comparisons among multiple cultures, quantitative approaches must be used. It is crucial, however, that respondents to a survey instrument actually report underlying values and assumptions (culture), not just superficial attitudes or perceptions (climate).

Two approaches are common for addressing this issue. One is to construct surveys based on ethnographic observation, so that the questionnaire items reflect the aspects of culture uncovered by the qualitative observation (see Enz, 1988; Schall, 1983; Siehl and Martin, 1990). Another way is to use a scenario analysis procedure, in which respondents report the extent to which written scenarios are indicative of their own organization's culture (Ouchi and Johnson; 1978; O'Reilly, 1983; Denison, 1990; Cameron and Freeman, 1991; Quinn and Spreitzer, 1991). The scenarios serve as cues— both emotionally and cognitively—that may bring to the surface core cultural attributes. The old proverb, "fish discover water last" (people are not aware of their culture until it is described for them), illustrates the philosophical basis of this approach. Respondents may be unaware of crucial attributes of culture until they are cued by scenarios on a questionnaire.

Dimensions

The third set of issues relates to the most appropriate dimensions of culture to assess in determining the relationships between culture and effectiveness. Since it may be impossible to assess *all* aspects of an organization's culture, it becomes necessary to focus on certain dimensions of an organization's culture more than others. At least two kinds of dimensions are relevant for assessment: content and pattern. Content dimensions refer to the aspects of an organization's culture that capture its substance—the assumptions, values, beliefs, and norms. They reflect what the culture *is*. Examples that have been used in research include internal-external focus, speed, riskiness, participativeness, clarity, power distance, masculinity, and individualism. Pattern dimensions refer to the interrelationships among these content dimensions, the patterns by which they manifest themselves. The most common pattern dimensions are cultural strength, cultural congruence, and cultural type.

The challenge in assessing content dimensions of organizational culture is to identify and assess the key archetypes that capture the culture's core dimensions. A variety of models of culture have been proposed, with dimensions and attributes being proposed by various authors (see Cameron and Ettington, 1988, for a review). These models each use a different rationale for their claims as a valid representation or core cultural dimensions. One attempt to assess core dimensions empirically, for example, was the application of a competing values framework to culture assessment (Cameron and Freeman, 1991; Quinn and Spreitzer, 1991; Yeung et al., 1991; Zammuto and Krakower, 1991). These authors argue that most individuals describe their organizational cultures according to the dimensions of this instrument (see Mason and Mitroff, 1973; Mitroff and Kilmann, 1976). Their approach assesses culture by way of a survey instrument, however, with the liabilities articulated earlier.

Although it is by no means a simple matter, assessing pattern dimensions of culture is less controversial than assessing content dimensions, because some consensus exists on the most important dimensions. Cultural strength refers to the dominance or preeminence of certain aspects of the culture in affecting everything that happens in an organization. It also reflects the intensity with which cultural values are held and clung to. It has been proposed as a key predictor of effectiveness. Deal and Kennedy (1982:5), for example, asserted that "a strong culture has almost always been the driving force behind continuing success in American business." Cultural congruence refers to the extent to which the culture reflected in one part of the organization is similar to and consistent with the culture reflected in another part of the organization. Congruence has also been hypothesized to be a major predictor or organizational effectiveness. For example, Nadler and Tushman (1980:75) found that, "other things being equal, the greater the total degree of congruence or fit between the various components [of an organization], the more effective will be organizational behavior at multiple levels." Cultural type refers to the specific kind of culture that is reflected in the organization (for example, an innovative, entrepreneurial culture). Cultural type reflects the extent to which certain cultural attributes or content dimensions dominate others in the organization. Cameron and Ettington (1988:385) found that "the effectiveness of organizations is more closely associated with the type of culture present than with the congruence or the strength of that culture." Each of these pattern dimensions, in other words, has been proposed as a key predictor of organizational effectiveness.

Because the measurement of both culture and organizational effectiveness is so difficult, reports of such relationships must be viewed with caution. Their value rests on the clarity and credibility of the theoretical linkages on which they are based and on whether the research focuses on meaningful and convincing aspects of cultures and effectiveness. It is highly unlikely that any study can encompass all of the complexities or eliminate all of the difficulties involved, so that progress in determining the relationship between culture and performance is likely to require some sacrifice of precision and control to reach insights and possible understanding about even parts of the whole picture.

Also, to fully assess the effects of cultures, we must take into account the dualities of their consequences. Since this volume addresses issues of improving human performance, the duality of positive versus negative consequences is especially pertinent. Although the examples cited at the beginning of this chapter and many others portray organizational cultures in terms of their positive effects on performance, it is clear that not all of the effects of cultures are positive or even benign. As already mentioned, existing cultures are often blamed for the failure of organizations to respond to changing circumstances. For example, many analysts saw IBM's culture as an impediment to needed change. Attempts to establish quality circles and participatory management often founder on the deeply held authoritarian values of management (Fitzgerald, 1988).

Scholars have identified other deleterious consequences of organizational cultures. On the basis of a careful and long-term study of a corporation in the high-tech industry, Kunda (1991) raised three concerns:

1. Do corporate cultures threaten individual autonomy with "a rather subtle form of domination, a culture trap combining normative pressure with a delicate balance of seductiveness and coercion" (p. 224)?

2. Do corporate cultures marginalize those not incorporated into the culture—temporary or contract workers, for example?

3. What effects will corporate cultures have on society "if their [members'] fundamental conceptions of themselves and their relationships to others are shaped in the corporate image" (p. 226)?

He then suggests that members should remember that organizations are instruments of social action and not ends in themselves, that social boundaries may have positive value, and that other arenas for self-definition exist and can be cultivated.

Another ethnographic study of managers in three large organizations found that the bureaucratic ethos evident in their cultures created "moral mazes." Managers' success was tied to pleasing their bosses and submitting to impersonal market demands (Jackall, 1988:191-192) rather than to adherence to any set of moral principles. Clearly, cultures can have various consequences that are not immediately obvious or necessarily desirable.

It is important to keep in mind the limits of both empirical evidence and theoretical development as we discuss the ways in which cultures may influence organizational performance.

CULTURE AND PERFORMANCE

Organizational cultures cannot directly affect performance because it is people who do the performing. Cultures must therefore somehow influence people in order to affect their individual or collective performance. To fully assess effects of culture on performance, we need to determine the paths by which culture affects people and how those effects are tied to their performance. Ideally, studies of the effects of organizational culture on performance would develop theories and evidence that links specific aspects of culture to specific aspects of performance through specified intervening variables. Unfortunately, only a very modest beginning has been made on this agenda. To identify all of the consequences for performance of any culture, we need to consider, as comprehensively as possible, the pathways by which cultures shape people's thoughts, feelings, and behaviors.

Culture affects performance because it affects how people think, feel, and act and helps to determine the situations in which they act. In more scientific terms, cultures influence people's cognitions, affective states, and behaviors, many of which have implications for work performance. Cultures also shape the contexts in which people work and the environments in which organizations operate and, in these ways, constrain individual behavior.

Cultures are clearly repositories of information and knowledge and, as such, can help or hinder work performance. Accurate information and valid knowledge will assist performance, whereas inaccurate information and superstitious knowledge are likely to detract from it (Daft and Weick, 1984; Feldman and March, 1981). Also, cultures provide cognitive frameworks through which people interpret what they observe and experience and provide language and referents to use in communicating with others (Wilkins and Ouchi, 1983). Research on strategic decision making has shown that different managers may interpret identical events as opportunities or threats and that these interpretations, in turn, are related to the actions taken (Dutton and Jackson, 1987). Cultures also contribute schemas and scripts that can affect performance by providing preexisting ways of understanding what is occurring, how to evaluate it, and what sequences of actions are appropriate to the situation (Lord and Foti, 1986; Wilkins and Ouchi, 1983).

Feelings through which culture is likely to affect performance include identification, loyalty, and commitment. Identification involves the linking of one's self-concept with membership in a culture. Such identification with an organizational culture may enhance performance if it enhances self-concepts and feelings of self-esteem. Athletes on a winning team are likely to experience such performance-enhancing identification. Identification could lessen performance if it leads to decreased self-esteem and worse self-concepts. Interviews with employees of the New York Port Authority revealed that they experienced such negative feelings as shame when their organization was subject to harsh criticism for its handling of the homeless (Dutton and Dukerich, 1991). Other instances in which identification with employing organizations probably led to negative feelings include the cases of Exxon employees after the oil tanker accident at Valdez, Alaska, and of Hooker Chemical Company employees after the contamination of the Love Canal area in Niagara Falls, New York, was revealed.

Loyalty and commitment both involve an emotional bonding between the individual and his or her cultural group and, as such, imply a willingness to exert effort and make sacrifices on behalf of that group (Druckman, 1994). Of course, whether or not loyalty and commitment are positively associated with performance desired by the organization may depend on what values and norms the target cultural group holds regarding performance. O'Reilly (1989) suggested that employees committed to an organization will be more dedicated because they care about their organization's fate, and their caring heightens the power of organizational norms to control their behavior. In this way, the ability of a culture to create commitment may affect its effectiveness in eliciting high performance from its members.

Another way in which cultures can affect performance is by programming people to behave in ways that are more or less effective in terms of performance. Swidler (1986) argued that cultures provide "tool kits" of stories, rituals, symbols, and world views that people often use to construct ways of ordering their behavior. She suggests (p. 277) that "people do not build lines of action from scratch, choosing actions one at a time as efficient means to given ends. Instead, they construct chains of action beginning with at least some prefabricated links. Culture influences action through the shape and organization of those links, not by determining the ends to which they are put."

In work organizations, various work-related skills, routines, and habits are culturally acquired and persist because they fit into valued strategies of action. By performing their work routines, organization members often get positive reinforcement and begin to internalize the routines as *the* way to do their work.

To the degree that culture programs people to behave in certain ways, it can have direct effects on individual performance. In many situations, however, performance is constrained by other factors. Also, individual performance does not always translate into organizational performance. Despite the consequent lack of certainty that a cultural intervention will affect performance in desired ways, astute managers take advantage of various levers available to them for managing their organizational cultures.

LEVERS FOR MANAGING CULTURES

Because cultures involve people's innermost thoughts and feelings, their ongoing relations with other people, and complex patterns of behavior, and because cultures take time to develop, they are not easy for managers to manipulate and control. There is also a spontaneous and indigenous side to cultures. On one hand, many of the informal subcultures that emerge in organizations develop without anyone's conscious intent or control. On the other hand, it seems obvious that, over time, various individuals have probably taken leadership roles in the creation and development of any culture, even those that are informal. To successfully manage their cultures, managers need to assume the role of cultural leader. Some, like Dan Daniels at the Lockheed L-1011 plant, may have intuitively developed a culturally sensitive style of managing from their experiences. Others may need to self-consciously learn to use the cultural levers available to them.

Theory suggests that cultures have leverage points—social mechanisms through which leaders and members can affect the culture in major or minor ways. These include selection, socialization, cultural forms, leadership, and subcultures. Research findings on each of these levers provide evidence supporting their effects on performance. Another leverage point, not usually under the control of managers or members, is the environment of the organization.

The idea of managers or other leaders controlling and managing cultures in organizations is very troubling to some observers (Martin and Powers, 1983; Georges and Jones, 1980; Kan, 1989; Alvesson and Berg, 1992) because they fear that those who succeed in managing cultures will use that ability to exploit others. It would be naive to ignore the ethical issues they raise and unrealistic to ignore the fact that, through their actions, managers *do* manage their cultures, more or less effectively, all of the time. The practical way to deal with ethical concerns about managing cultures thus becomes not a question of whether or not managers should manage their cultures, but rather one of how ethical concerns can be built into management efforts.

In most societies, managers of work organizations do not have unlimited control over their employees, who often find various ways to resist management control. Administrators and managers in some types of organizations do, however, have fewer societal limits on their control. Institutions like prisons and some mental hospitals, for example, have large amounts of control over their inmates and patients (Goffman, 1961). The military also has a larger degree of control over its members than do many other employing organizations (Janowitz, 1971). In high-control organizations, ethical issues become especially crucial in the management of culture.

Selection

One way to manage a culture is to select members so carefully that only those whose values and customary behaviors are consonant with the desired culture are admitted. Organizations vary in their ability to use selection, however. U.S. public schools, for example, are required by law to admit virtually all children, regardless of language skills, social skills, and physical handicaps. Furthermore, they cannot easily expel students who do not fit in. Private schools, in contrast, can be selective. Prisons, although they must take all criminals sent to them, have extreme sanctions available to shape prisoners' behaviors, if not their internal value systems. Prisoners can also be assigned to different types of prisons and different settings within the prison. Business and other employing organizations use various selection techniques—from interviews and psychological tests to lie detector and drug tests—to try to eliminate those candidates most likely to be disruptive in their cultures and to help them hire those candidates most likely to fit in and make positive contributions.

Socialization

What cannot be accomplished by selection, organizations can try to accomplish by socializing members to their culture after they are admitted. Organizations vary greatly, however, in the attention they pay to socialization and the tactics they employ (Van Maanen and Schein, 1979). Some tactics serve to shape recruits into the same mold as established members. The military uses many such techniques with its new recruits. Other techniques serve to develop less uniform and more individualized adaptations to the culture. These are usually reserved for roles that require autonomy and individual initiative. Training for higher ranks in the military employs these techniques.

The socialization tactics that organizations employ with new members can be classified along several dimensions (Van Maanen and Schein, 1979). Sometimes members are socialized in groups; at other times, they are socialized individually by old-timers or just by doing the job. Some socialization experiences are formal, in that the recruits are separated from others in the organization during the socialization process; others are informal, in that they occur in the regular work setting. Some socialization programs involve fixed sequences and timetables of activities and accomplishments; others allow for variability. Sometimes experienced members of the culture will be assigned to groom newcomers; at other times, newcomers self-select whatever socializing agents they can find. Finally, some socialization seeks to divest members of former roles that are seen as dysfunctional to organizational performance; other socialization accepts the current identities, skills, and values of entering members as appropriate and valued as it invests them in the new setting. Specific socialization experiences in actual organizations tend to combine these tactics in many different ways. Those that use more institutionalized tactics, with fixed sequences and timetables, are likely to encourage members to preserve existing cultural values and practices, and those that employ more innovative tactics, which are flexible and allow for variability, are likely to encourage recruits to develop innovative role orientations departing from past cultural prescriptions.

Organizations face trade-offs between selection and socialization (Wanous, 1980). They will find it easier to socialize new members into their cultures if the members they admit already hold beliefs and values consonant with their cultures and have learned behavioral routines consistent with their strategies and goals.

Western scholars were sensitized to the power of adult socialization when the Japanese established large numbers of factories or "transplants" in

North America and Europe in the 1980s. Japanese management is based on teamwork and unquestioned loyalty to the firm, whereas American and British management have historically stressed individual responsibility on the job and adversarial collective labor organizations to represent worker interests. Rather than resocialize individualist and union-oriented laborers, the Japanese have often selected "green-field" sites for setting up transplants (Abegglen and Stalk, 1985). Green-field sites are locations with no history of industrial organization, or sites where unemployment is high and unions are weak. In these settings the Japanese have been very successful in taking young workers and subjecting them to intense socialization experiences in order to instill in them loyalty to the firm and skill in teamwork practices such as quality circles (Oliver and Wilkinson, 1988).

Communication plays an important role in the socialization process. The communication that newcomers do or do not have with supervisors, coworkers, and others can affect their satisfaction with communication, role clarity, identification with the organization, organizational commitment, and the likelihood of staying or leaving (Jablin, 1987). Interview data on the types of socialization experiences that new graduates of business schools found most helpful in their initial jobs concluded that the most important aids to socialization were interactions with peers, supervisors, and coworkers (Louis et al., 1983).

Other research on the experiences of new business recruits found that both expectations and initial performance are important for later performance. In this research, company expectations were conveyed by the difficulty of the job to which a recruit was assigned (Berlew and Hall, 1966). Recruits who were put in more demanding jobs internalized more positive job attitudes and set higher standards for themselves. Both initially and subsequently, they also tended to perform better than recruits placed in less demanding jobs.

Other research has suggested that feelings about the self that are rooted in past experience are important moderators in the socialization process (Smith, 1968; Morrison, 1977; Weiss, 1978; Jones, 1983, 1986; Miller and Jablin, 1991). Differences in self-esteem, feelings of competence and confidence, and perceptions of self-efficacy are associated with different responses to socialization experiences. Negative feelings tend to produce avoidance strategies that constrain task immersion, information seeking, and social contacts, whereas positive strategies seem to facilitate learning how to act appropriately but do not necessarily ensure role acceptance (Jones, 1983; Miller and Jablin, 1991; Trice and Beyer, 1993).

Other researchers have also emphasized the active role that individuals play in their own socialization. Newcomers' information seeking has been theorized to influence a variety of cognitive and affective states that intervene between culture and performance, as discussed above. Chief among these are role clarity, role conflict, job satisfaction, and job tenure. Information-seeking tactics include testing limits, indirect questioning, surveillance, observing, disguised conversations, using third parties, and overt questioning (Miller and Jablin, 1991).

Both theory and the available empirical evidence indicate that socialization has many facets and that experiencing even some of these facets leads to better adjustment to organizational roles and cultures. Socialization must be viewed in terms of the adjustments that are required at various stages of membership in a group or organization. Socialization is an ongoing process that continues in some form throughout individuals' lives and careers.

Cultural Forms

Cultural forms are the concrete manifestations of culture. They consist of observable entities through which members of a culture affirm, express, and communicate cultural substance to one another. Dan Daniels used many cultural forms as levers to change the culture at the Lockheed L-1011 plant. He communicated his philosophy in colorful, easy-to-remember language and sayings (Snyder, 1988:197):

"Don't sell your integrity—it's the only thing that can't be bought."

"You may be *better at* something than some one else, but you are not *better than* they are."

"You don't have to make people do things your way to get performance."

He reinforced these messages by his own personal conduct—coming to work early, walking around, listening, and not criticizing others. He promoted people who could plan, treated their subordinates decently, and got results. He encouraged the managers working for him to emulate these behaviors. He developed a symbol of pride in the organization—blue flight jackets.

At the NUMMI plant, an abundance of cultural forms also served as levers for cultural change. Two were very basic: (1) the new union contract that embodied new levels of union-management trust and cooperation and (2) the production process itself, which embodied the highly successful Japanese way of producing cars. In addition, the very fact that Toyota sent 400 trainees from Japan to work with their U.S. counterparts was a symbol of Toyota's commitment to the joint venture. NUMMI's investing $3 million to send 600 employees to Toyota plants in Japan for training expressed a serious intent to change and the importance of learning new ways of doing things. Records posted in work team areas signified management's willingness to share information and the teams' responsibilities for finding ways to improve performance.

Many other examples of cultural forms could be given. They are all around us. Members of organizations and of occupational groups use specialized language, symbols, and signs. They wear uniforms and special clothes that signify their status. They tell stories to one another that express their work-related tensions and concerns (Martin et al., 1983). They practice rituals and taboos that help to reassure them in the face of uncertainty. They also engage in elaborate rites and ceremonies that have mixtures of practical and expressive consequences. Table 3-1 lists and illustrates six types of cultural rites that have been identified in both tribal societies and modern work organizations. Of the many cultural rites that probably occur in organizations, three have been documented: rites of creation (Turner, 1990), rites of transition (Deal and Kennedy, 1982), and rites of parting (Harris and Sutton, 1986). All involve a series of actions, sets of performers, and the use of artifacts that convey cultural meaning.

Subcultures

Organizations are rarely characterized by single cultures (Wilkins and Ouchi, 1983); instead, subcultures are pervasive and have important effects in most organizations (Gregory, 1983; Barley and Louis, 1983). There is still considerable controversy over whether it is misleading or helpful to look at organizations as having organization-wide cultures as well as subcultures (Martin, 1992; Meyerson, 1991; Schein, 1991; Trice, 1991). The sensible resolution of this controversy is to look for both in analyzing any particular organization. However, organization-wide cultures may not develop in all organizations because the conditions for their growth are not present. Also, organization-wide cultures are unlikely to maintain themselves in the face of some circumstances, especially the loss of many long-term members or rapid turnover among members. Thus, subcultures are probably more prevalent in organizations than are organization-wide cultures. When popular writers and journalists refer to *the* organizational culture, they are often describing only the managerial subcultures subscribed to by those at the top of an organization.

Since subcultures share all of the characteristics of the more encompassing concept of culture, many of the findings and theories related to cultures are equally applicable to subcultures. The important practical question for managers is to manage subcultures so that their values and goals are congruent with those of the overall culture. To enhance performance, subcultures must also accept organizational strategies for realizing those values and goals.

An example of how subcultures are employed to influence performance is provided by the United States Military Academy at West Point. West Point's stated purpose is "to provide the nation with leaders of character who serve the common defense" (United States Military Academy, 1993). West Point strives to achieve this purpose through a four-year experience designed around three distinct programs—intellectual, physical, and military development—as well as an overarching experience of ethical development that is integrated throughout each of the other programs.

The nature of followership that is learned by cadets at West Point is at least partly a function of the experiences they encounter during their plebe year, when they are subject in varying degrees to the authority of not only all commissioned officers but also all cadets of the upper three classes. The plebe system historically consisted of a socialization experience designed to strip new cadets of at least some of their previous characteristics and replace them with characteristics more acceptable to the military profession. In effect, they lose much of their old identities. The plebe system also made sure that all cadets, regardless of social status, started with the same opportunities. It served a useful purpose in leveling the playing field for all new cadets, in fostering cohesion and class bonding, in weeding out cadets who were unable to cope with an intellectually, emotionally, and physically demanding year, and in providing a powerful rite of passage into membership in what is called the Long Gray Line. However, the system required careful monitoring and was highly susceptible to unacceptable abuses.

More than once in its storied history, West Point officials have attempted to reform or do away with the plebe system (Lovell, 1979). Although the current cadet leader development system (USMA Cir 1-101, 1993) focuses on the overall four-year experience and deemphasizes the plebe experience, many vestiges of the plebe system remain. Constant vigilance on the part of leaders is necessary to prevent abuses similar to those all too familiar on civilian college campuses in the form of fraternity hazing. It is critical to the accomplishment of the Academy's purpose that developmental experiences encountered in this living laboratory be compatible with the espoused ideology relating to leadership and leader development.

Cadet companies are indeed fertile ground for subculture formation, because members interact more with each other than with anyone else, share powerful common experiences, and have many similar personal characteristics. The resultant subcultures have a powerful influence on their performance. Some companies have the reputation for being particularly demanding and strict in their enforcement of regulations pertaining to fourth-class duties; other companies are viewed as mellow or laid back with little concern for enforcing regulations. So long as the company subculture is enhancing (that is, concerned with issues that do not interfere with the desired culture), the company's tactical officer in charge is not likely to be concerned and may even encourage the subculture.

Serious, wide-scale abuses of the fourth-class system have almost al-

TABLE 3-1   Six Cultural Rites and Their Social Consequences

Types of Rites	Example	Evident Expressive Consequences	Examples of Possible Hidden Expressive Consequences
Rites of passage	Induction and basic training, U.S. Army	Facilitate transition of persons into social roles and statuses that are new for them.	Minimize changes in ways people carry out social roles. Reestablish equilibrium in ongoing social relations.
Rites of degradation	Firing and replacing top executive	Dissolve social identities and their power.	Publicly acknowledge that problems exist and discuss their details. Defend group boundaries by redefining who belongs and who doesn't. Reaffirm social importance and value of role involved.
Rites of enhancement	Mary Kay seminars	Enhance social identities and their power.	Spread good news about the organization. Provide public recognition of individuals for their accomplishments; motivate others to similar efforts. Enable organizations to take some credit for individual accomplish-ments. Emphasize social value of performance of social roles.

ways been associated with subcultural forms that are clearly counter to those espoused by the Academy. Academy officials are so mindful of the potential for disruptive subcultures that cadet companies are scrambled each year to forestall the development of strong subcultures that are extremely resistant to change. At the end of their sophomore year, cadets are assigned to different companies from those to which they were assigned during their first two years.

Some cadet companies develop subcultures that emphasize one of the developmental dimensions much more than the others. For example, a company may place priority of effort on physical excellence to the detriment of intellectual development. In such a company, very powerful norms may emerge causing cadets to focus discretionary time on physical fitness or training for an intramural sport instead of a more balanced use of time to

TABLE 3-1 Continued

Types of Rites	Example	Evident Expressive Consequences	Examples of Possible Hidden Expressive Consequences
Rites of renewal	Organizational development activities	Refurbish social structures and improve their functioning.	Reassure members that something is being done about problems. Disguise nature of problems. Defer acknowledgment of problems. Focus attention toward some problems and away from others. Legitimize and reinforce existing systems of power and authority.
Rites of conflict reduction	Collective bargaining	Reduce conflict and aggression.	Deflect attention away from solving problems. Compartmentalize conflict and its disruptive effects. Reestablish equilibrium in disturbed social relations.
Rites of integration	Office Christmas party	Encourage and revive common feelings that bind members together and commit them to a social system.	Permit venting of emotions and temporary loosening of various norms. Reassert and reaffirm, by contrast, the moral rightness of usual norms.

accomplish all developmental tasks to some satisfactory level. When the attention paid to one of the developmental experiences is so far skewed toward a single dimension that other developmental dimensions are not adequately addressed, the subculture is damaging overall performance.

This example illustrates how subcultures can have positive and negative impacts on intended organizational cultures and performance. Some subcultures are supportive or even enhancing of the overall culture; some pursue values that are orthogonal to the culture (the physical fitness enthusiasts), whereas other groups seem to be countercultural in the sense that they enact values (by hazing) that are contrary to those prescribed by current policy. Academy administrators are sensitive to these differences and try to manage them as best they can. But the impulses of subcultures cannot be totally controlled from the top of the hierarchy. For the shaping and maintenance of subcultural values that are congruent with those of the overall organizational culture, cultural leadership that communicates and reinforces congruent ideas and values is needed throughout the organization.

Cultural Leadership

In Chapter 4 we deal with how leaders influence the performance of the practical tasks of the organization. Here we focus on how the expressive side of leadership affects thoughts, feelings, and programmed behaviors that in turn affect performance.

Elements of cultural leadership that have been addressed in the literature include: the personal qualities of the leader, the situation as perceived by the leader and followers, the vision or mission of the leader, follower attributions about the leader and the situation, the performance of the leader, characteristic leader behaviors or style, administrative actions, the use of cultural forms, the use of tradition, and the persistence of consequences over time.

There are several views on the nature of the leader/culture interaction. Based on his observations as a researcher and consultant, Schein conceives of cultural leadership as emanating especially from the founders of organizations, whom he sees as imposing their cultural assumptions on the initial group of employees. As he puts it (Schein, 1992:212): "Leaders not only choose the basic mission and the environmental context in which the new group will operate, but they choose the group members and bias the original responses that the group makes in its efforts to succeed in its environment and to integrate itself." Founders use a variety of embedding mechanisms, he argues, to create what might be called the climate of the organization. At this stage the climate reflects only the assumptions of its leader. Through socialization, and over time, however, these assumptions begin to be internalized by the members.

Trice and Beyer (1993) see cultural leadership quite differently. They argue that cultural leadership is fairly common and can occur in many different groups and at many different places at the same time within a single organization. Thus, their approach addresses cultural leadership at the subcultural level as well as at the overall cultural level.

Ott (1989), building on Sathe's (1985) discussion of how organizational cultures tend to perpetuate themselves and using essentially the same mechanisms described by Schein, suggests that managers seeking to change organizational cultures must intervene appropriately in each of the important events or processes that influence the culture.

A useful typology describes four types of cultural leadership (Trice and Beyer, 1993):

1. Leadership that *creates cultures* occurs when leaders set social processes in motion to achieve their visions of what their organizations should be like and what they should try to accomplish. Founders often create cultures.

2. Leadership that *changes cultures* causes either the ideas or behaviors embedded in culture to become different than they were before. Dan Daniels, the manager of the Lockheed L-1011 plant, is a good example of a cultural change leader.

3. Leadership that *embodies cultures* represents, preserves, and nourishes an existing a culture. George Washington was an embodiment leader who represented relatively conservative values and principles as the first president of the United States.

4. Leadership that *integrates cultures* manages to keep some harmony among various subcultures while preserving their cultural differences. The Japanese managers who headed up the NUMMI joint venture during its early days must have had a flair for integrative leadership, for they had to reconcile the diverse interests of U.S. labor unions, General Motors management, and the Japanese managers of Toyota. Although these managers could not change the culture of the unions, GM, or Toyota, they managed to forge enough consensus to make the joint venture succeed.

Another way to look at the combination of culture and leadership is to assess how culture may facilitate or hinder leadership and its effectiveness. Because almost all organizations have subcultures, the presence of a strong overarching set of ideas and values, such as are embedded in military doctrine, greatly facilitates the exercise of leadership throughout an organization. When different leaders convey similar ideas and values throughout an organization, they are contributing to internal integration. When they manage to instill somewhat different ideas and values in their own units, they may be contributing to external adaptation by helping the organization to satisfy multiple, competing demands. Both types of cultural leadership can thus contribute positively to overall organization performance.

MANAGING ORGANIZATIONAL CULTURES

One implication of this discussion of cultural levers is that cultures develop inertia. The levers of selection, socialization, and cultural forms not only bring the culture to new members but also serve to reinforce culturally determined values and behaviors in those organizational members who are already acculturated. The stronger the culture—that is, the more pervasive it is in the organization—the more inertia it generates. Strong cultures are more resistant to managerial intervention than weak ones. The levers creating strong cultures may therefore lead to both effectiveness and ineffectiveness in organizations. Strong cultures, on one hand, can lead an organization to the "success breeds failure" syndrome in which organizations refuse, or are unable, to adapt to changing environmental demands. IBM's lingering overreliance on mainframe computer business is a well-known example. On the other hand, strong cultures also can lead organizations to a "success breeds success" situation in which a unique market niche and "brand identity" become associated with the organization because of its strong culture.

Organizations change as their environment, personnel, circumstances, and missions change. Culture serves not merely to slow the rate of change but also to keep change focused and in accord with current organizational operation; in strong cultures, change must be accommodated in order to avoid disruption and discontinuity. Therein lies the problem: those cultures most resistant to change, the strong ones, are precisely those in organizations in which culture is most influential in the organization's functioning. How can managers actually produce change in organizations with strong cultures?

Particular events sometimes occur that provide a window of opportunity for managing cultural change. Consider, for example, a telecommunications company located in a downtown business district. For a variety of financial and logistical reasons, the firm moved its entire operation to an outlying suburban area. The physical structure of the workplace changed. The balance of influence of subsections of the organization changed, e.g., technical support became more crucial at the time of the move than in routine day-to-day activities. Most important, there was a dramatic shift in personnel. Many employees who had relied on public transportation to get to the old central-city workplace were faced with a difficult commute to the suburbs. Others chose not to make the move and to resign rather than add hours to travel time and disrupt daily patterns of household organization. These difficulties affected employees across the organization, from front-line workers to supervisors to middle management. The move itself was accompanied by a pervasive and unprecedented turnover in personnel.

The use of levers to change culture was clearly at work in this case. Selection entered into the recruitment of a new workforce and socialization after they were recruited. The new site provided a vehicle for altering cultural forms as well, such as a new dress code for the suburbs, a new arrangement for lunches and breaks, and so forth. Subcultures were deconstructed and reassembled by the new physical arrangement of the move. Topology may not be destiny, but it was a major force in who talked to whom and how friendships and cohesive subunits formed (Festinger et al., 1950): friendships form from repeated casual contacts by people with similar interests and circumstances.

For a management desirous of managing organizational culture, a major move of this sort presents a fortuitous opportunity. However, such opportunities do not always arise as needed. Thus, an enduring problem for managers is how to employ cultural levers when such drastic environmental changes do not aid in moving organizational cultures in desired directions.

Unlike redesigning organizational structure or forming an organizational alliance, managing culture is fraught with ambiguity and uncertainty. Because culture is collective, emotional, historical, symbolic, dynamic, fuzzy— as well as largely unrecognized— it is difficult to pinpoint just what is to be managed or how. Well-known examples of culture management published both in the popular press and in the scholarly literature indicate that culture management takes at least three forms: creating culture purposely in a new organization, remodeling or reorienting an existing culture in an organization, and strengthening an organization's culture in the face of threats or pressures to change. Each of these three representations of culture management present its own challenges and issues as managers attempt to address them.

Creating Culture

When new organizations form, cultures are usually created within them. Cultures have a tendency to develop through predictable stages in the early part of an organization's life cycle, regardless of managerial intervention. Empirical research has been carried out in this area on government agencies, health care organizations, educational organizations, and the computer industry (see Cameron and Whetten, 1983; Cameron and Quinn, 1996, for reviews of the extensive research available).

In the earliest stages of development, organizations tend to be dominated by an "adhocratic" culture—characterized by an absence of formal structure, creativity and entrepreneurship, fluid and nonbureaucratic methods, and an emphasis on individuality, freedom, and flexibility among employees.

Over time, organizations supplement that orientation with a clan culture—a family feeling, a strong sense of belonging and dedication, personal identification with the organization, and a strong missionary-like zeal.

Organizational expansion eventually produces the need to emphasize structure, standard procedures, and control—that is, a hierarchy-focused culture. Such a shift makes members feel that the organization has lost the friendly, personal feeling that once characterized the workplace, and the focus on reduction of deviation, standardization, and restraint may give rise to escalating resentment or rebellion.

The fourth cultural shift is to a market-focused culture—a focus on competitiveness, achieving results, aggressiveness in customer relations, elaboration of structure, and an emphasis on external interactions. Market cultures are more typical of larger and more mature organizations than small or new organizations, and they are more typical of business organizations than service or educational organizations (Cameron and Freeman, 1991).

These life-cycle shifts in cultural orientation notwithstanding, forceful managers can have a powerful impact on the formation of a dominant culture that persists in their organizations. Almost four generations later, for example, IBM still reflects the culture created by founder Thomas Watson. Polaroid still reflects the culture created by Edwin Land, and Sony still reflects the culture created by Akio Morita. Among the mechanisms by which these powerful cultures were created are:

1. A unique and clearly articulated ideology,
2. The recruitment of like-minded employees,
3. The use of symbols to reinforce cultural attributes,
4. Repetitive socializing and training of employees in the key cultural values,
5. The appraisal and rewarding of behavior consistent with the desired culture, and
6. The design of an organizational structure that reinforces the key cultural values among all organization members.

These six levers are neither comprehensive nor unique to cultural formation, of course, but they are among the social mechanisms managers can initiate and largely control.

It is important note that there may be a liability associated with strong cultures. In the airline industry, for example, People Express Airlines effectively used cultural levers to develop a strong culture. It was patterned after the values of Don Burr, its founder and chief executive officer. Burr's explicit purpose was to form an airline that would be the model of customer concern, people sensitivity, and teamwork. People Express achieved almost unbelievably successful results during its first five years of existence, setting world records for income and profitability. However, a change in environmental demands brought about by the airline's purchase of Frontier Airlines, a unionized company, led to the rather swift demise of both companies. The strong culture of People Express was simply unable to adjust to the requirements of a radically different environment.

CHANGING CULTURE

Once an organization's culture is formed, tremendous pressure exists for it to persist. To change culture means that organization members become subject to ambiguity, disrupted patterns of interaction, a new reinforcement structure, different allocation procedures, and a different set of definitions of "how things are." Such a change is fearsome and disruptive, so organizational cultures tend to be very difficult to change. Often the more successful the organization, the more difficult the change.

That said, cultural change is sometimes necessary for organizational survival. A lack of fit may develop between the organization's culture and the demands of the competitive environment, or between the organization's culture and the demands of customers, or between the organization's culture and the style or personality of new leaders, or between the organization's culture and the cultures of other organizations with which alliances have been formed. In other words, mismatches may create conditions in which culture change is necessary for the organization to survive.

One well-known example of major culture change involved the U.S. Postal Service (Biggart, 1977: 417, 420):

> When Winton Blount was named postmaster general in 1972, he was charged with making the post office pay its own way. To do so he needed to discredit and destroy the old ideologies of dependency on Congress and of providing "service, service at all costs. . . ." To symbolize the new order, he replaced many established symbols and cultural forms with new ones. To signal the change of political status, the 200-year-old name of the post office was changed. A new logo, new typeface for all publications, and new postal colors were put in place. Nationwide birthday parties were held in every post office in the country, and a new stamp was printed with the new logo to commemorate the event. . . . The result of Blount's actions was the replacement of the old U.S. Post Office culture with a new U.S. Postal Service culture typified by more innovation and flexibility, service orientation, and efficiency.

Another example is the U.S. Army, whose culture changed not so much by the actions of a single leader but by a new policy instituted by Congress that replaced the former draft-based Army with an all-volunteer Army. The fact that volunteers now populated the Army led to several significant changes in the nature of the fighting force. Overall, the Army was able to attract more qualified recruits, with more formal education, higher skill levels, less drug and alcohol abuse, and less involvement in crime. Women joined the service in larger numbers than ever before. This new, more qualified workforce markedly changed the level of technological sophistication, improvements in quality, and efficiency of performance. The family responsibilities of military personnel and the relationships between the genders became critical issues for the Army, and ways of operating as well as some deeply embedded core values (e.g., men rule) changed as a result. Technical training became both a key motivator and a key incentive for Army service, and access to educational benefits became the single greatest motivator for Army enlistment. The formation of a joint chiefs structure led to more coordination and interchange among the services, resulting in less insularity and self-sufficiency.

The challenge faced by many managers of organizations is to actually lead a culture change effort themselves. The question is, how can culture change be purposively stimulated and managed in an organization? How can a profound and fundamental shift in the way the organization thinks of itself be induced?

Of the many approaches to systematically managing a culture change effort, one procedure, based on what is called the competing values framework, rests on the assumption that key dimensions of organizational culture can be assessed by way of a survey instrument (a controversial assumption, as pointed out earlier in the chapter). Highlighting the contradictory values and orientations that exist in all organizations, this framework identifies four types of organizational cultures (also see Yeung et al., 1991; Zammuto and Krakower, 1991; Quinn and Spreitzer, 1991; Hoijberg and Petrock, 1993, for empirical research on this framework).

Table 3-2 identifies the two dimensions that separate these different value orientations. As illustrated in the table, these dimensions produce quadrants that have been found to represent much more than value orientations. They identify congruent leadership styles, bonding mechanisms, and dominant theories of effectiveness (Cameron and Quinn, 1996). The two dimensions shown in the table, as well as the resulting quadrants and their attributes, have been empirically tested in multiple studies and have been found to have strong associations with organizational effectiveness (e.g., see Quinn and Rohrbaugh, 1983; Cameron and Freeman, 1991; Cameron and Quinn, 1996).

One dimension in the table differentiates values emphasizing flexibility, discretion, and dynamism from values emphasizing stability, order and control. This continuum ranges, in other words, from versatility and pliability on one end to steadiness and durability on the other end. The second dimension differentiates values emphasizing an internal orientation, integration, and unity from values that emphasize an external orientation, differentiation, and competition. This continuum ranges, in other words, from cohesion and consonance on one end to separation and independence on the other. Each of these culture types is based on different theories of organizational performance, values of goodness, leadership approaches, reward systems, core competencies, styles of management, and definitions of success.

The Dutch-based Philips Electronics used this framework to manage an intended culture change in a five-step process (see Cameron and Quinn, 1996). In the first step, the top management team reached consensus on the current organizational culture. This was done by constructing a culture profile based on responses to a survey instrument that assessed dimensions

TABLE 3-2   A Model of Cultural Congruence for Organizations

FLEXIBILITY

Type: Clan
Dominant Attributes: Cohesiveness,
   participation, teamwork, sense of family
Leader Style: Mentor, facilitator,
   parent-figure
Bonding: Loyalty, tradition,
   interpersonal cohesion
Strategic Emphases: Toward
   developing human resources,
   commitment, morale
	Type: Adhocracy
	Dominant Attributes: Creativity,
	   entrepreneurship, adaptability, dynamism
	Leader Style: Entrepreneur,
	   innovator, risk taker
	Bonding: Entrepreneurship, flexibility,
	   risk
	Strategic Emphases: Toward
	   innovation, growth, new resources

INTERNAL ORIENTATION ———————————— EXTERNAL ORIENTATION

Type: Hierarchy
Dominant Attributes: Order, rules and
   regulations, uniformity, efficiency
Leader Style: Coordinator, organizer,
   administrator
Bonding: Rules, policies and procedures,
   clear expectations
Strategic Emphases: Toward stability,
   predictability, smooth operations
	Type: Market
	Dominant Attributes: Competitiveness,
	   goal achievement, environment exchange
	Leader Style: Decisive, production- and
	   achievement-oriented
	Bonding: Goal orientation, production,
	   competition
	Strategic Emphases: Toward competitive
	   advantage and market superiority

STABILITY

Source: Cameron and Freeman (1991).

of culture consistent with the competing values framework. The consensus-producing discussion was an important clarification exercise in this step. In the second step, the top management team reached consensus on a "preferred" or future culture that they believed the organization had to achieve in order to become more successful. These two profiles, the current and the preferred cultures, were compared to identify discrepancies and to highlight needed changes.

The third step consisted of answering two questions regarding the observed discrepancies: (1) What does it mean to change? (2) What doesn't it mean to change? For example, a change toward a more team-oriented, participative culture and away from a controlling, directive culture meant that more value was placed on team performance, more decision authority was passed down to lower levels, and more sharing of leadership roles occurred. It did not mean that measurements were abandoned, that individual accountability was shelved, or that policies and procedures were ignored. The fourth step involved identifying specifically what was to be done, operationalizing the change agenda developed in the previous three steps. The fifth step involved implementing the newly developed culture change agenda by executing a model for managing change (e.g., Cameron and Ulrich, 1989; Galbraith and Lawler, 1993).

Of course, culture change did not occur quickly. Time frames for successful change are usually measured in years (even decades) rather than in months. The intent of any such model of culture change is simply to make the change management process systematic and rational rather than merely a product of historical or environmental inertia.

Reinforcing Culture

Despite the current emphasis on change, innovation, and transformation of cultures, it is equally important for managers to understand how to maintain and reinforce cultures. Some well-known organizations have found that they unwisely abandoned a culture that had proven successful in the past. Such abandonment may be gradual and unintended and occur more through neglect than conscious intent. It has been referred to as losing the organization's roots, abandoning core competency, and dishonoring the past (Wilkins, 1990).

For example, in the face of large market share losses to Japanese competitors, Harley-Davidson discovered the costs of abandoning the culture that had made it the premier motorcycle producer in the United States in the 1960s. The erosion of a sense of family and teamwork, the loss of feelings of employee involvement and empowerment, and the explosion of hierarchy and staff led to dismal quality, low morale, and poor management-worker relations. The former Harley family culture had gradually eroded, and it was exposed only by the threat of company extinction in the late 1970s. In addition to a number of major changes in manufacturing processes, supplier relations, and quality tools, a return to the core Harley-Davidson family culture was a significant reason why the firm recaptured market share and returned to profitability.

A contrasting example to this unwitting change in organizational culture is Hewlett-Packard (H-P). Despite severe profit erosion and an environment that trumpeted the value of downsizing and head count reductions, H-P maintained the culture during the 1970s and 1980s that had been created by its founders, Bill Hewlett and Dave Packard. "Instead of laying off some workers, they adopted a policy whereby their staff took a 10 percent pay cut and worked 10 percent fewer hours. H-P's keeping its full complement of staff, while other companies were taking lay-offs, conveyed the message that everyone on the team was valued and mattered to the company" (Wilkins, 1984:46).

An important question, of course, is how an organization can avoid culture drift in the face of pressures to change. One powerful device under the control of managers is what Trice and Beyer (1984) called cultural rites, already discussed as cultural forms (see Table 3-1). These organizational practices and ceremonies exemplify and thus reinforce the core values of the organization and create resistance to drift. Some rites and rituals are focused on individuals, whereas others are focused on the organization or group.

In addition to rites and ceremonies, selection and socialization are powerful levers to reinforce the culture. Aronson and Mills (1959) long ago illustrated that when people go through a great deal of trouble or pain to obtain something, they value it more highly and protect it more vehemently. Pascale (1990) pointed out that the process of entry into an organization can powerfully reinforce its culture. Providing barriers to entry into the organization, having people earn their place in the system, and extracting a price for membership help reinforce and maintain the existing culture by creating more attraction to it and protection of it.

A host of additional mechanisms exist, of course, to reinforce desired cultures. Cultural leaders can, for example, specify how the central vision of the organization is relevant to current goals (Cartright, 1968) and thus keep it relevant and vital. They can model the desired behaviors and preach desired values and beliefs. They can search out incongruent values and behaviors and work to eliminate them or bring them into alignment (Nadler and Tushman, 1980). They can identify subcultures whose values and behaviors exemplify the desired culture and broadcast their accomplishments. Finally, they can find and emphasize commonalties that override divisive conflicts. Imaginative managers can find almost unlimited opportunities to reinforce culture once they are sensitive to what culture is about.

Conclusions

The discussion of organizational culture in this chapter suggests the following observations:

1. Because cultures develop in work organizations, just as they do in other groups in societies, cultural processes underlie much of what happens in organizations.

2. Various levels of culture, including national cultures, occupational cultures, organization-wide cultures, and those of various work groups, influence performance in organizations.

3. Cultures consist of powerful and pervasive sets of ideas and related sets of behaviors that help people manage collective uncertainties and create social order, continuity, collective identity, and commitment. In organizations, cultures help managers and other members to deal with problems of external adaptation and internal integration.

4. Because cultures channel behaviors in some ways and not others, they are bound to affect individual and organizational performance.

5. The precise linkages between culture and performance have not been documented, however, because of lack of adequately precise criteria either for culture or for successful performance.

6. Past behavioral research and theory suggest that cultures can directly affect performance by leading to certain patterns of behavior, but they are more likely to influence performance indirectly through effects on those thoughts, feelings, and behaviors that contribute to members' performance at the individual and organizational levels.

7. Because cultures consist of ideas and behaviors that are implicit rather than conscious, managers may not be aware of how their statements, actions, and policies may be incongruent with the desired culture and thus undermine or weaken it.

8. Among the levers that managers can use to manage cultures in organizations are selection, socialization, and leadership. Managers can use each of these levers and other tools at their disposal to create, change, or reinforce cultures. Each of these forms of cultural management may be occurring at the same time in different parts of the organization.

4

Developing Leaders

Leadership is a term that has been defined in many ways by different theorists over the years. Most definitions involve a process of social influence wherein a leader exerts intentional influence over the cognitions, affect, and behavior of others (usually called subordinates or followers) to structure the activities and relationships in a group or organization. The leader is usually someone in a formal position of authority, although leadership can also be exerted informally or shared among different members of a group.

Most researchers evaluate leadership effectiveness in terms of the consequences for followers and other organization stakeholders. Researchers have used many different indicators of leadership effectiveness, including the short-term and longer-term performance of the leader's organizational unit, its preparedness to deal with challenges or crises, follower satisfaction and commitment, and the leader's successful advancement to higher levels in the organization.

The effectiveness of a leader depends on individual competencies, which include a variety of behaviors and skills. In this chapter, we first describe the competencies found to be related to leadership effectiveness. We then examine various types of training techniques and developmental activities that may be of use to increase these competencies and improve leadership effectiveness.

LEADERSHIP COMPETENCIES

Over the past half century, thousands of studies have been conducted to discover the underlying reasons for effective leadership.[1] Some progress has been made in discovering why some leaders are more effective than others, although the leadership literature is full of ambiguous theory and contradictory research findings. Two types of competencies associated with leadership effectiveness are behaviors and skills. Leadership behavior includes observable actions (e.g., making assignments) and cognitive activities (e.g., making conscious decisions). Skills include the leader's knowledge and ability to perform various types of activities.

Behaviors Related to Leadership Effectiveness

Early researchers focused on the distinction between task-oriented behavior and people-oriented behavior (Fleishman, 1953; Halpin and Winer, 1957). Even though these two values are sometimes incompatible, effective leaders find ways to integrate them in patterns of behavior that are appropriate for the situation (Blake and Mouton, 1982; Yukl, 1981, 1994). Many later researchers and theorists have proposed taxonomies with narrower, more specific categories of leadership behavior. These taxonomies differ in purpose, level of abstraction, and number of behavior categories, and there has been much confusion and disagreement about the most useful way to classify leadership behavior.

The accumulated research evidence suggests that a number of specific types of behavior are especially relevant to leadership effectiveness: (1) clarifying roles and objectives, (2) supportive leadership, (3) planning and problem solving, (4) monitoring operations and environment, (5) inspirational leadership, (6) participative leadership, (7) positive reward behavior, and (8) networking. These categories of behavior are not mutually exclusive, but instead overlap and interact in their effects on subordinates. Our decision to highlight these behaviors does not imply that other behaviors are not relevant. We have selected categories that seem especially meaningful for understanding leadership effectiveness and that also have sufficient empirical evidence from different types of research to confirm their relevance. The research includes correlational field studies, laboratory and field experiments, case studies, and content analyses of critical incidents.

Clarifying Roles and Objectives

An important leadership function is to ensure that subordinates know what work they are supposed to do and the expected results of this work. The communication of plans, policies, and role expectations to subordinates is called clarifying or directing. Examples include defining job responsibilities for subordinates, assigning tasks, setting performance goals, authorizing action plans for accomplishing a task or project, and providing instructions in how to do a task.

Overall, the research suggests that leaders who are effective clarify objectives and priorities for subordinates but allow them considerable discretion in determining how to achieve the objectives (see reviews by Bass, 1990; Fisher and Edwards, 1988). A serious crisis is one situation in which strong, confident direction by the leader is usually essential to guide and coordinate the response of the organizational unit (Mulder et al., 1970; Yukl and Van Fleet, 1982).

Supportive Leadership

Supportive leadership includes a variety of behaviors by which a leader shows consideration, acceptance, and concern for a subordinate's needs and feelings. Extensive research over several decades using a variety of research methods demonstrates that supportive leadership usually increases the satisfaction of subordinates with their leader and their job, regardless of the situation (see reviews by Bass, 1990; Fisher and Edwards, 1988). Results of research on the effects of supportive leadership on subordinate performance are less consistent, which may be due in part to the use of different definitions and measures from study to study (Yammarino and Bass, 1990; Boyatzis, 1982; Yukl and Van Fleet, 1982; Hand and Slocum, 1972; Latham and Saari, 1979; Porras and Anderson, 1981). It seems that supportive leadership contributes to higher performance in some situations, especially when it results in a more cooperative working relationship with subordinates.

Situational theories such as path-goal theory (House and Mitchell, 1974) and leadership substitutes theory (Kerr and Jermier, 1978) propose that less supportive leadership is necessary when job satisfaction and task commitment are already high (e.g., because the task is interesting and fulfilling, employees are experienced professionals, and coworkers provide a lot of support and encouragement). Most studies testing this proposition (see Indvik, 1986; Wofford and Liska, 1993) have found evidence consistent with it. However, even when subordinates are experienced and the task is interesting, a moderate amount of supportive behavior may still be appropriate.

Planning and Problem Solving

Planning and problem solving involve decisions about what to do and how to do it. Planning is more proactive and future-oriented, whereas problem solving is more reactive and immediate, and it is important to find an appropriate balance between them. Results from several types of studies indicate that effective leaders formulate flexible, pragmatic strategies and plans to accomplish their objectives (Carroll and Gillen, 1987; Howard and

Bray, 1988; Kim and Yukl, 1995; Kotter, 1982; Shipper and Wilson, 1992; Winter, 1979).

Leaders at all levels must also deal with unforeseen events and problems that disrupt the work, reduce efficiency, and require modification of plans. Results from a number of studies using different research methods suggest that effective managers take responsibility for identifying work-related problems, analyzing them in a systematic but timely manner, and acting decisively to implement creative, practical solutions (Boyatzis, 1982; Carroll and Gillen, 1987; McCall and Lombardo, 1983; Morse and Wagner, 1978; Peters and Austin, 1985). More problem solving is probably needed in dynamic, uncertain situations than in stable, placid situations in which there are few unanticipated events or external threats.

Monitoring Operations and Environment

Leaders need information from a variety of sources about the internal operations of their work unit (e.g., effectiveness of processes, status of projects, subordinates' competencies, quality of products and services) and relevant events in the external environment (e.g., the concerns of customers and clients, the capabilities of suppliers and vendors, the actions of competitors, market trends, economic conditions, government policies, and technological developments). Monitoring provides information needed to identify problems and opportunities, as well as to formulate and modify objectives, strategies, plans, policies, and procedures. Without adequate monitoring, a leader will be unable to detect problems before they become serious, provide appropriate recognition for subordinate achievements, identify subordinates who need coaching or assistance in accomplishing their work objectives, evaluate performance of subordinates accurately, and have a sound basis for determining allocation of rewards such as pay increases. Several types of studies provide evidence that monitoring is related to leadership effectiveness (Daft et al., 1988; Grinyer et al., 1990; Kim and Yukl, 1995; Komaki, 1986; Kotter, 1982; Larson and Callahan, 1990; Peters and Austin, 1985). However, it is essential for leaders to select appropriate forms and amounts of monitoring for subordinates and the situation. More internal monitoring is probably needed when subordinates are inexperienced, they have tasks that require close coordination, and the cost of mistakes is high. More external monitoring is probably needed when the environment is dynamic, competitive, or hostile.

Participative Leadership

Participative leadership can be defined broadly as including all forms of shared decision making with subordinates and delegation of authority to individual subordinates or groups of subordinates. The results of quantitative research (i.e., questionnaire studies, field experiments, laboratory experiments) on the effects of participation are summarized in several literature reviews and meta-analyses (Cotton et al., 1988; Leana et al., 1990; Miller and Monge, 1986; Wagner and Gooding, 1987). These reviews reveal that research evidence from the quantitative studies is inconsistent. Some studies found evidence that participative leadership resulted in higher subordinate performance, whereas other studies failed to find significant results. In contrast, findings from descriptive case studies of effective managers have been more consistently supportive of the benefits of participative leadership (e.g., Bradford and Cohen, 1984; Kanter, 1983; Peters and Austin, 1985).

Most of the quantitative research on participative leadership did not directly examine the possibility that consultation and delegation are effective in some situations but not others. To address this problem, Vroom and Yetton (1973) developed a theory specifying the necessary conditions for participative leadership to improve decision quality and subordinate commitment to the decision. Research conducted to test this theory has generally supported it (see Vroom and Jago, 1988; Yukl, 1994). The research indicates that a leader's use of participative decision making improves decision quality when subordinates have information and ideas not possessed by the leader and are willing to cooperate with the leader in finding a good way to achieve their shared objectives.

Delegation is a unique form of participative leadership that appears to improve subordinate performance when used in appropriate situations (Leana, 1986; Miller and Toulouse, 1986; Peters and Austin, 1985). Delegation is more likely to be successful when subordinates are competent, committed to organizational objectives, and willing to take on important responsibilities.

Inspirational Leadership

Inspirational leadership behavior is used is to motivate followers to exert exceptional effort and place the needs of the group or organization above their individual needs. Most studies on inspirational leadership suggest that it is one of the strongest predictors of subordinate commitment and performance (Avolio and Howell, 1992; Hater and Bass, 1988; House et al., 1991; Howell and Frost, 1989; Howell and Higgins, 1990; Podsakoff et al., 1990; Seltzer and Bass, 1990; Waldman et al., 1987; Yammarino and Bass, 1990; Yukl and Van Fleet, 1982).

According to most theories of inspirational and transformational leadership (e.g., Bass, 1985; Bennis and Nanus, 1985; Burns, 1978; Conger, 1989; Kouzes and Posner, 1987; Shamir et al., 1993; Tichy and Devanna, 1986), such leadership can enhance group performance in any situation, but it is especially important when major changes in the strategy and culture of the organization are necessary.

Inspirational leaders develop a clear and appealing vision of what the organization could accomplish or become. They interpret external events in a way that helps followers understand the challenges and opportunities facing the organization and the need for change (Bennis and Nanus, 1985; Tichy and Devanna, 1986). Inspirational leaders stimulate followers to think about problems in new ways and question old assumptions and beliefs that may no longer be valid (Bass, 1985). They build follower confidence and hope by acting confident and optimistic themselves, by expressing confidence that followers can attain challenging objectives, by communicating a credible strategy for achieving strategic objectives, by planning activities in a way that will ensure that progress is experienced early in the task, and by celebrating successful accomplishments by the group (Shamir et al., 1993; Kouzes and Posner, 1987).

Inspirational leaders use highly visible, symbolic actions to emphasize important values and demonstrate their own commitment to a vision, strategy, or change. Concern is demonstrated by the way a leader spends time, by resource allocation decisions made when there are trade-offs between objectives, by the questions the leader asks, and by the actions the leader rewards (Schein, 1992). The values espoused by a leader should be demonstrated in the leader's own behavior, and this must be done consistently, not just when it is convenient. Leading by example is especially important for actions that are unpleasant, dangerous, unconventional, or controversial.

Inspirational leadership is not simply a quality of the leader but is a quality of the relationship that develops between leaders and followers (Burns, 1978; Meindl, 1990). A leader's influence depends also on the perceptions and interpretations of followers. It is important to take into account the relations that develop among the followers and subordinates themselves. This social process affects the interpretations of followers and may be independent of influences that emanate from the leader's behaviors. It involves the thought processes of organizational actors and observers and has been modeled in terms of a social contagion process (Meindl, 1990). This approach alters the research focus from the leader per se to the larger contexts in which the leader functions.

Positive Reward Behavior

Positive reward behavior is usually defined as including two components: tangible rewards (e.g., bonus, merit pay increase) that are contingent on subordinate performance and (2) recognition (e.g., praise) for subordinate achievements and contributions to the performance of the leader's unit.

Podsakoff and colleagues (1984) reviewed research with questionnaire measures of leader behavior and found that positive reward behavior was correlated positively with subordinate satisfaction and performance. Similar results were found in most subsequent studies that included a measure of positive reward behavior (e.g., Podsakoff and Todor, 1985; Wikoff et al., 1983; Yammarino and Bass, 1990). Although the results were not significant in every study, they suggest that contingent rewards usually increase subordinate satisfaction and performance.

Recognition is easier to provide than tangible rewards, yet it is a form of behavior that is often underutilized by managers. Praise is more likely to be effective when it is clearly based on real contributions and sincere, instead of being used as a manipulative technique for the leader's own personal objectives (Yukl, 1994). Effective leaders actively look for behaviors and contributions to recognize, they recognize a variety of different types of achievements and contributions, and they find creative ways to provide recognition (Peters and Austin, 1985). The beneficial effects of recognition are likely to be greater when it is provided by a highly respected, trustworthy manager who holds a key position in the organization.

Networking

Research indicates that effective managers develop and maintain large networks of relevant contacts with people on whom they are dependent for information, support, or resources (Kanter, 1983; Kaplan, 1984; Kotter, 1982). Managers who use more networking also advance faster and further in the organization (Luthans et al., 1985; Michael and Yukl, 1993).

Internal networking is likely to be more important for large, complex organizations with a high degree of lateral dependence than for managers of autonomous subunits (Kotter, 1982; Stewart, 1982). External networking is likely to be more important when there is high dependence on external clients or suppliers, as when the work unit must change its products, services, or timetables frequently to accommodate the needs of clients and customers. Upper-level managers usually depend more on people outside the organization, and as a result they have more external contacts in their networks (Luthans et al., 1985; McCall et al., 1978).

Skills Related to Leader Effectiveness

Three basic categories of skills relevant to leadership effectiveness are technical skills, conceptual skills, and interpersonal skills (Katz, 1955; Mann, 1965). Technical skills include knowledge of products and services; knowledge of work operations, procedures, and equipment; and knowledge of markets, clients, and competitors. Conceptual skills include the ability to analyze complex events and perceive trends, recognize changes, and identify problems and opportunities; the ability to develop creative, practical solutions to problems; and the ability to conceptualize complex ideas and use models and analogies. Interpersonal skills include understanding of interpersonal and group processes; the ability to understand the motives, feelings, and attitudes of people from what they say and do (empathy, social sensitivity); the ability to maintain cooperative relationships with people (tact, diplomacy, conflict resolution skills); and oral communication and persuasive ability. A combination of specific technical, cognitive, and interpersonal skills is involved in the ability to perform relevant managerial functions such as planning, delegating, and supervising; this fourth category is referred to as administrative skills.

Research on skills relevant for leadership effectiveness generally supports the conclusion that technical skills, conceptual skills, interpersonal skills, and administrative skills are necessary in most managerial positions (Bass, 1990; Boyatzis, 1982; Bray et al., 1974; Howard and Bray, 1988; Mann, 1965). But only a limited amount of research has examined how situational differences moderate the relationship between skills and leader effectiveness. This research provides evidence that the relative importance of different types of skills depends on the type of organization, the nature of the environment, and the level of management (Boyatzis, 1982; Jaques, 1989; Katz and Kahn, 1978; Kotter, 1982; Kraut et al., 1989; Mann, 1965; McLennan, 1967; Pavett and Lau, 1983; Stewart, 1982).

Since the major responsibility of top executives is making strategic decisions, conceptual skills are more important at this level than at middle or lower levels (Jacobs and Jaques, 1987; Jaques, 1989; Katz and Kahn, 1978; Mann, 1965). Top executives need to analyze vast amounts of ambiguous and contradictory information about the environment in order to make strategic decisions and to interpret events for other members of the organization. Executives need to have a long time perspective (10 to 20 years) and the ability to comprehend complex relationships among variables relevant to the performance of the organization (Jacobs and Jaques, 1990). A top executive must be able to anticipate future events and know how to plan for them. Conceptual skills are needed to formulate a strategic vision to guide major changes in the organization in response to changes in the external environment (Wofford and Goodwin, 1994).

Unprecedented changes affecting organizations will make leadership in the 21st century even more important and difficult. To cope with these changes, leaders may require not only more of the same skills, but also new ones (Conger, 1993; Hunt, 1991; Segal, 1992). One competency that appears to be relevant for coping with increasing complexity and change is the ability to introspectively analyze one's own cognitive processes (e.g., how one defines and solves problems) and find ways to improve them (Argyris, 1991; Dechant, 1990). This competency (sometimes called self-learning) appears to involve the ability to develop better mental models, learn from mistakes, and change assumptions and ways of thinking in response to a changing world (Druckman and Bjork, 1994).

TECHNIQUES FOR ENHANCING LEADERSHIP COMPETENCIES

Two different approaches for developing leadership skills are training programs and learning from experience. Most training programs occur during a defined time period, are conducted by internal training professionals or outside educators, and take place away from the manager's immediate work site (e.g., a short workshop at a training center, a management course at a university). Experiential learning usually involves activities that are embedded within or related to operational job assignments, and they are often unplanned and informal. These experiences can take many forms, including coaching by the boss or coworkers, mentoring by someone at a higher level in the organization, special assignments embedded within the current job, special assignments on temporary leave from the current job, and a promotion or transfer that provides new challenges and opportunities for skill development. The effectiveness of training programs and developmental experiences depends in part on organizational conditions that facilitate or inhibit learning of leadership skills and the application of this learning by managers.

In the remainder of this chapter we examine features of both training programs and developmental experiences. We do not attempt to examine all training methods, aspects of development, and organizational factors that may facilitate or impede learning. For example, we do not attempt to evaluate self-development approaches, such as reading popular books for practitioners, viewing televised training programs and commercial videotapes, and using interactive computer programs designed to enhance management skills. There is almost no empirical research on the effectiveness of such approaches (Baldwin and Padgett, 1993). Our review focuses instead on the most promising training and development techniques about which there is at least some empirical research on effectiveness and facilitating conditions.

Training Programs

Most leadership training programs are designed to increase skills and behaviors relevant for managerial effectiveness and advancement. The training programs may attempt to increase self-awareness among participants, although they rarely try to change personality and values. Leadership training can take many forms, from short workshops that last only a few hours and focus on a narrow set of skills, to comprehensive programs that last for a year or more and cover a wide range of skills as well as their underlying rationale (e.g., a university master's degree in business administration program for executives).

The effectiveness of formal training programs depends greatly on how well they are designed. Their design should take into account learning theory, the specific learning objectives, characteristics of the trainees, and practical considerations such as constraints and costs in relation to benefits. The current state of knowledge about learning processes does not provide precise guidelines for the design of training. Nevertheless, training is more likely to be successful if it is designed and conducted in a way that is consistent with some important findings in research on learning processes and training techniques (see reviews by Baldwin and Padgett, 1993; Campbell, 1988; Druckman and Bjork, 1991, 1994; Howell and Cooke, 1989; Noe and Ford, 1992).

The training content should be clear and meaningful. The activities should be organized and sequenced in a way that will facilitate learning. The choice of training methods should take into account the trainee's current skill level, motivation, and capacity to understand and remember complex information. Trainees should actively practice the skills to be learned (e.g., practice behaviors, recall information from memory, apply principles in doing a task). They should receive relevant feedback from a variety of available sources, and feedback should be accurate, timely, and constructive. The instructional processes should enhance trainee self-efficacy and expectations that the training will be successful.

Organizational Conditions Affecting Training Success

Research on the success of leadership training provides mixed results, and it is evident that the training is not always successful (Burke and Day, 1986; Latham, 1988). Sometimes the training is not worth the cost of providing it. The amount of learning that occurs within formal training programs and the application of learning back on the job depend greatly on several conditions in the job environment. The motivation to acquire and use new skills is increased by an organizational climate and culture that support personal development and continuous learning (Rouiller and Goldstein, 1993; Tracey et al., 1995).

One factor is how much choice employees have about attending training programs. Motivation to learn appears to be higher when participation in a training program is voluntary rather than compulsory (Facteau et al., 1995; Hicks and Klimoski, 1987) and when employees receive the training they prefer (Baldwin et al., 1991). Another factor is the extent to which bosses and coworkers promote and support the training. Several studies have examined how support from people in the manager's immediate environment influences application of learned skills after the training is completed (Facteau et al., 1995; Fleishman et al., 1955; Ford et al., 1992; Hand et al., 1973; Huczynski and Lewis, 1980; Kozlowski and Hults, 1987; Noe and Schmitt, 1986; Rouiller and Goldstein, 1993; Tracey et al., 1995). Application of skills is more likely when bosses provide opportunity, encouragement, support, and reinforcement. Also, skills learned in a short training program can be enhanced by planning follow-up activities such as refresher sessions, progress review sessions, and specific projects related to the training.

Some progress has been made on documenting the importance of organizational factors for the application of training, but we still know little about the specific conditions facilitating application of different types of skills after training and the critical time periods for their maximal effect. To date, most of the research on organizational conditions consists of correlational studies that measure perception of the training environment and self-reports of skill application shortly after the training is completed. We need more longitudinal research on a wider variety of managerial skills, with better measures of learning, environmental conditions, and skill application (Baldwin and Ford, 1988; Tannenbaum and Yukl, 1992).

Training Techniques

A large variety of training methods have been used for leadership training (Bass, 1990; Burke and Day, 1986; Tetrault et al., 1988). Lectures, demonstrations, procedural manuals, videotapes, equipment simulators, and interactive computer tutorials are used to teach technical skills. Cases, exercises, business games, simulations, and videotapes are used to teach conceptual and administrative skills. Lectures, case discussion, videotapes, role playing, and group exercises are used to teach interpersonal skills. Two promising techniques that are becoming widely used for leadership training are behavioral role modeling and large-scale simulations.

Behavior Role Modeling

Behavior role modeling is a training method widely used to enhance the interpersonal skills of managers. In behavior role modeling training, small groups of trainees observe someone demonstrate how to handle a particular type of interpersonal problem (e.g., provide corrective feedback, provide coaching), then they practice the behavior in a role play and get nonthreatening feedback. The effective behaviors are usually shown on a videotape that lasts from 3 to 10 minutes. In most programs the trainer explains the learning points prior to the modeling demonstration, then trainees observe them enacted in the video. Sometimes learning points also appear in the video as the behaviors occur.

The learning points can be practiced by trainees in a role play conducted in front of the class or in small groups that allow several trainees to practice the behaviors concurrently. Trainees can obtain feedback from a variety of sources, including the trainer, other trainees who serve as observers, and from videotapes of their own behavior in the role plays. In most programs, trainees are asked to plan how to implement the behavior guidelines back on the job. After writing their plans, trainees can discuss them in dyads, in small groups, or with the trainer privately to do some reality testing and obtain guidance and encouragement.

Burke and Day (1986) conducted a meta-analysis of studies evaluating behavior role modeling and concluded that it was one of the most effective training methods for managers. Subsequent reviews also support the utility of this training method (e.g., Latham, 1989; Mayer and Russell, 1987; Robertson, 1990), although most of them expressed concerns about the limitations of the research. Few studies have measured behavior change back on the job or subsequent performance improvement in addition to immediate learning of behaviors in the training session. Despite the positive results found in most studies on the effects of behavior role modeling training, we still know little about when and why the training is effective.

Large-Scale Simulations

Large-scale simulations are being used increasingly in training programs for managers (Kaplan et al., 1985; Van Velsor et al., 1989). This technique can be used to help participants practice and learn administrative skills, interpersonal skills, and leadership behaviors. The simulations typically involve a single hypothetical organization with multiple divisions (e.g., a bank or plastics company). Participants are assigned to a different positions in the organization and carry out the responsibilities of the executives for a period of one or two days. Participants read extensive background information about the organization and their position (e.g., prior history, products and services, financial information, industry and market conditions, organization chart, position duties and responsibilities). Each participant also has copies of recent correspondence (e.g., memos, reports) with other members of the organization and outsiders. Participants have separate work spaces, although they are allowed to communicate by various media and to schedule meetings. During the simulation the "managers" make strategic and operational decisions just as they would in a real organization.

Participants receive feedback about the group processes and individual skills and behaviors. Feedback is usually provided by other participants and by observers who track the behavior and decisions of the participants.

Additional feedback can be provided by videotaping meetings among the participants. The facilitators help the participants understand how well they functioned as executives in collecting and processing information, analyzing and solving problems, communicating with others, influencing others, and planning strategy and operations.

There is increasing evidence of the utility of simulations for leadership development, although the research literature on simulations is still very limited (Keys and Wolfe, 1990; Thornton and Cleveland, 1990; Wolfe and Roberts, 1993). More research is needed to determine what types of learning occur and the conditions that facilitate learning. Some serious limitations in most large-scale simulations that need to be addressed include the short time period available to make effective use of behaviors that necessarily involve a series of related actions over time and the lack of appropriate follow-up activities to facilitate transfer of learning back to the job (Druckman and Bjork, 1994).

Learning from Experience

Much of the skill essential for effective leadership is learned from experience rather than from formal training programs (Davies and Easterby-Smith, 1984; Kelleher et al., 1986; Lindsey et al., 1987; McCall et al., 1988). In recent years there has been increasing interest in studying how managers learn skills and values from their experience. Researchers have begun to investigate what is learned, how it learned, and the necessary conditions for successful development of leadership competencies.

The extent to which leadership skills and values are developed during operational assignments depends on the type of experiences afforded by these assignments. Research on aspects of job experience related to leadership development (Lindsey et al., 1987; McCall et al., 1988; McCauley, 1986) found that growth and learning were greatest when challenging situations or adversity forced a manager to come to terms with personal limitations and overcome them. The research also found that challenge was greatest in jobs that required a manager to deal with change, take responsibility for high-visibility problems, influence people without authority, handle external pressure, and work without much guidance or support from superiors.

More learning occurs during operational assignments when people get accurate feedback about their behavior and its consequences and use this feedback to analyze their experiences and learn from them. However, useful feedback is seldom provided within operational assignments, and, even when available, it may not result in learning. Feedback is more likely to result in development when there is external pressure for the person to change, combined with strong social support (i.e., acceptance, assurance of self-worth, sincere desire to help the person) (Kaplan, 1990). The extent of learning from feedback may also depend on some characteristics of the manager (Bunker and Webb, 1992; Kaplan, 1990; McCall, 1994). More learning is likely for managers who are receptive to feedback, willing to experiment, reflective about the reasons for outcomes, and concerned about people as well as the task (Kelleher et al., 1986).

A key source of feedback and coaching for most managers is the boss, but sometimes the boss does not provide them (Hillman et al., 1990; London and Mone, 1987; Valerio, 1990). A person is unlikely to get much feedback and coaching from a boss who does not understand their importance, who is preoccupied with immediate crises, or who is mainly concerned with his or her own career advancement. Another potential source of feedback and coaching for managers is peers and subordinates (Kram and Isabella, 1985; London et al., 1990). Peers and subordinates may be especially important as a source of feedback, advice, and support for managers when superiors are unavailable or unwilling to provide it.

Organizational Conditions Affecting Learning from Experience

As in the case of training, some conditions within an organization help to determine how much job challenge occurs, how much feedback is provided, how mistakes and failure are interpreted, and how much the managers are motivated to learn new skills. Not much research has been conducted on these situational conditions.

The amount of management development during operational assignments is influenced in part by prevailing attitudes and values about development. More development is likely when executives in an organization have strong values about the importance of development for the effectiveness of the organization and are aware of the developmental opportunities in operational assignments (Hall and Foulkes, 1991). At present, most organizations do not make job assignments that explicitly provide adequate developmental opportunities and a logical progression of learning (Baldwin and Padgett, 1993).

The learning climate, culture, and reward system within the organization may also influence development. More leadership development is likely in an organization in which top management values it highly and perceives it to be important for organizational effectiveness. In an organization with a learning climate that values continuous learning, more members of the organization will be encouraged to seek opportunities for personal growth and skill acquisition (Kozlowski and Hults, 1987).

Even when the organization has a strong culture to support the value of individual development, it is not easy to achieve. Planning of developmental experiences for individual managers is likely to be haphazard and unsystematic if passed on from boss to boss. McCall (1992) suggests the need to make particular individuals or committees responsible for planning and coordinating the overall process of management development for the organization.

The U.S. Army may be a model for leadership development programs. Although there is no system-wide program, a number of Army training facilities and bases have designed programs that include many of the elements suggested by McCall. Many of the programs help soldiers to define goals and consider ways to achieve them. At the Army War College, students engage in data gathering and self-reflection, set goals, develop a learning plan, obtain feedback, and have periodic reviews. At Fort Leavenworth, students assess their own performance as part of a Leadership Assessment and Development Program. They are also given opportunities to consider performance requirements for tasks at higher levels in the organization's hierarchy. Missing, however, from many of these programs are assessments of how they impact the careers of participants. (See Druckman and Bjork, 1991:Ch.5, for a discussion of these and other Army programs in the context of a framework for career development.)

Developmental Techniques

A number of techniques can be used to facilitate the learning of relevant skills from experience on the job. These planned techniques can be used to supplement informal coaching by the boss or peers. The sections below briefly discuss special developmental assignments, job rotation, mentoring, after-action reviews, multirater feedback workshops, developmental assessment centers, and action learning.

Special Assignments. Special assignments are sometimes used to develop leadership skills, behaviors, and values. Some special assignments can be carried out concurrently with regular job responsibilities, whereas others require taking a temporary leave from one's regular job. Research on the effectiveness of developmental assignments is still very limited. Longitudinal research at AT&T (Bray et al., 1974; Howard and Bray, 1988) provides evidence that diverse, challenging assignments early in one's career may facilitate advancement. However, the relationship found between advancement and job challenge provides only indirect evidence about special assignments. The research does not evaluate the consequences of using special assignments as a separate developmental technique distinct from regular job responsibilities. Research at the Center for Creative Leadership and elsewhere suggests that different skills are learned from different types of challenges and hardship experiences (Field and Harris, 1991; Lindsey et al., 1987; McCall et al., 1988; McCauley et al., 1995; Valerio, 1990). However, this research relies on managers' retrospective reports of their development, not on a systematic comparison among different types of assignments using measures of competencies taken before and after the assignment. Moreover, since selection for assignments is not random, it is difficult for analysts to separate the effects due to the assignment per se from those due to the characteristics of the people being assigned. More research is needed to determine what types of assignments are effective for what type of skills and what type of people.

McCauley and colleagues (1995) have suggested some ways to improve the use of special assignments for developing managers. Before making assignments, it is important to identify the challenges and learning opportunities they provide and relate them to the manager's developmental needs and career aspirations. Managers need to become more aware of the importance of developmental assignments, and they should share in the responsibility for planning them. The challenges afforded managers and what they learn from them should be tracked, and this information should be related to career counseling and succession planning. Similar recommendations are made by White (1992), who in effect is suggesting the integration of special assignments with mentoring and multirater feedback. Dechant (1994) suggests that learning from special assignments can be facilitated by the development of a concrete learning plan.

Job Rotation Programs. Job rotation programs with substantive assignments in different subunits of an organization offer a number of developmental opportunities. Managers face the challenge of quickly learning how to establish cooperative relationships and deal with new types of technical problems for which they lack adequate preparation. They can learn about the unique problems and processes in different (functional or product) subunits and the interdependencies among different parts of the organization. Job rotation also provides managers the opportunity to develop a large network of contacts in different parts of the organization.

Despite widespread use of job rotation in industry and the military, only a few studies have been conducted to evaluate this developmental technique. A study by London (1989) on scientists and engineers found that they benefitted in several ways from a job rotation program. Participants reported having higher mutual respect for other functions, a greater appreciation of the need for collaboration, and a stronger belief in the value of viewing problems from different perspectives.

A survey by Campion and colleagues (1994) of employees in a variety of organizations examined the costs and benefits of job rotation. Participants reported that job rotation resulted in increased managerial, technical, and business skill and knowledge. Amount of job rotation was positively correlated with rate of advancement, but the direction of causality was not clear. To clarify the relationship of job rotation to skill acquisition and advancement, we need longitudinal research with repeated measurement of key variables at appropriate intervals.

The study by Campion et al. (1994) showed that job rotation also has some costs. One cost is lower productivity for the rotated individuals, which is due to the normal learning curve for a new type of job. We still have little knowledge about how long it takes to become effective in a different type of managerial position, or how long it takes for the desired learning to occur. Research is needed on the costs and benefits of job rotation, how much rotation is desirable, and how long managers should remain in each position.

Mentoring. In the last decade there has been increasing interest in the use of formal mentoring programs to facilitate management development (Noe, 1991). Mentoring is a relationship in which a more experienced manager helps a less experienced protégé; the mentor is usually at a higher managerial level and is not the protégé's immediate boss. Research on mentors (Kram, 1985; Noe, 1988) finds that they provide two distinct types of functions for the protégé: a psychosocial function (acceptance, encouragement, coaching, counseling) and a career facilitation function (sponsorship, protection, challenging assignments, exposure and visibility).

Mentors can facilitate adjustment, learning, and stress reduction during difficult job transitions, such as promotion to the first managerial position, a transfer or promotion to a different functional unit in the organization, an assignment in a foreign country, and assignments in an organization that has been merged, reorganized, or downsized (Kram and Hall, 1989; Zey, 1988). Several studies show that mentoring results in more career advancement and success for the protégé (Chao et al., 1992; Dreher and Ash, 1990; Scandura, 1992; Turban and Dougherty, 1994; Whitely and Coetsier, 1993).

Some of the research suggests that informal mentoring is more successful than formal mentoring programs. For example, Noe (1988) found that personality conflicts and lack of mentor commitment were more likely to occur with assigned mentors. The difference between formal and informal mentoring may be due primarily to the way a formal program is conducted, including the selection and training of the mentors. The success of a formal mentoring program is probably increased by making participation voluntary rather than required, by providing mentors some choice of a protégé, by explaining the benefits and pitfalls, and by clarifying the expected roles and processes for both mentor and protégé (Chao et al., 1992). Protégés need to be aware of the developmental benefits of mentoring, because they can influence the amount of mentoring they receive (Hunt and Michael, 1983). Turban and Dougherty (1994) found that protégés were more likely to initiate mentoring relationships and get more mentoring if they had high emotional stability, internal locus of control orientation, and self-monitoring.

Mentoring is also affected by demographic factors such as age, gender, and race. Women and minorities have special problems finding successful mentoring relationships (Ilgen and Youtz, 1986; Ohlott et al., 1994; Noe, 1988; Ragins and Cotton, 1991, 1993; Ragins and McFarlin, 1990; Thomas, 1990). Common difficulties women encounter in mentoring relationships include stereotypes about appropriate behavior, concern about intimacy with men, awkwardness about discussing some subjects, lack of appropriate role models, resentment by peers, and exclusion from male networks. Some of these difficulties persist even when women mentor women. Despite the difficulties, some recent studies found no evidence that gender affects the success of mentoring (Dreher and Ash, 1990; Turban and Dougherty, 1994).

In general, the research suggests that mentoring can be a useful technique for facilitation of career advancement, adjustment to change, and job satisfaction of protégés. However, there is little research yet on the ways mentors actually facilitate development of leadership competencies (Tannenbaum and Yukl, 1992). More research is needed to identify the skills, values, and behaviors most likely to be acquired or enhanced in a mentoring relationship, the learning processes, and the conditions facilitating development.

After-Action Reviews. Learning from experience is more likely when a systematic analysis is made after an important activity to discover the reasons for success or failure. The after-action review or postmortem is a procedure for improving learning from experience by making a collective analysis of processes and resulting outcomes for an activity conducted by the group. This approach for evaluating activities and planning improvements is pervasive now in the Army but much less common in civilian organizations.

After-action reviews are usually focused on technical aspects of tactics and strategy rather than on leadership issues. There is potential for providing useful feedback to individuals about effective and ineffective leadership behavior, but some obvious constraints tend to limit the occurrence of this type of feedback. Many subordinates are afraid to point out mistakes make by a powerful leader or to suggest ways the leader could be more effective in the future. Many leaders are reluctant to have their actions and decisions critiqued by subordinates in an open meeting.

There has been little research to evaluate the benefits of after-action reviews for increasing leadership development. Additional research is clearly needed to determine the conditions and procedures appropriate for using after-action reviews to improve leadership skills and processes.

Multirater Feedback Workshops. The use of behavioral feedback from multiple sources has become a popular method for management development. This approach is called by various names, including 360 degree feedback and multirater feedback. In a feedback workshop, managers receive information about their skills or behavior from standardized questionnaires filled out by others, such as subordinates, peers, superiors, and occasionally such outsiders as clients. Feedback about how others view the manager is usually provided in a written report to each participating manager. In the feedback report, ratings made by others are usually compared with self-ratings by the manager and to norms for other managers. An experienced facilitator helps each manager interpret the feedback and identify developmental needs.

Accurate feedback depends on gaining the cooperation of a representative set of respondents who interacted frequently with the manager over a period of time and had adequate opportunity to observe the behaviors in the questionnaire. Respondents are more likely to provide accurate ratings if they understand the purpose of the survey, how the results will be used, and the procedures to ensure confidentiality of answers. Ratings are more likely to be accurate if the feedback is used only for developmental purposes and is not part of the formal performance appraisal process (London et al., 1990).

Despite the widespread use of feedback workshops in recent years, only a few studies have assessed their impact on management development. Three studies found that feedback workshops can result in improvement of management skills and changes in managerial behavior (e.g., Hazucha et al., 1993; Nemeroff and Cosentino, 1979; Wilson et al., 1990). Although multirater workshops appear to be a promising approach for leadership development, more research is needed to determine what form of feedback is most useful, the conditions under which behavioral feedback is most likely to result in beneficial change, the types of skills or behavior most likely to be improved by feedback workshops, and the types of managers who will benefit most from participating in feedback workshops.

Developmental Assessment Centers and Workshops. Traditional assessment centers use multiple methods to measure managerial competencies and potential for advancement. Such methods include interviews; achievement, personality, and situational tests; short autobiographical essays; and speaking and writing exercises. Information from these diverse sources is integrated and used to develop an overall evaluation of each participant's management potential. The assessment center process typically takes two to three days, but some data collection may occur beforehand. In the past, most assessment centers were used only for selection and promotion decisions, but in recent years there has been growing interest in using assessment centers for developing managers (Boehm, 1985; Goodge, 1991; Rayner and Goodge, 1988; Munchus and McArthur, 1991).

Only a few studies have examined the effectiveness of developmental assessment centers. A study by Papa and Graham (1991) found that participation in a developmental assessment center resulted in more performance improvement after two years when managers received specific skill training afterward based on the feedback they received about skill deficiencies. Engelbracht and Fischer (1995) conducted a study of managers who participated in a developmental assessment center and received subsequent coaching and developmental assignments from their boss (who received a copy of the manager's feedback and recommendations for improvement). The managers were rated by superiors on skills and performance three months after the developmental assessment center, and the ratings were higher than those for a control group. Neither study provides a clear indication of the unique effects of the developmental assessment center, because other developmental activities such as skill training and special assignments were used in conjunction with it.

When combined with studies on participant perceptions about assessment centers (e.g., Fletcher, 1990; Iles et al., 1989; Jones and Whitmore, 1992), the research suggests that this developmental technique can enhance self-awareness, help to identify training needs, and facilitate subsequent development of leadership skills. However, we still do not know much about the underlying learning processes in developmental centers and workshops, or about the necessary conditions for successful development.

Action Learning. Action learning is an approach used widely in Europe for combining formal management training with learning from experience (Margerison, 1988; Revans, 1982). A typical program of action learning is conducted over a period of several months and includes field project work interspersed with skill training seminars. Individuals or teams of managers conduct field projects on complex organizational problems requiring use of skills learned in the formal training sessions. The emphasis is on developing cognitive and interpersonal skills rather than technical knowledge. The managers meet periodically with a skilled facilitator to discuss, analyze, and learn from their experiences.

Few studies have been conducted to evaluate the effects of action learning, and these studies have relied on self-reported benefits rather than objective indicators of behavior change and performance improvement. In a study by Prideaux and Ford (1988), participants reported that they increased their self-awareness, emotional resilience, interactive and team skills, analytical skills, and learning skills. Marson and Bruff (1992) studied Federal Aviation Administration supervisors who carried out six short, individual projects after classroom training, with coaching and support from their bosses; few of the supervisors reported any skill improvement. McCauley and Hughes-James (1994) had school superintendents rate the benefits derived from individual developmental projects; the percentage of participants who reported increased skills was low. Overall, the results from research on effects of action learning are inconclusive. It is difficult to determine the unique benefits from developmental projects without an experimental study that includes a control group, which has not yet been done.

UNANSWERED QUESTIONS

Many specific research questions have been identified in earlier sections of this review. At this point we point out some more general research questions about leadership training and development. Research on each of the following questions would greatly enhance our understanding about increasing leadership competencies in large organizations:

1. How should we conceptualize and measure the skills, competencies, and behavior needed by current and future leaders?

2. What types of experiences are most useful for developing different types of leadership skills?

3. What training techniques are effective for different types of leadership skills and behavior?

4. What skills and values are needed for shared leadership in teams, and what is the best way to develop these skills?

5. What is the contribution of self-help activities to the development of leadership competencies, and how can the benefits be increased?

6. To what extent are underlying values and personality traits influenced by developmental techniques, and what experiences and conditions are necessary for beneficial change to occur?

7. How is leadership development related to other human developmental processes and life stages?

8. How will changes in technology provide new challenges and opportunities for training and developmental activities in organizations?

9. How can we achieve a better integration between formal training and development from operational assignments and self-development activities?

10. How can we create and maintain the type of organization culture that will support, nurture and facilitate increased leadership development?

CONCLUSIONS

Considerable progress has been made in identifying the competencies related to leadership effectiveness. Nevertheless, ambiguity in the conceptualization of leadership competencies and measurement difficulties have impeded faster progress. Increasing environmental change and new challenges suggest that more skill and perhaps some new competencies will be needed for success in the 21st century. New forms of organization and increasing skill requirements for leaders are likely to make shared leadership increasingly important. Organizations of the future will rely more on teams of leaders and the sharing of leadership functions by more members of the organization. As yet we know much less about this type of leadership than about leadership by individual managers in traditional, hierarchical organizations.

Training of leadership skills is a multibillion-dollar business conducted by universities, consulting companies, and in-house organization training centers. Despite the massive volume of training that exists, there has been only a small amount of research on its effectiveness, and much of it relies on self-serving judgments and subjective feelings. Informal self-learning by reading books and viewing videos is also a big business, but we know little about the benefits derived from these activities or the extent to which they can substitute for formal instruction. Guidelines for the design of training are available from several decades of research on human learning, but little of this research involved leadership training. Relatively new techniques such as behavior role modeling and simulations appear very promising for leadership training, but we need to find out more about how to use these techniques effectively. Organizational conditions, such as the degree of support from bosses and the learning climate, appear to be a major determinant of the application of training on the job, but there has been little research on how to create and sustain favorable conditions.

After years of preoccupation with formal management training, researchers have finally acknowledged the importance of learning leadership competencies from experiences on the job. Research on the conditions facilitating development of leadership competencies has made considerable progress in the past decade, yet mapping of relationships between specific experiences and enhancement of specific competencies has just begun. Several developmental techniques for increasing experiential learning on the job appear very promising, including mentoring, special assignments, job rotation, multirater feedback workshops, developmental assessment centers, after-action reviews, and action learning. However, the amount of research on these developmental techniques is still very limited. We have much to learn about the optimal conditions and timing for them, including what competencies will be enhanced, when the techniques should be used, how the techniques should be used, and for whom. It is evident that organizational conditions enhance or inhibit leadership development, but we need to learn more about how to create and sustain favorable conditions. We also need to learn more about the impacts of leader decisions and actions on those conditions. These concerns can be addressed by a framework that considers leader development as part of an organizational system.

Preliminary evidence suggests that formal training, development on the job, and self-development are much more effective when coordinated with each other and supported by a strong learning culture in organizations. However, we have just begun to think about how to integrate these different elements. More attention to this issue may be spurred by the growing realization that leadership development may be as important strategically as product development, marketing, and customer service for long-term organizational effectiveness (Hall and Seibert, 1992; McCall, 1992).

NOTE

[1]The committee has made no attempt to review this vast literature. We concentrate on studies designed to explore influences on leader competencies and training approaches. Many of these studies were conducted from a social-psychological perspective. For classic early treatments of leadership functions from a sociological perspective, see Bernard (1938) and Selznick (1957).

5

Interorganizational Relations

Two medium-size banks in a large U.S. metropolitan area recently came to the same conclusion: each was too small to withstand the market power of its larger competitors. Neither had the resources to compete or to grow and, moreover, both were prime takeover targets for large banks wanting a presence in their metropolitan market. Faced with a future of stagnation at best, and dismemberment at worst, the two banks decided to merge. Today, the combined institution is twice the size of the former banks and is one of the largest savings banks in the United States. The new bank has the size to be a major player in its market and is now pursuing efficiencies of scale and scope never before possible.

This type of interorganizational relationship, and other forms of organizational collaboration and linking together, represent an increasingly common strategy for the survival and growth of corporations as they seek to defend against competitive attack, enter into new markets, and gain access to developing technologies. Interorganizational cooperation, although largely reported as a Wall Street phenomenon, has by no means been confined to the business community, however. New roles for the military in the post-cold war era, such as peacekeeping missions and disaster relief, have increased the importance of multinational operations and posed a significant challenge to the military's cooperation with local relief agencies such as the Red Cross and local government agencies (as the next chapter discusses). Even nations, traditionally concerned with issues of sovereignty, have entered into collaborations with each other in the belief that cooperation in both political and economic ventures is often better than independent action. The North American Free Trade Agreement (NAFTA) and the European Union (EU) represent a new level of international interdependence among neighboring states.

Although corporations, local agencies, military forces, and nations have long attempted to cooperate with or co-opt each other, it is only in the last two decades that relations between organizations have become recognized as a critical tactic for organizational survival, growth, and success in a hostile or challenging environment (Harrigan, 1985, 1986; Gomes-Casseres, 1988; Paré, 1994; Fligstein, 1990; Bleeke and Ernst, 1995).

At least three factors are contributing to this increase in partnerships, networks, consortia, and federations, in addition to mergers and acquisitions. First, businesses compete in a global context today, and the trend is not expected to abate. With this kind of competition—more challenging and rapidly changing—organizational leaders are seeing wisdom in joining forces. Second, there is greater competition for scarce resources today, so more and more are competing for less and less; sharing costs, risks, and scarce resources is making sense to many organizational leaders. Third, there is growing recognition that collaborative behavior, in contrast to competition and individualism, may often (but not always) be a better way to operate.

Today, firms, government agencies, and states are apt to be seen by both researchers and practitioners as involved in a complex web of organizational relations, formal and informal, intended and unintended, that can help or hinder their ambitions. With this awareness has come an explosion of research and conceptualization, if not theory, by social scientists and management scholars that has attempted to understand the forces that prompt organizations to connect with each other and the conditions under which interorganizational relations are likely to succeed or fail. Although at this point there is more theory than evidence, the data suggest that differences of situation, orientation, purpose, culture, and power can affect the outcome of an ostensibly good match.

In this chapter, we characterize the voluminous writings on interorganizational relations of all types. This body of work is large and growing but can be divided into two distinct literatures: (1) macro environmental studies of the political and competitive aspects of relations between and among organizations and (2) micro studies of the processes by which organized groups relate to each other and the factors that are likely to lead to a successful collaboration. We should point out that this chapter is based primarily on literature generated in the United States. There is an equally large and growing body of literature on interorganizational relations that is more international; see, for example, such recent sources as Gerybadze (1994), Kuman and Rosovsky (1992), and Yoshino and Rangan (1995).

The chapter begins with a characterization of the environmental research, including the history of the analysis of interorganizational relations, the ways in which researchers have conceptualized organizational environments, and the forces that increasingly push organizations to collaborate with each other. It then goes on to discuss the research concerning the processes of interorganizational relations, including the wide range of reasons that organizations collaborate, a taxonomy of types of interorganizational structures that are possible, life-cycle stages in cooperative relations, and a number of other relevant factors, including culture, leadership, evaluation, intergroup relations, and boundary stresses. Finally, we consider the conditions under which various forms of organizational connections are likely to succeed or fail. We end with questions for further research and the committee's conclusions in this area.

ENVIRONMENTAL ASPECTS OF
INTERORGANIZATIONAL RELATIONS

Early theories of management were intent on perfecting the modern production organization by developing principles of efficient management and applying scientific analysis to organizational problems (Perrow, 1992). Although several schools of thought developed over the first half of the twentieth century, they all had in common a focus on the organization as an independent entity to be managed. Successive theories shifted the focus from the production system to the social system, but for the most part they proceeded from a belief that management science, properly applied, could control the forces necessary to maximize productivity.

This focus on the organization as the unit of analysis, with manipulable variables, began to shift after World War II when systems theory, taken from biology, was applied to organizations. Systems theory encouraged researchers to look first at organizations as cybernetic systems capable of self-regulation and eventually as systems that interact with their environment, for example by processing information and other resources from the environment (Boulding, 1956). This "open systems" perspective on organizations encouraged a new focus for research about organizations and their environments. As Scott put it, "The environment is perceived to be the ultimate source of materials, energy, and information, all of which are vital to the continuation of the system. Indeed the environment is even seen to be the source of order itself" (1987:91). It became clear to researchers and practitioners that much of what an organization needs to succeed is outside the organization itself.

An awareness of the world outside a particular organization has led researchers to realize that much of an organization's environment consists of other organizations. A focus on organizations and their environments stimulated research on how organizations sharing an environment as either competitors or potential allies are affected by their neighbors in organizational space. Although some of the research is abstract, much of it has prescriptive implications for organizations attempting to manage their relations with other organizations in order to ensure survival, gain market power, and otherwise improve their performance.

Conceptualizing Organizational Environments

Organization Sets, Fields, and Networks

In the 1960s and 1970s, organizational scholars began conceptualizing relations between organizations in order to study them. Several levels of analysis have become standard ways of discussing interorganizational relations. The first, the *organizational set*, is an application of a social psychological model, the role set, to an organization. Just as an individual has a set of different roles he or she plays with other people—spouse, parent, worker, friend—an organization is conceived as having a set of relations with other organizations (Blau and Scott, 1962).

Organizational set analysis concentrates on the relationships of a single organization to see how those relationships affect its activities and performance. In many situations, however, organizational outcomes are the consequences of groups of organizations acting in ways that affect each other. Variously called, with somewhat different meanings, the action set (Aldrich and Whetten, 1981), the interorganizational field (Warren, 1967), and the industry system (Hirsch, 1975), this unit of analysis looks at relationships among groups of organizations that interact over time in ways that affect each other.

Hirsch's comparative analysis of the recording and pharmaceutical industries demonstrates the impact of the structure of an *interorganizational field* on the overall performance of an industry (1972; see also 1975). Although both pharmaceutical and recording companies have important similarities, for example, gatekeepers (physicians and disc jockeys) who mediate between themselves and their customers, the drug industry has been far more successful than recording companies in protecting their interests in patent protection, distribution, and pricing. Hirsch's study points to the superior collective efforts of drug companies in pursuing common interests, compared with the disorganized and misdirected efforts of recording companies that attempted to bribe disc jockeys in what became known as the payola scandals. He attributed at least some of the drug industry's higher profitability to the character of the relationships among organizations in the industry. Similarly, Miles and Cameron's study of the cooperative strategies employed among the Big Six firms within the tobacco industry (1982) demonstrates the effects on profitability of organized efforts among ostensible competitors.

Although organizational sets and interorganizational fields are still important conceptual categories, much recent research utilizes the concept of an *organizational network*. Network analysis differs from organizational set and industry analysis in seeking not only to identify the relationships among organizations but also to examine the character and structure of those relationships, usually by modeling them mathematically (Nohria and Eccles, 1992). The premise is that the networks within which an organization is embedded both constrain and provide opportunities for action. Organizational actions, and hence performance possibilities, are to a large degree explained by an organization's position within a network of organizations.

One body of research looks primarily at nonprofit community service organizations (Laumann and Papi, 1976; Galaskiewicz, 1979; Knoke and Rogers, 1979) and has the advantage of looking closely at the multiple and overlapping ties between organizations in a community, usually a geographically bounded setting. These studies tend to show how interdependencies among organizations that exchange money, people, political support, and other resources come to shape possibilities for action. Focusing on a geographic region, however, limits researchers' ability to assess the impact on performance of forces and organizations outside the region.

Much of the recent interest in strategic alliances, joint ventures, and other forms of interorganizational relationships came about as an attempt to facilitate or manage network relations, increasingly possible since the Reagan administration's weaker enforcement of antitrust laws and the passage of legislation permitting some forms of research consortia. Another important factor shaping network research is the observation that new high-technology industries, notably biotechnology and electronics, are characterized by intense patterns of formal and informal network relations. Barley and colleagues (1992:317) note that, in these industries, scientific advances come so quickly that "even well-heeled corporations cannot hope to track, much less fully exploit, relevant scientific advances by relying solely on the published literature and their own research operations. Instead, relevant technical knowledge is more efficiently obtained by direct access to research conducted elsewhere" and made available through interorganizational relations.

The authors note, too, that whereas some high-technology industries such as electronics build on scientific communities such as chemistry and physics that have been integrated into industrial manufacturing since the nineteenth century, biotechnology is founded on a wholly new community of participants. Recent advances in recombinant DNA and hybridoma cell formation suddenly brought cutting-edge molecular biology into the center of the pharmaceutical and agricultural industries. In biotechnology, far more than electronics, however, strategic alliances between small research firms and well-funded larger corporations are common because of the expense of clinical trials necessary for government approval of biotechnology products. They conclude that "the way in which a firm participates in the network is integral to its strategy for survival and growth" (p. 343).

Another and perhaps most important factor in prompting research on organizational networks is the observation that business networks have been widely successful in the global economy. Whereas the U.S. economy is based on a belief that competitive individualism is the appropriate principle for exchange relations among economic actors—a principle that is institutionalized in laws and practices such as arms-length bidding relations between suppliers and buyers, antitrust regulation, and insider-trading laws (Williamson, 1992; Biggart and Hamilton, 1992)—this principle does not exist in many other successful economies.

Regime Analysis

Another approach to analyzing interorganizational cooperation, international regimes, was developed from the need to understand cooperation in the less structured global system. An international regime is a set of explicit or implicit principles, norms, rules, and decision-making procedures around which actor expectations converge and that help coordinate actor behavior (Krasner, 1982; see also Mayer et al., 1993). Some examples include the regimes surrounding nuclear nonproliferation, the law of the sea, and the nascent international environmental regime (Young, 1989). Regime analysis represents a movement away from purely institutional analysis (Kratochwil and Ruggie, 1989) to one that looks at broader and sometimes less formal patterns of cooperation (Kahn and Zald, 1990).

Organizations play several roles in the regime. Certainly, cooperation among organizations can be the driving force behind the development of an international regime or define its structure; an example is the coordination among national health agencies, nongovernmental organizations, and the World Health Organization. Yet organizations, and cooperation among them, can also be the *consequence* of or institutionalized manifestation of coordination between different groups or states in the world. International cooperation can also occur outside or independent of organizations, providing the analyst with a broader conception of behavior than is present by a pure concentration on institutional behavior. A focus on organizations and cooperation is also enhanced by understanding the broader milieu in which organizations operate and cooperation emerges (Haas, 1980). The limitations of the regime framework, however, include its difficulty with accommodating change, its being too issue-specific to permit generalizations, and its limited applicability to more structured, less anarchic environments than global politics (for a more detailed critique of this approach, see Strange, 1989).

Collaboration as an Organizing Principle

Although competition, not collaboration, has historically been the organizing principle for organizations and markets, particularly in the United States, there is growing evidence of collaboration and other forms of managed interdependence among firms and not-for-profit organizations in the United States. Firms in a market are more likely to compete, and not collaborate, when the market is stagnant or declining and resources are increasingly scarce (Porter, 1980). Competition is also more likely in situations in which institutional factors—such as a legal system that supports antitrust regulation—or deeply rooted distrust among members of an industry, militates against collaboration.

A number of forces, many of which are on the increase around the world, prompt organizations to collaborate with each other. Resource dependency theory (Pfeffer and Salancik, 1978) argues that, because a focal organization must depend on other organizations for the inputs it needs to survive, it may be in its interest to attempt to manage the organizations on which it is dependent. They argue that mergers and acquisitions, which represent total control of another organization, are only the most extreme of an array of strategies that organizations can employ to coordinate with or impose their interests on other organizations. They may use a series of "bridging strategies" (Scott, 1987:209) to lock in the supplies or support of another firm, including contracting, strategic alliances, and co-optation, the incorporation of important external agents into the firm, for example by forming interlocking boards of directors (Palmer, 1983; Mizruchi and Schwartz, 1986).

Transaction cost economics (Williamson, 1992) argues that, under conditions of high uncertainty and small numbers of alternative suppliers, collaboration can improve cost-effectiveness and therefore improve the profitability and competitive performance of an organization. Other economists argue that collaboration weakens an organizational field by reducing competition (Scherer, 1980; Caves, 1982), thus leading to higher prices and less innovation. Ouchi and Bolton (1988), however, found in a study of microelectronics and other industries that participation in collaborative research and development (R&D) ventures strengthened the firms' global competitiveness.

Although much of the recent impulse for mergers and acquisitions was fueled by the development of the junk bond market in the 1980s and the use of purely financial criteria to mate corporate partners, a decade of failed alliances has made organizational executives less sanguine about entering into this type of long-term, permanent acquisition. In fact, research suggests that as many as half of all domestic mergers and acquisitions are financial failures (Paré, 1994). It is now clear that successful collaborations among organizations, even those with ostensibly good financial or strategic reasons to collaborate, are difficult to achieve. Financial synergy may be a necessary component of a successful relationship for a market-based firm, but compatible leadership style, strategic orientation, and culture are necessary as well, as discussed below (Sankar et al., 1995; Fedor and Werther, 1995). This is no less true of not-for-profit organizations, especially those with a strong missionary culture such as religious organizations and the military, in which value clashes can doom an alliance (Wallis, 1994).

FRAMEWORKS FOR UNDERSTANDING INTERORGANIZATIONAL PROCESSES

Reasons for Collaborating

Both research and practice show that organizations enter into relations with each other for a wide range of reasons: (1) long-range survival (Burke and Jackson, 1991); (2) gain in market power (Porter, 1990); (3) synergy (Kanter, 1989); (4) risk sharing (Bleeke and Ernst, 1993; Harrigan, 1986); (5) cost sharing; (6) subcontracting and outsourcing (Porter, 1990); (7) technology sharing (Harrigan, 1986); and (8) knowledge of a market.

As steps toward linking up with another organization begin, the parties involved are faced with at least two clear yet perplexing paradoxes, ones of vulnerability and control (Haspeslgh and Jemison, 1991). Organizations have to decide how much they will cede control to their partner.

The paradox of vulnerability—trust versus self-preservation—is concerned with whether or not the recent proliferation of interorganizational collaborations represents a new spirit of cooperation or a new level of cost-cutting and market exploitation. From one perspective, collaboration is valuable in and of itself, opening gateways to such activities as organizational learning and transformation. To facilitate this transformation, however, partners must openly share information about strategic objectives, organizational resources, and internal challenges, which paradoxically increases vulnerability to acquisition, loss of market share, proprietary control of valued resources, and other sources of strategic advantage. Thus, collaboration can be seen as both promoting and threatening an organization's long-term stability and viability. Nevertheless, an avoidance of collaborations may also represent a costly choice, with inefficiencies and insufficient learning possibilities. The challenge is to find the right partner (one with complementary resources, compatible business and cultural characteristics, and similar philosophies regarding business goals and the collaboration's role in achieving them) yet not to be so protective of organizational resources that the collaboration becomes impossible.

The paradox of control—stability versus synergy—concerns the tension faced by managers of interorganizational relations between the impulse to control the outcome of the collaboration and the potential synergy that can result from the absence of tight controls and management. Although a clear division of authority and decision making in interorganizational relations may reduce potential conflicts arising from partners' differing strategies, cultures, and work systems, a clear division may also reduce the likelihood that genuinely new perspectives and possibilities will emerge from the relationship. An organization therefore risks undermining the synergistic objectives that led it to enter a collaboration in the first place when it institutes tight controls that may be intended to guarantee success. This is especially true when a collaborating organization uses less measurable objectives for indicating success, such as organizational learning and management and work styles.

A PARTIAL TAXONOMY OF
INTERORGANIZATIONAL GOVERNANCE STRUCTURES

As a guide to understanding interorganizational relations, we present a taxonomy of interorganizational governance structures, based on work by Kahn (1990) and Harrigan (1986). Although not all-encompassing, it is comprehensive enough to provide a road map for how to understand interorganizational relations. The following taxonomy moves from relatively less interdependent relations to relations in which interdependence and its management are key.

• *Mutual Service Consortia; Research and Development (R&D) Partnerships.* Organizations pool their resources to procure access to information, technology, or some other service too costly to acquire alone (Kanter, 1994). Tasks (including financial support) are distributed among the participants, and the proceeds are returned to participants according to the terms of the agreement. No separate entity is created for the management of this relationship.

• *Cross-Licensing and Distribution Arrangements.* Organizations enter into agreements formalizing the limited sharing of technology or other product attributes such as brand names or markets. These arrangements are strictly contracted and bounded in scope and duration.

• *Joint Ventures.* Two or more organizations ("owners") combine varying resources to form a new, distinct organization (the "venture") in order to pursue complementary strategic objectives. This new organization is jointly owned and managed, and proceeds are distributed between the venture and owners according to a formula agreed on by the owners.

• *Strategic Alliances.* Similar to ventures, two or more organizations combine resources in pursuit of mutual gain. However, in a strategic alliance, a new firm is not created. Although interdependence is, of course, required for a joint venture to work effectively, the characteristic of interdependence is essentially the same as that required for any organization, whereas for a strategic alliance to work effectively, two distinct organizations must learn to cooperate and depend on each other.

 • *Value Network Partnerships.* Organizations join forces to capitalize on potential efficiencies in the production and/or distribution process (Porter, 1990). Whereas each participating organization is responsible for one area of the production system, the participating organizations are highly dependent on one another for the ultimate delivery of their product. This form of collaboration concerns the alliance of certain organizational functions such as production, and typically not multiple functions that encompass more of a particular business or business units as in a strategic alliance.

 • *Internal Ventures.* An organization acts independently to create a distinct entity, from within its own ranks, for the purposes of expansion, innovation, or diversification. These are often established with the goal of capitalizing quickly on entrepreneurial initiatives coming from members of the organization's work force. When action is then taken to establish a joint venture with another organization, the description above of a joint venture would then apply.

 • *Mergers/Acquisitions.* A special case of interorganizational relations; when they are established, problems of interdependence between organizations become issues of within-group functioning and are directly related to organizational performance. Acquisitions are preferred to ventures and alliances when shared ownership of initiatives is not desired.

Table 5-1 presents the types of interorganizational relations, along with some of the situational determinants of their formation and their likely outcomes (Harrigan, 1986; Porter and Fuller, 1986).

Situational Determinants

In the design of an interorganizational relation's governance structure, three questions are key: (1) What are the reasons for collaborating? (2) How will both risks and benefits be distributed? (3) What will be the indicators for successful achievement of participants' mutual goals? The responses to these three questions suggest the degree of managed interdependence appropriate to the relationship between partners and, indirectly, the ideal governance structure for the relationship.

TABLE 5-1   Taxonomy of Cooperative Interorganizational Relationships

Degree of Managed Interdependence	Inter-organizational Relationship	Strategic Purpose	Ownership/ Division of Proceeds
Least managed	Market (competitive)		
	Mutual Service Consortium, Research & Development Partnerships	Contracted pooling of resources for shared access to valued commodity: market, technology, process	No shared ownership/ negotiated division of proceeds
	Cross-Licensing and Distribution Arrangements	Limited sharing of technology and markets	No shared ownership/ negotiated distribution of proceeds
	Strategic Alliance	Reciprocal exploitation of resources for less specified mutual gain	Varying shared ownership and managerial control/negotiated distribution of proceeds between owners
	Joint Venture	Reciprocal exploitation of resources for specific mutual gain in presence of compatible strategic objectives	Varying shared ownership and managerial control/ negotiated distribution of proceeds between venture and owners

Issues/Obstacles	Boundary Characteristics	Key Psychological Phenomena Affecting Viability	Milestones for Success
(Limited or unmanaged interfirm cooperation in marketplace)			
Possible development of competitive conflict (shared product/market)	Stable, contained interface, high constituent power, committee, slow-moving	Perceptions of equity, competitor benefits	Negotiated distribution of consortium outputs, quantifiable, static
Loss of control of knowledge re technology and markets	Stable, contained interface, high constituent power, comittee, slow-moving	Perceptions of equity, competitor benefit	Performance of both organizations
Firms risk ownership and organizational identity, because relationship leveraged by equality/inequality of shared investment/commitment and distribution/evolution of bargaining power	Boundary-spanning project team(s), multiple interfaces, varying constituent power, high-stress on boundary-role persons	Perceptions of equity (need measurement systems), perceptions of power, compatibility of cultures, intergroup trust and competition, resistance to cooperation at operational level	Venture performance, value added to owners is negotiated, benchmarked, monitored, revised (monitoring and control systems needed)
Conflict between owners, between owners and venture likely to develop as each organization's performance, priorities, and environment change Firms risk valued assets, because relationship leveraged by equality/inequality of shared investment/commitment and distribution/evolution of relative bargaining power	Hybrid organization/culture buffers cooperating partners, venture identity distinct from parent organizations, varying constituent power as a function of dependence and bargaining agreement constraints	Perceptions of equity (need measurement systems), perceptions of power, compatibility of cultures (including management style, work norms, and values), owner-venture competition, resistance to cooperation at an operational level	Venture performance, value added to owners is negotiated, benchmarked, monitored, revised (monitoring and control systems needed in owner organizations and in venture)

Dilemmas of control and synergy

TABLE 5-1   Continued

Degree of Managed Interdependence	Inter-organizational Relationship	Strategic Purpose	Ownership/ Division of Proceeds
	Value Network Partnership	Reduce environmental variability, streamline production and delivery systems (raise competitor entry costs)	No shared ownership/ contracted provision of products, services
	Internal Venture	Capitalize on internal entrepreneurial initiatives, exploit opportunities requiring faster response without sharing resources	Negotiated internally
Most managed	Merger/ acquisition	Merger with/ acquisition of competitor or affinity organization in support of strategic objectives	No shared ownership/ division of proceeds

Strategic Purpose

Some collaborative initiatives are extremely limited in objective and scope. They involve a relatively passive pooling of resources for the participants' mutual benefit. For instance, participants might share information regarding a particular technology or economic developments in a specific market or region. In the private sector, relationships of this kind usually take the form of mutual service consortia or R&D partnerships.

Issues/Obstacles	Boundary Characteristics	Key Psychological Phenomena Affecting Viability	Milestones for Success
Possible lock-in with standardization/competitive pressures for innovation Conflict re cost-effectiveness of provided product services, allocation of profit	Multiple interfaces: sharing of systems, information, processes, and resources Varying constituent power, high stress on boundary role persons	Perceptions of equity (need measurement systems) Perceptions of power Compatibility of cultures Intergroup trust and competition, resistance to cooperation at operational level	Market share, profit margins, other markers of organizational performance and efficiency Partner relations persons and perceptions
Dilemmas of control and maximized return Conflicts re management control, resource provision and output distribution	Multiple interfaces: sharing of systems, information processes, and resources Varying constituent power, high stress on boundary role	Intergroup competition and envy, resistance to cooperation at operational level	Venture performance Value added to owners is negotiated, benchmarked, monitored, revised (monitoring and control systems needed)
Interorganizational dynamics become intraorganizational challenges	Boundary expansion/ subsumption	Perceptions of power, perceptions of implications for performance and related impacts on cooperation, compatibility of cultures	Organization performance

Note: Adapted from R.L. Kahn (1990) for concept of managed interdependence dimension and Harrigan (1986) for strategic functions of most relationship types.

Relationships involve relatively little risk on the part of the participants. They are bounded in scope and often in time as well. Mutual service consortia and R&D partnerships can provide extremely valuable resources to their participants but demand very limited cooperation.

Similarly, when an organization shares a specific asset with another organization, as in cross-licensing or distribution arrangements, the interface between participating organizations is relatively specific and contained. Cross-licensing and distribution arrangements usually involve the licensed use of another organization's technology, production or distribution methods, or brand name, with the purpose of bolstering organizational performance.

A more complex and interdependent relationship is necessary when a collaboration involves reciprocal exploitation of resources in pursuit of mutual gains. There are two related models for such a relationship: the joint venture and the strategic alliance. Joint ventures involve the creation of a distinct organizational entity for managing the overlapping goals of the sponsoring organizations. Strategic alliances attempt to avoid potential conflicts by limiting the power of the (new) organization responsible for the founders' mutual gain, but relations of this type often have the effect of exacerbating tensions between the founders (Harrigan, 1986).

Attempts to capitalize on linkages in the value network by strengthening relationships among suppliers, producers, distributors, etc., take the form of value network partnerships. Relationships of this type are undertaken to increase organizational efficiencies. For business organizations, they have the added indirect benefit of increasing industry competitiveness by raising the costs of competitor entry (Porter, 1990).

When an organization wishes to capitalize on internal initiatives or to sponsor pursuit of a goal that is not supported by existing systems, internal ventures can serve as valuable models. In an internal venture, a new endeavor can be sponsored without the sharing of resources with outside organizations. The paradox of control is especially important to internal ventures, as organizations struggle to sponsor initiatives that are by definition beyond their typical realm of expertise.

Moves to gain control over competitors or affiliates by expanding organizational boundaries clearly fall under the acquisition model. Similarly, the conditions under which mergers are to be emulated is straightforward— mergers involve the creation of a new organizational entity through the dissolution and recombination of previously existing boundaries.

Ownership of Responsibility

The more a relationship is managed, the more ownership of responsibility and the division of proceeds are shared. The exception to this statement is the case of a merger or acquisition in which the former separate ownership becomes one. In the middle of the continuum are joint ventures and strategic alliances. According to Yoshino and Rangan (1995), there are basically three types of ownership structures in strategic alliances: (1) nonequity, in which neither partner owns a part, (2) equity stake in the other partner, and (3) a separate alliance company, a joint venture that both partners fund (usually 50/50). They suggest that the best ownership structure for an alliance is one that fits the overall strategy of the collaboration—if goals are limited, then the ties can be comparatively loose. If the alliance is critical to long-term success, then a tighter structure is warranted. The point is that the degree of ownership and the division of proceeds should be linked directly to the mission and strategy of the respective partners.

Obstacles to Cooperation

Issues and obstacles to cooperation between and among interorganizational relationships can be far-ranging. This is true both in practice as well as in the literature. Oliver (1990) has identified five critical contingencies that affect different types of relationships, such as trade associations, joint ventures, and corporate-financial interlocks. The five are asymmetry, reciprocity, efficiency, stability, and legitimacy. We can use her schema to consider briefly issues and obstacles to cooperation:

- *Asymmetry.* A potential obstacle is an imbalance of power and control between or among the partnering organizations. This is the case when one of the partners wants to dominate the other so that desired resources can be controlled by the dominant partner.
- *Reciprocity.* More or less the opposite of asymmetry, the assumption being that cooperation and collaboration are emphasized as opposed to domination; obstacles will arise if there is perceived inequity in, for example, sharing of resources; trust is key to this relationship aspect. Reciprocity more often occurs when the partners are pursuing a new venture rather than merely sharing resources (see, for example, Pfeffer and Nowak, 1976).
- *Efficiency.* Often relationships are formed to improve internal efficiencies for one or both of the organizations; a strategic alliance between two hospitals, for example, might result in the purchase of one high-technology diagnostic tool instead of two and thereby reduced costs. Again, both hospitals must experience better efficiencies for this dimension of the relationship to be perceived as equitable; otherwise, there is a major obstacle.
- *Stability.* When one of the partners, for example, copes with its external environmental uncertainties far better than the other, then there is the potential for imbalance in the relationship. If one of these partners spends more time, energy, and money on market research in order to reduce uncertainty in the external environment, then the possibility of an obstacle to the relationship arises.
- *Legitimacy.* The partners are attempting to enhance their reputations, images, and prestige in their environments by joining together; with the passage of time, one of the partners may benefit more than the other, which sets up an obstacle to further cooperation.

These categories of Oliver's are informed by and summarize many studies and so contribute to a better understanding of interorganizational relationships. In practice, there are other ways of categorizing potential obstacles to effective relationships, e.g., cross-cultural barriers. Furthermore, over time in a relationship things change, often as a consequence of the rapidly changing environment.

Likely Outcomes

The choice of organizational governance structure—joint venture, consortia, merger, etc.—has profound effects on many aspects of the collaborating organizations. We explore briefly the consequences of these choices according to (1) boundary characteristics, (2) psychological dynamics, and (3) milestones for success.

Boundary Characteristics

As the structure chosen for an interorganizational relationship shifts from least managed to most managed, boundaries of interdependence between and among the partners become less distinct. Boundary roles can be seen in terms of two forms of negotiation: the bargainer and the representative (Druckman, 1977; Walton and McKersie, 1965). At the least managed end of the continuum, the individuals who are relating across organizational boundaries have two duties—to represent and to bargain. Moving toward more managed interdependence, bargaining becomes even more salient. At the merger stage, the bargainers do their jobs and then "blend or integrate themselves out of role existence."

Psychological Dynamics

Findings from cognitive psychology contribute to our understanding of interorganizational relationships. For example, Schwenk (1994) points out that the biases of decision makers can heavily influence the degree of success in interorganizational relations, for example, through overconfidence (see also Nisbett and Ross, 1980).

Perceived equity may be an issue. In a recent merger of two financial firms, the early slogan was that it was a "merger of equals." Members of each firm would be treated fairly and end up in the merged organization with parity. A few months following the merger, it was clear that the assumption of equity was violated. Of the top 19 executive positions, 16 were filled by members of one of the previous firms, and only 3 came from the other organization. This outcome, as might be expected, caused a significant setback in the progress of the merger. Had the original position been one of acquisition instead of merger, different expectations and perceptions regarding equity would have been established. Being acquired does not, as a rule, create expectations of parity. In a joint venture, issues of equity are typically specified clearly. As we move toward the least managed end of the continuum, matters of equity are easier to manage because the partners do not interact with one another as intensively.

Milestones for Success

For commercial enterprises, the milestones are expressed in financial terms, such as increased market share, new products developed as a result of the collaboration, an expansion of the distribution systems, etc. For consortia or R&D partnerships, milestones are much more varied. Increasing the talent pool, accumulating more knowledge faster, having access to information formerly unavailable, and saving on costs of conducting certain lines of research are but a few of the possible indicators for success in collaborations outside the commercial sector.

LIFE-CYCLE STAGES IN COLLABORATIONS

Regardless of the eventual structure of a particular cooperative agreement between organizations, clear patterns characterize the process by which two organizations negotiate an interorganizational arrangement. The movement through these processes can be thought of in terms of a life cycle of interorganizational relations. Figure 5-1 presents a schema for such a life cycle, based on observation of a number of organizations; the shaded boxes indicate processes that occur continuously during the life of an agreement between organizations.

Preengagement Stage

The preengagement stage refers to the state of the organizations prior to the initiation of a particular collaborative endeavor. In business relations, this stage usually involves the voluntary selection of another organization with which to collaborate. In the public sector, it is far more likely that collaboration is mandated, as in the case of peacekeeping efforts between allies or the coordination of disaster relief efforts by state and local agencies. Private-sector firms sometimes find themselves forced to collaborate, however; for example, corporate headquarters in pursuit of a particular goal might mandate that a subsidiary collaborate with another subsidiary or with an outside organization.

When collaboration is a voluntary option, an organization's leaders have the luxury of assessing collaboration as a means for achieving long-term

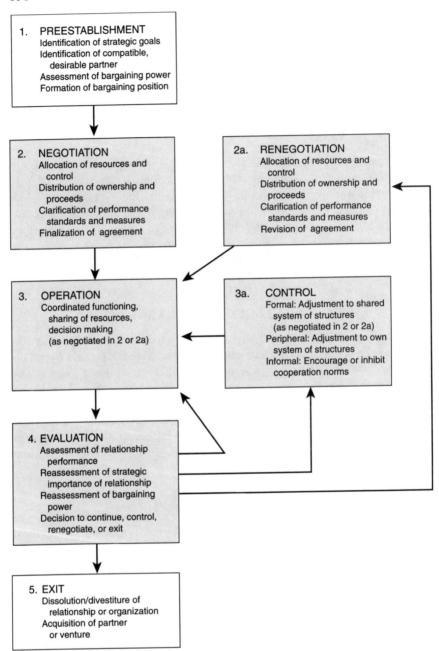

FIGURE 5-1   Life cycle of cooperative interorganizational relationships.

goals. An organization may also be on the receiving end of an offer to collaborate, prompting reassessment of their organizational strategy in order to respond to a proposal. The approached organization also enters the preengagement stage.

Potential or mandated partners should then be evaluated for compatibility. The first approach to evaluation assesses similarities of management and business philosophies, abilities to communicate, and interpersonal trust; the second approach is an assessment of the organizations' relative bargaining power in the relationship. Intangible factors, including each partner's perceptions of the other's reliability, trustworthiness, and culture, will exert an influence on initial bargaining positions. When the choice to ally with another organization is voluntary, intangible factors weigh more importantly in deciding whether or not to proceed with a relationship. Even when the relationship is not mandated, however, evaluation during the preengagement stage can identify areas of concern that might be addressed in the formal governance agreement created by the partners.

These assessments will affect each organization's perception of the distribution of power, dependence, and control in the relationship and thus the choice of bargaining position as the agreement concerning governance of the relationship is negotiated. Because in this initial stage partners may not be entirely forthcoming with one another about their formulas for determining the strategic value of the relationship, many partners may not even come to realize that their respective assessments of the relationship's value and potential arise from widely differing evaluation systems. As a result, partners who may be quite compatible may never proceed to negotiation or may fail to capitalize on these potentials as they enter their relationship. Similarly, partners who initially appear compatible may proceed to negotiate a relationship that, upon closer examination, would be deemed inappropriate.

Negotiation Stage

If partners advance to the point at which they discuss formally the allocation of responsibilities, resources, and authority that would exist in the relationship, they have begun, at least informally, to manage their interdependence. In the negotiation stage, the provision of inputs to and the division of proceeds from the relationship being created is negotiated. If either inputs or proceeds are relatively intangible (for instance, if one organization is offering to teach a participative management style as one of many inputs, and the counterpart organization offers insight into marketing to a new segment), then specific measures by which to assess the relationship's performance have to be created. These measures will need to be true to the interests of the participating parties, but also relevant to the performance of the collaboration and not so difficult to measure that they overburden the new system with excessively bureaucratic monitoring and measurement systems. The negotiation stage thus demands the management of the paradox of control; systems that support the achievement of collaborative objectives must be created, yet these systems must be flexible enough to allow both expected and unforeseen benefits of the collaboration to emerge.

Negotiators on behalf of the partnering organizations are in the difficult position of protecting the interests of their host organizations as well as the viability of the partnership (Adams, 1976). Cultural differences, and other differences in perspective, will have a considerable impact on the effectiveness of negotiations in satisfying these dual objectives (Bontempo, 1991). Differences in cultural expectations regarding negotiation behavior, measurement, record keeping, and control systems and in approaches to strategic planning can all be expected to clash at the negotiation table. Furthermore, characteristics of negotiators' host organizations will have an influence on the course of negotiations; cultural characteristics such as need for control, trust of outsiders, and perceptions of relative power will influence both the expectations placed on negotiators and the range of negotiating behaviors available to them (Druckman and Hopmann, 1989).

Operation Stage

After the agreement has been finalized, the collaboration proceeds to the third stage, operation, in which the agreement is implemented. The relationship now consists of an exchange of resources across organizational boundaries; if the relationship is a joint venture, the owners work with the venture as an independent system rather than a theoretical entity. Even if a new formal organization has not been created, the reality of working across organizational boundaries at many functional levels is likely to be quite different from the experience of courtship and negotiation. In order to facilitate cooperation at managerial and operational levels of the organization, employees need to be informed of the strategic value of the collaboration (Kanter, 1994), criteria for evaluating the relationship's success, and the relationship of their jobs to these criteria. New behavior by managers and other employees also needs to be structurally supported and systemically rewarded. Managers and operational employees are in a situation similar to that in which negotiators found themselves, with their loyalties at least partially divided between fulfillment of their responsibilities to their home organization and support of the collaboration. This tension can result in a serious threat to the collaboration's viability, especially if employees are receiving mixed signals about their roles in the collaboration or about senior management's commitment to its success.

Several other cultural and psychological phenomena can be expected to influence cooperation between collaborating organizations. Compatibility of work norms has a powerful effect on cooperation between the groups. The degree to which work-related behaviors such as timing, quality, and sharing of information and other resources are met influences employees' willingness to cooperate in the future.

The perceptions that members of the participating groups have of each other also affect their likelihood of cooperation. When group relations are characterized by a climate of trust, group members are more likely to help one another; if there are perceptions of competitiveness or ill will, discrimination against outgroup members is far more likely (Flippen et al., 1995). Smith and Berg (1987) indicate that a focus on the mutual stake that interdependent groups share helps to reduce intergroup resentments.

Evidence of the importance of perceived future achievement in mitigating resistance to intergroup cooperation (Haunschild et al., 1994), supported by social identity theory (Tajfel, 1981, 1982), suggests that members' perceptions of interorganizational endeavors coincide with their own goals. This can be achieved through the use of communication systems that reinforce the strategic importance of the interorganizational effort. Social identity theory research also points to factors that increase people's positive feelings about dissimilar groups. The works of Singer et al. (1963), Fishbein (1963), Druckman (1968), and Brewer (1968) can be taken together to indicate that more favorable attitudes are expressed toward dissimilar others from groups that are perceived to be (1) allies, (2) similar to one's own group, (3) comparably skilled or advanced, and (4) interested in membership in one's own group (Druckman, 1994). Intraorganizational communications can support the likelihood of intergroup cooperation by highlighting or encouraging any of these factors.

Evaluation

Regardless of specific criteria, though, evaluation of a multiorganizational relationship's performance occurs continuously on an informal basis, and it should be undertaken formally by all participant organizations on a periodic schedule. However measured, mutually satisfactory performance lays the groundwork for ongoing cooperation. Whenever possible, evaluation measures should be shared between collaborating organizations in order to reduce erroneous attributions regarding causes of successes and deficits in performance.

Renegotiation, Control, or Exit

If managers from each of the collaborating organizations are satisfied with the evaluation and decide that no response is necessary, the collaboration will probably continue as before, with managerial attention once more focused on the operation phase of the relationship life cycle. Given the dynamism of today's economic and political environment, and the fact that learning occurs almost inevitably as a result of collaboration experience, evaluation will probably indicate either major or minor opportunities for adjustment. If the need for adjustment is large, and the bargaining agreement permits, managers can approach their partners for renegotiation of the relationship. Objectives of the renegotiation are identical to those of the negotiation stage. Psychological aspects of this phase are similar also, except that all parties to the negotiation have a better idea of the likely behavior of their counterparts in the relationship; these experiences supplement their organizations' culturally determined approaches to cooperation and collaborating, which influenced behavior during negotiation.

When renegotiation is not an option, or in situations in which more minor adjustments to the collaboration are indicated, participant organizations can use control mechanisms to influence the functioning of the collaboration. Control mechanisms can be invoked either to promote or to inhibit the collaboration's effectiveness.

Many relationships, especially between public organizations, are bounded by a specific time duration or for the purposes of accomplishing a joint project and dissolve when these criteria have been satisfied. If the relationship was not specifically bounded in this way, and partnership performance is unsatisfactory to a partner with sufficient bargaining power to terminate it, or if the environment has changed so radically that the collaboration is no longer relevant to the participants' strategic goals, the cooperative interorganizational relationship will end.

In relationships between public organizations, success or failure in the accomplishment of mutual goals can have effects on the sponsoring organizations and *their* relationships (see Figure 5-1). When organizations have even a remote possibility of future collaboration, the importance of an amicable exit should be clear, given the role of group relations in laying the groundwork for cooperation. Of obvious importance in the dissolution of interorganizational relations is the avoidance of unduly scapegoating a particular partner for its shortcomings. The role of responsible and factual systemic analysis of problems and widespread communication of both findings and corrective action taken cannot be overemphasized.

OTHER FACTORS

Culture Clash and Change

Differences in values, expectations, and behavioral norms of communication and negotiation impact the possibility of cooperation during any contact between two organizations. Because corporate culture can be expected to exert a stronger effect on work behavior than either national or ethnic culture (Kotter and Heskett, 1992), cultural differences may be a factor in both domestic and international relationships between organizations. Thus, international relationships between organizations are more (but not exclusively) subject to the issues of difference that are present in any negotiated relationship between two or more organizations. Similarly, those who wish to improve the viability of domestic collaborations can apply much of the work regarding national and ethnic cultural differences.

In designing collaborations, then, managers should be well informed about a number of cultural variables that will impact relationship viability. Especially when more interdependent relationships are being considered, they should possess as much information as possible regarding their own organization's corporate and national/ethnic culture: which characteristics are relatively stable and which more ephemeral, how these characteristics might augment or impede achievement of strategic goals, and how members of other cultures view their own.

Leadership

Organization leaders play a critical role in the success of any collaborative relationship between two organizations in a number of ways. First, leaders' assessments of their strategic goals and the best ways to pursue these goals will constrain the type of partner sought, as well as at what point in an organization's and industry's life cycle such collaborations are pursued. Second, the personal styles and business philosophies of organizational leaders can play a critical role in initial negotiations of collaboration as well as the partner ultimately chosen. In this sense, leaders can be seen (at least partly) as manifestations of, and actors on behalf of, their own organizational culture. Whereas interpersonal compatibility among leaders may be a good indicator of success, this is probably so because it bodes well for the effectiveness of contact among the organizations they represent rather than because of their own working relationships. The leader is an important symbolic element of the organizational community, and the success of a relationship between organizations will depend on his or her clear communication of goals and expectations for the collaboration, as well as the strategic value of the collaboration. Such communication throughout all participant organizations will be critical to operational success (Kanter, 1994). Appreciation of the relationship among leadership, culture, management behavior, and ultimate performance can vastly improve an organization's chances of embarking on and maintaining a successful relationship with other organizations (see, for example, Burke and Litwin, 1992; Burke and Jackson, 1991).

Evaluation

Successful management of interorganizational relations must therefore often include the possibility of review and renegotiation of agreements regarding strategic objectives, investments, provision of other resources, distribution of ownership, and division of proceeds. However, in order to avoid conflict, the organizations must agree on measures of the outcome variables on which these decisions will be based before the collaboration begins to operate. New measures can be added to the relationship system during subsequent negotiations, and ineffective ones removed. This clarification of measurement systems supports circumspect and well-founded decision making regarding collaboration management. Once again, the paradox of control emerges as a challenge during the creation of performance measures that reflect the interests of all involved parties—measures should support the system, not choke it. Nevertheless, appropriately chosen measures can help to reduce the likelihood of inaccurate appraisals of poor or solid performance, as well as the perceptions of inequitable distributions of inputs and proceeds between the participating groups.

Intergroup Relations

Intergroup relations are typically examined and understood in the context of conflict and competition for scarce resources (e.g., Levine and Campbell, 1972; Alderfer, 1977; Rice, 1969). However, in the creation of collaborative alliances, organizations are attempting simultaneously to manage this competition and their shared or overlapping interests. The work of group relations theorists can contribute to the identification of phenomena that may help to overcome this challenge. For instance, organization members' perceptions of other organizations and *their* members can be expected to exert a strong influence on their abilities to cooperate with members of those organizations, as well as on their abilities to exploit opportunities and resources offered by those organizations. Although perceptions of members of other organizations as outsiders may be inevitable, at least in initial stages of contact, the experience of that "outsider-ness" can be either potentially threatening and undermining or potentially enhancing and thus valuable. Perceptions of outsiders can thus impact the viability of any collaborative endeavor undertaken by two organizations.

These perceptions can be modified or controlled in a number of ways. First, information about the potential benefits accruing to the organization as a result of the collaboration must be widely available. Second, dissemination of the performance indicators discussed above can help reduce what may be unfounded perceptions of discrepancy in cost-benefit yields, thus facilitating cooperation between group members.

Finally, Haunschild and colleagues (1994) have demonstrated that group members' expectations about how contact with another group will impact their own performance exert a strong influence on the group's openness to reframing its identification to include another group. Wilder (1986) has indicated that biases against another group can be weakened by individuating outgroup members, encouraging cross-categorization (these objectives can be achieved by forming work groups that cut across previously existing boundaries between groups), introducing a common enemy or overarching goal (i.e., highlighting the strategic importance of cooperation between groups), and removing situational cues associated with group membership. Managers can thus shape the meaning of the collaboration by focusing on expected performance benefits, making structural and systemic adjustments to support the achievement of these goals, and removing cues that detract from cooperation.

Stresses on Boundary Role Persons

The paradox of vulnerability and maintaining a climate of trust, open communication, and information sharing while at the same time protecting the host organization's autonomy and security presents a challenge for executives charged with managing interorganizational relationships.

Those performing in boundary positions are also responsible to both constituents in their host organizations and to their counterpart boundary managers in other organizations. Negotiation and the transfer of information and other resources across organizational boundaries occur within a boundary transaction system (Adams, 1976), wherein actions taken by constituents within organizations, as well as those taken by boundary managers, can have effects on the outcomes experienced by both organizations. Synergies resulting from the relationship depend largely on an organization's openness to influence from its own employees operating in clearly defined boundary roles. If there is resistance to the exercise of this influence, the relationship will be effectively contained, and potentially valuable information will not be distributed throughout the organization.

Conditions for Failure and Success

Obstacles to the success of relationships between organizations are real indeed, but they are not insurmountable. Organizational leaders who hope to capitalize on the opportunities available through collaboration and also to develop their organization's reputation as a desirable partner should consider both conditions that lead to failure and those that contribute to success.

Conditions for Failure

- First and foremost, if there is insufficient clarity about goals and how to measure progress toward these goals, the relationship is doomed.
- Should power and control between the partners be imbalanced, the relationship is not likely to last; that situation would indicate that an acquisition or a dissolution of the arrangement is in order. It may be that, in certain matters, one partner has more power and control than the other. Such an imbalance in certain areas may be acceptable as long as the imbalance is favorable to the other partner in other areas.
- If one partner has more expertise, status, and/or prestige than the other, the relationship is likely to be short-lived.
- If one or more of the partners is overly confident and unrealistic about the future success of the relationship, believing that he or she has sufficient control over variables external to and within the partnership, then conditions are ripe for failure.
- If things change without contingency plans, especially for renegotiating the relationship, the partnership is likely to deteriorate. Flexibility is key.
- A lack of perceived equity in the relationship of any kind—a fair distribution of important jobs to both partnering organizations, for example—will lead to serious problems.

These six conditions are neither discrete nor complete. Nevertheless, they represent some of the most significant conditions for failure in interorganizational relations.

Conditions for Success

The most important condition for success in an interorganizational relationship is having a goal or a set of goals that is clear and achievable only through the cooperative efforts of both partners. Social psychologists who have studied intergroup competition, conflict, and collaboration point to the critical function of what has come to be called a superordinate goal—a goal that neither partner could achieve separately but by joining together they can.

It is also imperative that this goal or set of goals be measurable. The question that must be answered is, "How will we know that we are making progress toward goal achievement, for example, a year from now?" Other important conditions include:

- A balance of power and control in the relationship—if one of the partners is too dominant, then the consequences are more like an acquisition, with one absorbing the other and the other as an entity essentially going out of existence;

• Mutual gain—each partner benefits from the relationship; the gain for each may be quite different—e.g., one obtains needed technology, the other realizes significant cost savings—as long as both clearly benefit;

• Committed leaders—when leaders of the partnering organizations demonstrate a strong belief in the efficacy of the relationship and show cooperative, collaborative behavior, others in the respective organizations are likely to follow suit;

• Alignment of rewards—making certain that organizational members are rewarded for cooperating, for partnering-type behavior;

• Respect for differences—like individuals, no two organizations are the same; organizational members must therefore work hard to overcome biases and stereotypes and be rewarded when they do;

• Good luck—things change, and partnering organizations sometimes have some control over the changes and sometimes not; a natural disaster can, for example, destroy a budding joint venture in agriculture. Thus, the importance of contingency plans and maintaining a degree of flexibility and a willingness to renegotiate is clear.

UNANSWERED QUESTIONS

If recent newspapers and magazine articles are indicative, the trend toward some form of interorganizational relationship will continue and probably even increase. More and more industries, especially the mature ones (e.g., chemicals, pharmaceutical, banks, etc.), are consolidating and therefore many additional mergers and acquisitions can be expected. There also appears to be a growing reliance on other, less permanent forms of relationships, such as networks and alliances. If this shift from a more permanent relationship (e.g., merger and acquisition) to less permanence (e.g., network, consortium, or alliance) is indeed true, why such a shift? Understanding more about this trend would be an excellent research agenda.

Assuming a shift to less permanence in relationships, two reasons to examine them via research present themselves. First, experience with and observation of a number of organizations suggests that most mergers and acquisitions prove to be unsuccessful, and economies of scale and promised synergies are not realized. The two (or more) cultures remain untouched and, eventually, what looked like a promising synergy becomes a disappointment. Why enter a relationship that is likely to be unsatisfactory? With consolidation occurring in many industries, ultimate survival is a primary reason. Also, mergers and especially acquisitions mean that more control by senior executives can be exercised. These are strong attractions for permanent relationships. Understanding these different dynamics—that is, why mergers and acquisitions continue unabated when a successful outcome is questionable—would be a useful addition to our knowledge of interorganizational relations.

Second, to compete effectively in a turbulent, global marketplace, to keep the peace in a volatile society that may be falling apart, or to consolidate resources in a city that is losing industries and key professional and technical people, organizations today have to be highly flexible. Decisions must be made quickly and then perhaps changed in a matter of months if not days. This growing need for rapid decision making and adaptability flies in the face of permanence.

Research is needed, particularly research that is based on methods of rapid data gathering and analysis, to gain a better understanding of these trends and how ongoing they are likely to be.

In her review of key articles in the literature, Auster (1994) proposed five more specific needs for future theory and research: (1) conceptual clarity, (2) broadening units of analysis, (3) expanding the time frame of analysis, (4) investigating the complementarity of structure and process, and (5) expanding levels of analysis. These five areas for further study suggest rather clearly where the gaps are in the research literature so far, and consequently where more research is needed. Practice has outrun theory and research in this field, and there is a growing mountain of popular books and articles on strategic alliances, joint ventures, and the like. These publications can suggest executives' concerns and important areas for research. This literature is built largely on anecdotes and consultants' experiences. Scholarly research can subject many of these ideas and beliefs to systematic evaluation.

CONCLUSIONS

The discussion in this chapter suggests the following conclusions:

1. The success of firms may be tied to how well they are linked with other firms in their environment. Industries like tobacco, pharmaceuticals, and electronics are profitable in part because competitors collaborate, within legal limits, in pursuing issues of common interest.

2. The performance of an organization may be linked to its position in a network of relations—whether, for example, it is able to tap into networks for information or whether it is relatively isolated.

3. The best unit of analysis for research on business performance—especially in Asia, some parts of Europe, and in highly networked industries like biotechnology—may be the network and not the individual firm.

4. Organizations typically enter into alliances either to accomplish a goal that cannot be achieved alone or to distribute costs.

5. Successful collaborations are the result of a well-managed process that is negotiated through predictable stages, from a preengagement state, to an evaluation stage, and possible renegotiation or exit from the relationship. The chances of success are increased to the extent that the process passes through all of these stages.

6. Collaborations are more likely to fail when goals for the alliance are not clear or measurable, when there is a power or expertise imbalance between the organizations, and when organizations are inflexible in the face of changing circumstances.

7. Political and military organizations are often forced to collaborate with partners for reasons other than the choice of organizational leaders. Research is necessary to understand how best to prepare these organizations and their personnel for alliances and alien forces, states, and organizations that may be very different culturally and operationally and with whom they do not have a predisposition to ally.

8. Research is needed to understand the conditions for successful collaboration between nonmarket organizations in which financial measures of success are not available and issues of ideology and mission are especially salient in the overall political environment or context.

PART II

Organizational Change and the Case of the Army's Changing Missions

6

New Military Missions

Organizations must adapt to environmental change. A prime instance is when their central purposes or missions are dramatically altered. The other chapters of this book highlight the challenges faced by organizations when they undergo a significant change in their missions, whether the change is the addition of new missions, the abandonment of old missions, or the modification of existing ones.

Unlike the previous chapters, which review the literature on organizations broadly and draw conclusions pertaining generally to many types of organizations, this chapter and the next concentrate attention on the case of a single, complex organization—the U.S. Army—as it undergoes fundamental changes in its missions. Although the arguments developed apply as well to other types of organizations, we are focusing here on the particular circumstances of the Army. Appendix A provides a brief discussion of the ways in which military organizations differ from other organizational forms.

CHANGING MISSIONS IN A POST-COLD WAR ERA

Although the basic purpose of U.S. Army—the successful waging of land warfare—has not changed, its missions have broadened for it to function in the post-cold war world. The unforeseen and precipitous end of the cold war and the attendant reordering of international society have altered some of the basic missions, training, and orientations undertaken by that organization (McCalla, 1994). The first major change is the shift in focus from one central enemy (the Soviet Union) to a potential multiplicity of enemies or no enemy at all. With the breakup of the Soviet Union, the

United States military no longer can consider actions in a bipolar setting, but may face many different enemies consisting of many states or even subnational groups; some of its missions may even render traditional conceptions of enemy and ally irrelevant. Second, the "new world order" may place less significance on nuclear weapons and traditional conventional military firepower. In many new missions, such heavy weaponry is inappropriate or even counterproductive to the goals that must be achieved; restraint of military force may be necessary, replacing traditional notions of battlefield superiority.

Third, the fixed deterrent deployment of the U.S. Army, so common in Europe, Korea, and elsewhere during the cold war, must be transformed to deal with quickly emerging crises in many parts of the world. The need for the development and refinement in the military of smaller-sized rapid deployment forces has accelerated with the diminution of the Soviet/Russian threat and the emergence of new hot spots in Somalia, Bosnia, and elsewhere; the Army must now adopt more flexible, ad hoc deployment strategies. Fourth, the activities that the Army may be called on to perform have increased both in number and scope.

Finally, the end of the cold war has led to the creation of more multinational military operations. Previously, the U.S. Army was involved in joint operations only with close allies. Now the Army faces the prospect of participating in actions that (1) may involve a large number of different state actors, not all of whom may support American goals, (2) may not include well-defined procedures for coordination, and (3) may involve United Nations (UN) or foreign command over its forces. (This change was officially recognized in President Clinton's National Security Strategy released by the White House in February 1995.) Many of the benefits and problems of interorganizational cooperation noted in the previous chapter are thus directly applicable to the U.S. Army in performing its new missions. However, these missions differ from the kinds of joint ventures and mergers discussed in Chapter 5. They are almost always temporary, imposed on the Army without the organization's consent, and involve a variety of governmental and nongovernmental organizations whose tasks overlap rather than complement one another, as in the cases of corporate collaboration described earlier. Here we consider the kinds of coordination issues that occur in the context of the new Army missions.

In the post-cold war era, the U.S. Army has had to adapt to a broadened and more extensive set of missions and requirements. This chapter describes this new range of missions and develops a typology useful for analyzing the similarities and differences among them. In light of that analysis, we go on in the next chapter to identify the skills needed for the different missions.

CLASSIFYING AND COMPARING MISSIONS

Beyond its traditional roles in the defense of the United States and its national interests, the U.S. Army has been or may be called on to perform a variety of other missions. The term *peacekeeping* has been popularly used to designate a wide range of phenomena, often improperly referring to any international effort involving an operational component to promote the termination of armed conflict or the resolution of long-standing disputes. In the interest of conceptual clarity, we offer the following taxonomy of different missions qualifying as *operations other than war*, which is the designation that the military uses for nontraditional operations and includes peacekeeping operations as well as missions that fall well outside that realm. The taxonomy does not include all possible missions (for such a list might be infinite), but rather represents those missions that the Army or other foreign militaries have been called on to perform recently or historically, are on the agenda for possible peacekeeping missions by the United Nations, or have received serious consideration in American and international policy-making circles. In providing this taxonomy as a prelude to an analysis of appropriate training and skills, we are not offering a judgment about the wisdom or viability of these missions, but only recognize that such missions will be the product of government decisions and preparations should proceed as if they might be implemented.

The categories below are also not mutually exclusive, since a given military operation may include more than one of the missions outlined, either simultaneously or sequentially (there may be instances, however, in which the missions are fundamentally incompatible with one another). Such mixing of missions may not even be designed or anticipated at the outset or even during the course of a mission. Mission change and adaptation may occur very rapidly on a micro level during the performance of a specific operation, much as it does at the macro level when fundamental changes in missions can occur.

A Taxonomy of Operations Other than War

1. *Traditional peacekeeping* is the stationing of neutral, lightly armed troops with the permission of the host state(s) as an interposition force following a cease-fire to separate combatants and promote an environment suitable for conflict resolution. Traditional UN peacekeeping troops were deployed in Cyprus beginning in 1964 and southern Lebanon starting in 1978 (Diehl, 1994).

2. *Observation* consists of the deployment of a small number of unarmed, neutral personnel with the consent of the host state to collect information and monitor activities (cease-fire, human rights, etc.) in the deploy-

ment area, sometimes following a cease-fire or other agreement (Wainhouse, 1966). The UN observer mission in the Middle East (UNTSO), first deployed in 1948, is an example.

3. *Collective enforcement* is a large-scale military operation designed to defend the victims of international aggression and restore peace and security by the defeat of aggressor state forces (Mackinlay, 1990; Mackinlay and Chopra, 1992; Downs, 1994). The multinational operations in Kuwait in 1991 and Korea in the 1950s fit this profile; so too would a "collective security" operation, as envisioned by the UN Charter, carried out by an international army.

4. *Election supervision* consists of observation and monitoring of a cease-fire, disarmament, and a democratic election following a peace agreement among previously warring internal groups; this function may also include the assistance of local security forces (Beigbeder, 1994). UN operations in Namibia in the late 1980s and Cambodia in the early 1990s are examples.

5. *Humanitarian assistance during conflict* involves the transportation and distribution of life-sustaining food and medical supplies, in coordination with local and international nongovernmental organizations, to threatened populations during a civil or interstate war (Minear and Weiss, 1993; Natsios, 1994; U.S. Department of the Army, 1994). Operations in Somalia and Bosnia during the 1990s are examples.

6. *Disaster relief* involves the transportation and distribution of food and medical supplies as well as the rebuilding of infrastructure and maintenance of basic services following a natural disaster (Gordenker and Weiss, 1991; Cuny, 1991). The U.S. Army relief operation after Hurricane Andrew in 1992 is an example.

7. *State/nation building* includes the restoration of law and order in the absence of government authority, the reconstruction of infrastructure and security forces, and facilitation of the transfer of power from the interim authority to an indigenous government (Kumar, 1995; U.S. Department of the Army, 1994; Boutros-Ghali, 1992; Cox, 1993). The United Nations carried out some of these functions in the Congo in the early 1960s, but it was unable to do so in Somalia after the deployment of forces in the early 1990s. The U.S. Marine involvement in the Caribbean during 1920-1930 is another example of nation building.

8. *Pacification* consists of quelling civil disturbances, defeating local armed groups, forcibly separating belligerents, and maintaining law and order in an interstate war, civil war, or domestic riot, especially in the face of significant loss of life, human rights abuses, or destruction of property (U.S. Department of the Army, 1994). The international community was reluctant to take this kind of action after the start of the Bosnian conflict in the early 1990s, despite the high level of casualties and ethnic-cleansing campaigns.

9. *Preventive deployment* consists of stationing troops between two combatants to deter the onset or prevent the spread of war (Mackinlay and Chopra, 1992; Diehl and Kumar, 1991; Urquhart, 1990; U.S. Department of the Army, 1994). The UN-sponsored troops in Macedonia, deployed in the early 1990s to deter the spread of war in the former Yugoslavia, are examples of this type of nontraditional use of military force.

10. *Arms control verification* includes the inspection of military facilities, supervision of troop withdrawals, and all activities normally handled by national authorities and technical means as a part of an arms control agreement (Krepon and Tracey, 1990; Mandell, 1987; Jurado and Diehl, 1994). Multinational peacekeeping troops performed some of these functions in the Sinai operation that followed the 1979 Egyptian-Israel peace agreements.

11. *Protective services* includes the establishment of safe havens, "no fly" zones, and guaranteed rights of passage for the purpose of protecting or denying hostile access to threatened civilian populations or areas of a state, often without the permission of that state (U.S. Department of the Army, 1994). International actions in the 1990s to protect the Kurds in Iraq (Operation Provide Comfort) and the Muslims in Bosnia are consistent with this purpose.

12. *Drug eradication* consists of the destruction of narcotic-producing vegetation and processing facilities and the monitoring of international transit points for narcotics trafficking; it may or may not involve coordination with the governments of narcotics-exporting states (Rikhye, 1991; U.S. President, 1992). Some U.S. efforts in concert with the Colombian government over several decades are related to this nontraditional military mission.

13. *Antiterrorism* involves using the military to strengthen facility security and assist in training programs, replacing or supplementing traditional civil or paramilitary forces in these roles. Some actions may even include counterterrorism roles, such as assisting in hostage rescue or negotiation (Diehl, 1994; Rikhye, 1991). The Israeli military performs many of these functions.

14. *Intervention in support of democracy* is a military operation intended to overthrow existing leaders and to support freely elected government officials or an operation intended to protect extant and threatened democratic governments; activities may include military action against antidemocratic forces and assistance in law, order, and support services to democratic authorities. The United States invasion of Panama in the 1980s and the 1994 intervention in Haiti (at least until General Cedras agreed to relinquish power) are illustrative of such missions.

15. *Sanctions enforcement* is the use of military troops (air, sea, and land) to guard transit points, intercept contraband (e.g., arms, trade), or punish a state for transgressions (e.g., human rights abuses) defined by the

international community or national governments in their imposition of sanctions (U.S. Department of the Army, 1994). A blockade of North Korea or other nuclear weapons-seeking states to punish them for violations of the Nuclear Non-Proliferation Treaty would be an example. The U.S. blockade of Cuba in 1962 is another example.

16. *Aid to domestic, civilian populations* consists of the use of military forces in their native country for enhancing the well-being of the population in several areas (Nunn, 1993):

- *Human capital development* is assistance in the improvement of educational, personal, and vocational skills among different segments of society. The U.S. Civilian Conservation Corps' program during the 1930s is an example. The proposed National Guard Youth Corps and the YESS program in Michigan are other examples.
- *Public health assistance* is the assistance of public health authorities in meeting emergency needs and chronic problems associated with the health of the population. The Military Assistance to Safety and Traffic Program already incorporates some of this mission and is available in several states.
- *Rehabilitation of infrastructure* is the restoration and construction of public facilities (e.g., roads, schools, housing). Although a foreign example, Operation Provide Comfort in Iraq provided road and housing construction similar to what might be done domestically.
- *Firefighting* consists of the use of military troops to support civilian efforts in controlling forest fires and wildfires. The 1994 deployment of U.S. troops to fight fires in the Pacific Northwest is an example.

This taxonomy provides an initial classification of operations other than war by reference to the purposes of these 16 missions. In order to develop efficient training programs and strategic planning, there have been attempts to classify these missions further along several dimensions, identifying similarities across types. One method has been to consider the timing of the intervention vis-à-vis the stage of armed conflict (Thurman, 1992); operations are classified according to whether they are deployed before hostilities occur (such as some forms of preventive deployment), during low-intensity conflict, during full-scale war, or following armed conflict (such as election supervision). Another method (Mackinlay and Chopra, 1992) is to arrange operations according to the level of risk (generally the intensity of conflict) and the military assets necessary for the operations; observation and enforcement missions generally represent the ends of this continuum. Still other classifications implicitly combine mission function, timing, and level of coercion to derive the popularly used categories of peacekeeping, peacemaking, peace building, and peace enforcement (although the actual meaning of these terms varies widely) (Boutros-Ghali, 1992; U.S. Department of the Army, 1994).

Such categorizations can be misleading because of their imprecision; they are often not useful because they lump together seemingly disparate missions, which involve very different characteristics, actions, and training. As an alternative to the traditional continuum of peace operations, we offer a new method of classification based on characteristics drawn from the academic literature on international conflict management.

Similarities and Dissimilarities Among Missions

The classification developed by the committee describes each mission in terms of 11 contextual characteristics that are related to its deployment (Table 6-1). These characteristics vary considerably in the degree of control that military planners and commanders can exercise over conditions. Some characteristics are inherent in the operation and determined by political decisions or extant factors; these include the roles played by the military force, the extent to which national constituencies accept the costs and possible losses incurred by the mission, and the ease with which success can be judged. Other characteristics are subject to greater manipulation or modification by the military. Some involve greater military influence, such as whether procedures for the mission are clear. Others can be only partly influenced by the military themselves, such as the ease of exit and the likelihood that the mission expands beyond expectations, referred to as "mission creep." Certain contextual factors may be relatively fixed at the outset, such as the clarity of the relationship with the host country, but might change over time as a result of the strategy and behavior of the military

TABLE 6-1   Contextual Characteristics of Missions

Characteristic	Categories
Role of peacekeeper	Primary, mixed, or third-party
Clarity of relationships with host country	Clear, clear on some tasks but vague on others, or vague
Clarity of procedures	Clear, fluid, or vague
Clarity of goals and desired outcomes	Clear, somewhat clear, or vague
Conflict management process	Distributive, mixed, or integrative
Level of control over conflict	Much, moderate, or little
Ease of exit from mission	Easy, moderate, or difficult
Possibility of mission creep	High, moderate, or low
Assessment of mission success	Easy, moderate, or difficult
Tolerance of costs by constituencies	Low, moderate, or high
Prior experience for Army	Much, some, or little/none

force. In addition to these contextual characteristics, the missions can also be described in terms of the Army's experience with this or a similar kind of operation.

Mission Profiles

By describing the missions in terms of the characteristics listed in the table, we can construct a profile of each mission. For example, traditional peacekeeping may be described as follows: the soldier's role is that of third party, relationships with the host country are clear on some tasks but vague on others, procedures are fluid, goals are clear in the short term but vague in the long term, the process is primarily integrative, soldier control is relatively low, exiting from the operation is difficult, the chances for mission creep are moderate, the assessment of success is moderately difficult, constituencies have little tolerance for costs, and, with regard to traditional Army experience, there are few analogues.

We note that a number of other characteristics, which do not affect the mission profiles, are also certainly relevant to military planning and may impact the kinds and degree of training required for a given mission; many of these characteristics are context specific and cut across different mission types. They include the likely degree of interaction anticipated with the local population, the dispersion of forces and the relative autonomy granted different parts of the operation, the physical conditions (amenities, level of privacy, facilities) in the area of deployment, the degree and type of communication access, logistical dependence, clarity of relationships with allies, and level of support for the mission among military personnel, to offer several examples. These characteristics must be considered for each mission, since they may serve to modify the training requirements for the mission types developed below.

To create mission profiles, three expert analysts were asked to rate the 16 missions using the characteristics listed in Table 6-1. The analysts included an academic specialist on peacekeeping who is a member of the committee, a major in the Canadian armed services with long experience in peacekeeping operations, and a retired U.S. ambassador with expertise in international conflict management. For each mission, the analysts rated all the characteristics in terms of three possibilities, usually distinguishing among high (or clear), moderate (clear on some tasks, vague on others), and low (vague). To develop consensus ratings, differences among the analysts' ratings were resolved through discussion or, in some cases, by using the middle category as a kind of compromise decision. The final ratings, which took the form of codes ranging from 1 to 3, were used as data for a scaling analysis that reveals similarities and differences among the mission profiles.[1]

Scaling Analysis

This exercise and the resulting statistical analyses were designed to discover a pattern of relationships among the missions, one that might serve to organize the discussion of training requirements that follows in the next chapter. The pattern that emerges should be regarded as a hypothesis, since other dimensions could also be discovered. We are interested to know whether the pattern that emerges is useful in distinguishing among the various missions.

The pattern is based on correlations calculated for each possible pair of missions: in this case, all the possible pairs total 120.[2] The correlation coefficient expresses the extent to which two missions are similar in terms of the judgments made across the set of 11 characteristics. In a separate analysis, we were also able to assess the extent to which the characteristics correlated with one another individually. For example, the analysis provides information about the characteristics that relate most strongly to the ease of assessing mission success. This variable was found to correlate positively with clarity of goals (.56) and negatively with mission creep (–.61) and with tolerance of costs (–.48).

It seems that the clearer the mission's goals, the easier it is to assess its success. And the less likely the possibility of mission creep and the more tolerance constituents have for costs, the more difficult it is to assess mission success. These findings suggest, not surprisingly, that a clear statement of goals provides criteria for judging success. They also suggest that it is easy to judge failure in light of mission creep and high costs, but not easy to assess success when mission creep is less likely and costs are low.

Using a technique referred to as multidimensional scaling, we can capture the complete set of relationships among the missions. (See Kruskel and Wish, 1990, for a discussion of the procedures and applications.) The technique reveals an underlying structure for the complete set of correlations. That structure takes the form of a two-dimensional space that provides coordinates for locating the missions: more similar missions are located in closer proximity in the space.

Broadly speaking, the scaling analysis is used to identify meaningful groupings of the missions and the dimensions along which they are grouped. Although a larger number of dimensions is possible, we limited the number to two, based on satisfying criteria of interpretability, ease of use, and stability. These dimensions organize the missions in terms of relationships and processes that are emphasized in the literature on conflict management. The exercise provides a basis for organizing the discussion in the next chapter on the challenges and skills needed to perform effectively and places it in the context of the research literature. These skills are broadly applicable to a wide variety of conflict situations, including those confronted often by military peacekeepers.

Results of the Analysis

Results of the scaling analysis are shown in Figure 6-1. Two results are of particular interest for our purposes: one is the dimensions themselves, which appear as the north-south and east-west axes of the figure. The other is the clustering of the missions in constellations across the four boxes of the figure.

Dimensions. The distinction between primary and third-party roles clearly divides the missions from north to south. Soldiers in primary roles are principals in the conflict, whereas those in third-party roles are not direct parties to the conflict, but rather mediators or conciliators. Most of the missions in the north quadrants—disaster relief (F), sanctions enforcement (O), drug eradication (L), antiterrorism (M), collective enforcement (C), protective services (K), and intervention in support of democracy (N)—were coded as primary roles for soldiers. Most of the missions in the south quadrants—election supervision (D), arms control verification (J), observa-

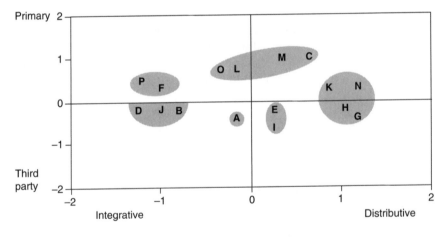

A Traditional peacekeeping	I Preventive deployment
B Observation	J Arms control verification
C Collective enforcement	K Protective services
D Election supervision	L Drug eradication
E Humanitarian assistance during conflict	M Antiterrorism
F Disaster relief	N Intervention in support of democracy
G State/nation building	O Sanctions enforcement
H Pacification	P Aid to domestic, civilian populations

FIGURE 6-1 Missions across characteristics.

tion (B), traditional peacekeeping (A), and preventive deployment (I)—involve third-party roles for soldiers.

Two missions—humanitarian assistance during conflict (E) and pacification (H)—were regarded as having elements of both primary and third-party roles; they are located at the "border" between the southeast and northeast quadrants. Only two missions appear to be misplaced: the mixed mission of aid to domestic populations (P) is located in the northwest quadrant with primary missions, and the primary mission of state/nation building (G) is located in the southeast quadrant with third-party missions. A strong correlation between the role variable (each mission coded as primary, mixed, or a third-party role) and the dimension plots supports this interpretation. (The correlation is .70.)

The distinction between integrative and distributive processes divides the missions from west to east, although it is not as clear a distinction as the north-south one. The distinction between distributive and integrative bargaining was made originally in the context of labor-management negotiations by Walton and McKersie (1965). Distributive bargaining refers to processes in which parties attempt to increase their own outcomes (usually money, territory, positions, or power) at the other's expense. By integrative bargaining, we refer to processes in which parties attempt to achieve mutually beneficial solutions to a problem (which may involve either tangible or intangible resources). Parties are concerned with relationships and search for enduring resolutions.

Most of the missions in the west quadrants consist of integrative processes—traditional peacekeeping (A), observation (B), election supervision (D), disaster relief (F), arms control verification (J), and aid to domestic civilian populations (P). The only exceptions are sanctions enforcement (O) and drug eradication (L). Of those in the east quadrants, only state/nation building (G) is integrative; humanitarian assistance during conflict (E) and pacification (H) are mixed; and all the others are regarded as being characterized primarily by distributive processes. The correlation between the mission codes for process (as distributive, mixed, or integrative) and the dimension plots is a moderately strong .51.[3]

Clusters. The way in which the missions are grouped or clustered in the space may indicate similarities, reducing the 16 missions to fewer, more general types. Using traditional peacekeeping as a point of reference, the clusters of missions can be seen to fan out to the west, north, and east. Five distinct groupings are apparent. To the west (in the southwest quadrant), election supervision (D), arms control verification (J), and observation (B) are grouped together. These missions have in common a *monitoring function* and are relatively passive. Also to the west but in the northwest quadrant are two nonconflict missions intended specifically to deal with *emer-*

gencies: aid to domestic populations (P) and disaster relief (F). To the north (spanning the northwest and northeast quadrants) are the combat-oriented *coercive* (or *offensive)* missions: sanctions enforcement (O), drug eradication (L), antiterrorism (M), and collective enforcement (C). To the west and spanning the north and southwest quadrants are missions whose purpose is to *restore countries to functioning civil societies*: protective services (K), intervention in support of democracy (N), pacification (H), and state/nation building (G). Finally, to the near west are two missions intended to *limit damage* to conflicting societies: humanitarian assistance (E) and deterrent deployment (I); both these types of missions characterize the United Nations peacekeeping operations in Bosnia and Macedonia in the early 1990s. The five groupings can be viewed as different kinds of challenges to soldiers, each calling for similar sets of trained skills, which we discuss in further detail in the next chapter.[4]

NEEDED SKILLS FOR NEW MISSIONS

The distinctions we make among missions call attention to the variety of operations other than war that can be performed by military forces. The various tasks are also likely to call for a somewhat different mix of skills needed to accomplish the mission, although this is not always accepted by the U.S. Army, which states that the "first and foremost requirement for success in peace operations is the successful application of war-fighting skills" (U.S. Department of the Army, 1994:86). In the next chapter, we discuss the kinds of skills that are needed for the various kinds of missions.

NOTES

[1]The experts were used as a consensus panel for judging each of the missions in terms of their characteristics. Our only concern is whether the expert judgments are accurate, and we have reason to believe that they are. The analysis used these judgments to develop and then evaluate the mission profiles (16 missions on 11 characteristics) in terms of similarities and dissimilarities. The relevant N's for the scaling analysis are the 16 missions by the 11 characteristics, not the three experts.

[2]Although some variables were coded in terms of a three-step scale going from "much" to "little," others were coded in discrete categories such as whether the soldier's role was primary, mixed, or third party (see Table 6-1). For this reason, we decided to use a correlation coefficient based on categorical rather than scaling assumptions. This is the gamma coefficient. Interested readers may consult Goodman and Kruskal (1954) for details.

[3]It should be noted, however, that the distributive/integrative variable correlates also with the north-south dimension as well as with the primary/third-party variable. Thus, although these dimension names usefully distinguish among the missions, they are used only for heuristic purposes.

[4]Another scaling analysis was performed on the 11 characteristics across the 16 missions. Results suggest a distinction in terms of "control." Characteristics in the western quadrants are those over which soldiers have limited control (for example, role, tolerance of

costs, analogous past experiences). Those in the eastern quadrants are characteristics over which they have at least some degree of control, for example, process as distributive or integrative, clarity of procedures, relationships among goals, control over conflict.

7

Conflict Management Training for Changing Missions

Our analysis of the Army's new missions calls attention to the kinds of skills that are needed to conduct them effectively. In this chapter, we identify the combat and contact skills needed for peacekeeping and operations other than war (OOTW) activities, then review current military training programs for the applicability of their skills training to mission requirements. Training programs worldwide devote relatively little time to the development of contact skills. We therefore propose a number of ways to improve conflict management training for particular missions. We also discuss factors that limit the effectiveness of this kind of training, interfere with the evaluation of the training, or limit mission effectiveness.

PREPARING FOR OPERATIONS OTHER THAN WAR

Combat and Contact Activities

A useful way to think about needed mission skills is to make a distinction between those used in combat operations and those involved in contact with individuals and groups. By combat skills, we refer to basic military skills used in situations in which there is a physical threat, weapons discharge, combat engagement, or internal security operation. By contact skills, we refer primarily to communication skills involved in exchange and liaison duties, interviews and public relations, negotiations and related discussions, civil-military cooperation, mediation of disputes, and interagency cooperation. Missions are likely to differ in terms of their mix of combat and contact activities; they also differ according to the rank and duties of the military personnel involved in the operation. A chief difference among missions is whether the soldier's role is that of primary party or third party, as shown in Figure 6-1.

A recent survey conducted by the Lester B. Pearson Canadian International Peacekeeping Training Center (Last and Eyre, 1995) used the distinction between combat and contact activities. Canadian soldiers in the Bosnian (N = 197) and Croatian (N = 185) United Nations (UNPROFOR) operations were asked a number of questions about their experiences during the time period November 1993 to April 1994. Ninety-six questions, arranged in nine groupings, were asked of samples at three ranks: enlisted soldiers, noncommissioned officers (NCOs), and officers. Of these, 50 questions were relevant to the combat-contact distinction: 32 deal with combat activities, 18 with contact activities. From the answers, profiles were constructed for each operation. These profiles show the relative balance of combat and contact experiences for the two missions and how these experiences vary by rank.

The results show that combat skills are important at all levels, but that contact skills are more significant with increasing rank. The proportion of combat and contact experiences for the enlisted and NCO ranks was roughly equal for both operations. Officers reported about twice as many contact (about 40 percent) as combat (20 percent) activities in the Bosnian operation and almost three times as many contact (40 versus 15 percent) activities in the Croatian operation. The most frequent combat experiences reported were being a target for rocks thrown, encountering mines, coming under small-arms fire, being restrained, and being held at gunpoint. The most frequent contact experiences reported were working with interpreters, negotiating with civilian police and belligerent factions, and interacting with local civilians.

With regard to activities involving negotiation, almost all officers and many senior NCOs reported experiences with a soldier or officer of one of the warring factions; only 29 percent of the enlisted group reported having these experiences. A smaller percentage of officers (60 percent) reported negotiating with civilian leaders of one of the factions; an even smaller percentage of the enlisted group reported these experiences (about 15 percent). With regard to mediation or conciliation, about 50 percent of the officers and senior NCOs had these experiences, compared with only about 10 percent of the enlisted soldiers.

This leads to the conclusion that developing contact skills is clearly essential for officers, and it may be important to develop them even at the lower levels. It is also apparent that contact skills are increasingly important in many of the newer operations other than war. In traditional peacekeeping operations, only senior officers could be expected to have direct interactions with the protagonists and thus require some contact skills. Junior officers and enlisted personnel might never have to use such skills, as they might be stationed as part of an interposition force in an area of low population density (e.g., the Sinai Desert). Operations other than war such as election supervision and humanitarian assistance require military personnel at all levels to be prepared to interact directly with the local population, perhaps on a daily basis.

If contact skills are important, then it is important to know to what extent training programs emphasize these skills. The Canadian survey is a first attempt to document what is actually done in OOTW missions. Nevertheless, it is largely limited to one type of mission, which we referred to above as limiting damage. The survey documents that these missions are characterized by a mix of combat and contact experiences and that the relative emphasis on these skills varies for the different ranks. These types of missions may consist of more combat activities than monitoring missions and more contact than coercive missions. The different missions may also entail different mixes of contact and combat skills in the training packages for the different ranks. Such comparisons await the results of similar surveys conducted in conjunction with other types of missions. The Canadian effort is a useful model for those surveys.

Training Programs

The combat versus contact distinction can also be used to depict what is being done in programs that train military personnel for operations other than war. The committee considered 79 programs worldwide that are summarized in a September 1994 training catalog issued by the Inspector General's Office of the Department of Defense (DoD). The catalog is divided between U.S. and international (33 countries) training activities; the U.S. programs are further divided into DoD (and its separate services) and non-DoD programs. Following a general description of the program, the specific topics taught in courses or addressed in roundtable discussions are listed. For example, elective courses dealing with peace operations at the Army War College are listed as "collective security and peacekeeping," "peace operations exercise," and "conflict resolution and strategic negotiation." Examples of subject areas included in the training packages at the Army Command and General Staff College are "non-combatant evacuation," "humanitarian assistance/disaster relief," "combatting terrorism," and "arms control." This information was used to assess the extent to which the programs emphasized the training of contact and combat skills.

Using keywords to identify contact skills, we calculated a ratio of the number of contact to combat skills included in each program's training curricula.[1] The ratio consisted of the number of contact skills divided by the total number of topics listed for each program. The results of this analysis indicate:

- Across the 79 programs, including both U.S. and international, an average of 13 percent of the topics or activities listed involved contact or interpersonal skills.
- For the 59 programs in which at least one contact skill was mentioned, an average of 25 percent of the topics involved the use of contact or interpersonal skills.
- There is little variation among the programs in terms of the number of contact skills included, with a range for most programs from 0 to 5 (or 0 to 25) percent. There is little difference between U.S. and foreign programs, nor is there much difference between the DoD and non-DoD programs or among the programs sponsored by the different services.
- The program that includes the most contact skills—five—is conducted by NATO. The program with the highest percentage of contact relative to combat skills is the U.S. central command.[2]
- With regard to the total number of skills being taught, there is considerable variation, with a range from 0 to 21. Among the more encompassing programs are the Air Command and Staff College (21 skills), NATO (16), Uruguay's Navy course (15), the United Nation's military observer training in the United Kingdom (14), the United Nation's soldier training courses (14), and specialized training in the Philippines (14).

Taken together, the results of the two analyses make it apparent that a gap exists between the skills being trained and the activities that occur in peacekeeping and related missions. Fetherston also recognized this gap, noting that "at best only a small fraction of course time is spent on [conflict resolution or cross-cultural orientation skills]—approximately 5 percent in any of the programs [that devote the most teaching hours to contact skills], either national or regional" (1994:208).

There is a diversity of opinion among U.S. military and foreign officers about whether traditional military skills are sufficient for most operations other than war. Nevertheless, it is evident that current training programs are skewed more in the direction of the view that combat skills are adequate for most personnel, regardless of mission. Yet it is apparent to the committee that a significant gap in the training of contact skills exists. The gap is accentuated further by uncertainty with regard to which skills are most pertinent to which types of missions. Having reached this conclusion, however, leads to the questions of what specifically should be trained and how the training should be done. These questions are addressed in the sections that follow.

Developing Contact Skills

There is a large literature on approaches to developing communication and related interpersonal skills. Fetherston (1994) considered training issues in the context of theory and practice—she views training as a critical link between them. She depicts the link in terms of a cyclical framework in which "conceptual analysis leads to developments in training which lead to changes in practice. . . . (T)hese changes then initiate testing and revising which finally feed back into the conceptualization process" (1994:164-165). The process is visually represented in Figure 7-1. She illustrates the links with examples from cross-cultural training and concentrates on skills and attitudes that relate to effective interactions between members of different cultures.

Drawing on a review of literature by Hannigan (1990), Fetherston emphasizes the general communication skills of listening, entering a dialogue, initiating interaction, dealing with misunderstandings, language, and interaction management (see also Harbottle, 1992). She notes that although subject-matter expertise is important, it is insufficient without these communication skills. These are also the skills needed for effective third-party intervention in general. The review of literature also identifies attitudes that relate to cross-cultural effectiveness. In addition to positive attitudes and respect for the host culture, she notes that "a critical aspect of intercultural interaction [is] to be able to judge when it is best to be flexible and when it is better to be persistent" (1992:168). This is also a critical aspect of all international negotiations, as illustrated in the recent collection of papers on flexibility edited by Druckman and Mitchell (1995).

With regard to approaches used in developing these skills, Fetherston distinguishes among six types of training methods: fact-oriented training,

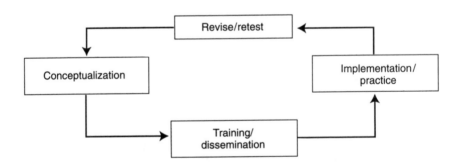

FIGURE 7-1 Cyclical development of the theory and practice of peacekeeping. Source: Fetherston (1994:165). Copyright A.B. Fetherston. Reprinted with permission of St. Martin's Press, Incorporated.

attribution training, cultural awareness training, cognitive-behavior modification, experiential learning, and interactional learning. She agrees with an earlier judgment made by Grove and Torbiorn (1985) that fact-oriented training is inappropriate because it does not allow for changes in one's usual patterns of interacting with others. These authors favor experiential learning because of its emphasis on learning through actual experience, allowing the trainee to notice the impact of his or her behavior on others.[3] That impact is likely to be understood better if the trainee can internalize the host's values, which is a goal of attribution training (see Brislin, 1986; Danielian, 1967). Indeed, it is likely that a combination of methods works best.

Although it is important to develop general communication and interaction skills, it is also necessary to know when to use them. Some skills may be more useful for certain types of missions or for certain stages of a particular mission. Insufficient attention has been paid to this issue, due at least in part to a lack of differentiation among missions or among stages of missions. With regard to missions, the taxonomy described above contributes to distinctions among types of missions. With regard to stages, Fisher and Keashly's (1991) contingency model of conflict escalation, refined further by Fetherston (1994), has implications for thinking about developmental processes within peacekeeping missions. (See also Grove and Torbiorn's [1985] adjustment-cycle model of cross-cultural experience, which is discussed below.) And with regard to developing specialized skills, Johnson and Layng (1992) present an approach that builds skills that can be elicited in response to specific occasions or challenges.

Focusing on the conflict process, Fisher and Keashly (1991) developed a typology of conflict escalation that distinguishes among four stages: discussion, polarization, segregation, and destruction. At each stage, the relationship between protagonists changes significantly. The preferred method of conflict management by the parties themselves becomes increasingly competitive, going from joint decision making in Stage 1 to outright attempts at destruction in Stage 4. Intervention activities also change in terms of goals and intervention strategies: assisting communication through negotiation in Stage 1, improving relationships through consultation in Stage 2, controlling hostility through muscled mediation in Stage 3, and controlling violence through peacekeeping in Stage 4. (See the summaries in Fetherston, 1994:Appendices 3 and 4.) Interestingly, peacekeeping is used in this model only after a conflict has escalated to a destructive stage.

These models describe developmental processes. Each specifies the conditions under which certain processes are likely to occur as well as the intervention or training strategies that are appropriate. The Fisher and Keashly (1991) model links intervention approaches to steps on a ladder of escalation. Grove and Torbiorn (1985) link training methods to periods of adjustment. These are complementary models. The former has implications for the military mission; the latter addresses issues that are relevant to the individual soldier. Both models are useful for identifying the kinds of interventions or adjustment problems for which training is needed. Neither model suggests, however, how the training or preparation ought to be done.

Guidance for training programs is provided by the research literatures on cross-cultural training and on conflict management. Fetherston (1994) reviews the literature on cross-cultural training and communication skills, and, as we noted above, uses this work as an example of linking theory with practice. She devotes less attention to the research on conflict management strategies. That body of research is also an example of linking theory with practice and deals with third-party intervention strategies in a more direct way than the cross-cultural training research. Of course, these skills have broad applicability, allowing us to draw on a large research literature for relevance to OOTW missions.

CONFLICT MANAGEMENT TRAINING

Training in conflict management skills is recognized as an important part of preparation for peacekeeping and other OOTW missions. Despite the absence of these skills that we noted in many of the training programs worldwide, there is a noticeable trend toward incorporating units on negotiation and mediation in courses at the United Nations and at various military colleges and training facilities in the United States and Canada.[4] One of the more systematic approaches to the training of negotiation skills is the course designed by the UN Department of Peacekeeping Operations. Its training strategy covers four aspects of negotiation: its aim, the principles of negotiation, the elements of negotiation, and negotiation phases (including preparations, negotiation proper, closing, and reports and follow-up). Using a mix of lectures and role-playing exercises, the trainers provide advice about how to negotiate, and the trainees experience the process and the impact of their moves on that process. The advice given is to proceed in steps. With regard to the negotiation proper: start with tension-reducing gestures, understand all parties' limits of concession, narrow down differences, use persuasive skills, be correct and impartial, and request renewed negotiation.

Although such training is useful, it does not link the training to distinctions among types of missions. Nor do the programs distinguish among the missions in terms of primary versus third-party roles or distributive versus integrative relationships. Making these distinctions would tailor training to the kinds of skills needed for particular missions. To further improve the training programs, we suggest the use of up-to-date material and progressive in-class simulations.

First, we suggest that the classroom material presented to the soldier be brought up to date, so that it reflects the current state of knowledge in the field. The current material is quite dated, having a strong orientation to distributive and primary-party processes. Also, mediation and other third-party processes were at times confused with negotiation. Second, we suggest that in-class training be more extensive as well as varied and attempt to equip the soldier with a broad set of contact skills. The ideas here are quite basic: a soldier learns by doing, and the more varied the practice, the more flexible and effective the soldier will be (see also Druckman and Bjork, 1994:Ch. 3).

We suggest a confidence-building approach to skills acquisition. For some specific examples, consider primary-party (negotiation) training. It should move from a simple arena to a more difficult one—for instance, from negotiations over a fixed sum to negotiations with integrative potential. There could be one-trial negotiations, followed by multiple trials. Initially, issues could be simple, followed by negotiations over more complex issues. Some issues could be on divisible items, others not. With such progressions, the negotiations can be moved from simple to more complicated arenas, giving the soldier not only negotiation experience but also experience in increasingly varied and difficult contexts. In terms of other relevant forms, the negotiation experiences could move:

- from low emotion issues to high emotion issues,
- from familiar (car purchase) to unfamiliar negotiations (Dutch auction),
- from no alternatives to the negotiation to both sides having alternatives,
- from no power difference to high power difference,
- from no constituencies to multiple constituencies,
- from one opponent to several opponents, and
- from an ethical to an unethical opponent.

We suggest a similar approach for teaching the soldier third-party (mediation) skills. Initially, the soldier needs to be exposed to current knowledge on mediation and schooled as to when third-party versus primary-party approaches are required. Subsequently, the soldier should participate in increasingly varied and difficult third-party simulations. Specifically the simulations could move:

- from conflicts over one issue to conflicts over multiple issues,
- from conflicts with fixed outcome solutions to those with integrative solutions,
- from conflicts with two parties to those with multiple parties,

- from conflicts in which there are no alternatives to ones in which disputants have multiple alternatives, and
- from mediations requiring no strategies to those that do.

The conflict management research that would be drawn on for this instruction is divided between studies that deal more with distributive issues or bargaining processes and those more relevant to integrative or problem-solving processes. These are distinct approaches to negotiation, one primarily tactical, the other problem solving. As such, they can be thought of as techniques used to train negotiators. In the following sections, we describe these approaches, summarize key studies, and note both strengths and weaknesses with each approach, including attempts made to evaluate them.

Distributive Processes

Recall that our scaling exercise produced two dimensions along which the 16 missions were categorized. One was the distributive/integrative dimension and the other was the primary/third-party dimension. Consider now the distributive end of the first dimension. The emphasis of this approach is on moving an opponent to one's own preferred position. To the extent that tactics can be scripted or consist of procedures that are easily learned, the approach is somewhat mechanistic and manipulative, focusing on what the soldier can do to move the other party toward his or her desired outcome. The bargaining literature (both popular and academic) is replete with descriptions of various tactics that are intended to be used to influence the other to accept one's terms in competitive situations.

This approach is suited to missions in which adversarial parties are clearly defined, gains and losses to the parties can be calculated, the main goal is to achieve a settlement (rather than a longer-term resolution), and efforts are not made to turn over control (in the short term) to the disputing parties themselves. Examples are collective enforcement, preventive deployment, pacification, and antiterrorism. In addition to the combat skills needed for these missions, the soldier, in the role of primary or third party, is often faced with highly partisan disputes that require hard bargaining. The research literature suggests a number of bargaining tactics that can be used to encourage settlements of competitive disputes:

- Concede first on small issues, using this to make the case for later reciprocation by the other on larger issues (Fisher, 1964; Deutsch et al., 1971);
- By conceding less and infrequently early in the negotiation, a bargainer creates expectations for agreements on his or her terms (Druckman and Bonoma, 1976);

- Commit yourself to a position by presenting clear evidence that indicates you cannot offer any more concessions (Schelling, 1960);
- Persuade the opponent of rewards in making concessions, making it clear that the concession should not be viewed as compromising a commitment to a larger principle (Schelling, 1960);
- Increase the size of a demand after tabling a concession (Karrass, 1974);
- Take actions that prevent the other from losing face. Face loss often leads to rigid positions, even those that incur material losses (Brown, 1977);
- Propose a deadline to force action especially when the terms on the table are favorable (Carnevale and Lawler, 1986);
- Develop acceptable alternatives to negotiated agreements. They reduce a decision-making dilemma in the face of deadlines (Fisher and Ury, 1981);
- By shifting the talks to higher levels, the bargainer can relieve his or her reluctant adversary from taking responsibility for making the needed concessions (Druckman, 1986); and
- By avoiding the appearance of being tactical, the negotiator may avoid imputations of mistrust and antagonism (Snyder, 1974).

Among its strengths, this approach is based on a large body of empirical research dating from Siegel and Fouraker's 1960 book on bargaining behavior. Their work provided a paradigm for experiments on the impacts of alternative concession-making strategies on outcomes. Important reviews of this literature are Walton and McKersie (1965), Kelley and Schenitzki (1972), Rubin and Brown (1975), Pruitt and Kimmel (1977), Hamner and Yukl (1977), and Pruitt (1981). A recent meta-analysis illustrates the cumulative nature of the studies and distinguishes among strong and weak influences on bargaining behavior (Druckman, 1994).

Among the problems with the distributive approach are that it (a) assumes the "other" is receptive or responds in a passive manner to one's use of tactics, (b) says little about whether the other is playing a similar or different tactical game, (c) has little to say about continuing or repeated interactions among the parties or their relationships, (d) reduces opportunities for creative problem-solving by focusing only on the distributive issues, (e) ignores the deeper sources of conflict that may overshadow the interests at stake, and (f) may leave parties feeling that they fell short of their goals or leave them with the uncomfortable feeling that they were manipulated or manipulated the other party into accepting their positions. Furthermore, by encouraging intransigent posturing, this approach provides few incentives that would encourage the other to be flexible.

Many of the self-help books and seminars approach negotiating from the viewpoint of the tactician bent on maximizing returns. Popular examples are the books written by C. Karrass (1974), G. Karrass (1985),

Cohen (1980), and Nierenberg (1968). These books are used often as texts in seminars conducted by the authors. One well-known seminar titled "Negotiate to Win" highlights strategies for getting the best deal in competitive situations (Cooper Management Institute, 1993). Using role-playing exercises, the trainer provides opportunities for seminar members to experience the "seven commandments of good negotiating": trade every concession, start high, make smaller concessions especially at the end, "krunch" early and often (with examples of how to do this),[5] be patient, nibble at the end, and look for creative concessions to trade. When these well-known tactics are taught, trainees are alerted to the importance of face-saving and the need to create a positive atmosphere through the use of "soft" language.

Unfortunately, few attempts have been made to evaluate effects of the training on negotiating performance over time. Nor are the trainers favorably disposed toward such evaluations—when asked about evaluations, trainers often remark that their success is indicated in the marketplace, where subscribers "vote" and profits result. Little thought goes into whether the training improves performance. Considerable attention is given to ways of marketing the seminars to attract new customers. Although accepting the distributive bargaining approach, these trainers largely ignore the insights from the research studies cited above.

Integrative Processes

The emphasis of this approach to training is on a search for high joint-payoff solutions that endure. Bargaining is eschewed in favor of creative problem solving. A premium is placed on establishing a cooperative atmosphere, on acknowledging the other's plight or the reasons he or she takes particular positions, and on diagnosing the sources of conflict, rather than executing tactics to win.

Some of the features of this approach involve the way roles are defined and the kinds of behavior that is enacted:

• The approach is less concerned with settlements than with enduring resolutions and improved relationships.
• While searching for sources of conflict, the parties also identify factors that aggravate the conflict or contribute to tensions among themselves.
• While emphasizing process activities, the approach recognizes the importance of a thorough understanding of the substantive issues at stake.

This approach contrasts to the distributive bargaining approach in several ways: (a) it focuses on conflicts that result primarily from misunderstandings and stereotyped perceptions rather than interests, (b) it seeks to create relationships based, at least to some extent, on interdependence, (c) it emphasizes the importance of developing mutual trust, (d) it assumes that positive interpersonal relations (and understanding) will produce enduring resolutions of the conflict, and (e) it downplays the fact that many conflicts are matters of interest resolved through compromise rather than by finding integrative solutions.

This approach is suited to missions for which the parties (which often include the local population) have common goals and seek to prevent further losses, the main goal is to achieve long-term solutions or stability, and attempts are made to turn the situation over to the local population as soon as possible. Examples are disaster relief, election supervision, aid to domestic populations, and in some respects, observation. These missions are characterized less by conflicts of interest than by conflicts over the best way to solve the common problem confronting the population. Challenges include organizing the local population, coordinating with nongovernmental organizations, and knowing when to turn the operation over to the local population. The contact skills needed to meet these challenges are those discussed in the literature on integrative problem solving.

Although the research to date on integrative processes has been limited, there are some significant studies that have identified conditions for effective problem solving. For example, with regard to negotiators, Carnevale and Pruitt (1992) found that problem solving is more likely to occur when negotiators show significant concern for the other's outcomes as well as their own, when the parties exchange information about their underlying priorities and needs, and when both sides are convinced that their conflict has integrative potential (outcomes that are best for all parties). With regard to a mediative process, Kressel and his associates (1994) identified a problem-solving (integrative) style that contrasts with a settlement-oriented (distributive) style. The former was a more active approach that progresses through stages involving searching for the sources of conflict, generating hypotheses and diagnoses, and shifting responsibility to the disputants for generating and feeling a sense of ownership for solutions. It produced more frequent and durable outcomes than the settlement-oriented style, even though it was used less frequently by the participants in their study. It also produced a more favorable attitude by disputants toward the mediative experience. (Mediative processes are discussed below in the section on the third-party role.)

Among its strengths, the integrative approach identifies the skills needed for a satisfactory and lasting solution to conflicts.[6] By emphasizing the cognitive demands of problem solving, the approach calls attention to the realization that there are unlikely to be quick fixes to the resolution of conflicts. It includes skills useful for negotiators as well as those needed by mediators, whose goal is to achieve a constructive resolution of conflict. Included among those skills is the need to defend oneself against unwarranted accusations or anger directed at oneself as well as the detection of bluffing (Druckman and Bjork, 1991:Ch. 9).

Among its weaknesses, the approach does not distinguish between sources of conflict (interests, values, needs) and factors in the situation that aggravate the conflict (e.g., competitive orientations, hardened constituencies, simplified images, media coverage). It assumes but has not demonstrated that improved interpersonal relations and understanding lead to enduring resolutions. This may be particularly critical, in that some operations other than wars will be deployed when conflict participants have relatively clear perceptions but fundamental and perhaps irreconcilable differences in interests or preferences. Furthermore, efforts have not been made to distinguish between general and situation-specific third-party skills, and little has been done regarding the transferring of resolutions achieved with small groups to other groups or organizations.

With regard to practical contributions, the approach gained popularity with the 1981 publication of Fisher and Ury's *Getting to Yes* (see also Fisher et al., 1991). These authors called attention to deeper interests than those revealed by the positions of disputants in negotiation. In a sequel, Fisher and Brown (1988) emphasized the importance of relationships, making the distinction between agreements that may serve immediate needs and relationships that may be either helped or hindered by the negotiation process. Carrying this theme further, Saunders (1991) stressed the importance of developing international relationships as a goal of foreign policy decision making. The relational theme in international relations has gained momentum in post-cold war theorizing, largely as a reaction to realist approaches (Stern and Druckman, 1995). It is central to problem-solving approaches to conflict management and to the debate about participation in OOTW activities.

The approach is also reflected in various attempts to deal with deep-rooted conflicts between nations and ethnic groups. A set of techniques, referred to loosely as the problem-solving workshop, has evolved from early versions (Burton, 1969; Doob, 1970; Kelman, 1972) to refined interventions with strong claims for effectiveness, especially in the context of the Middle East conflict (e.g., Rouhana and Kelman, 1994) and elsewhere (e.g., Fisher, 1994). Little has been done to advance a methodology for assessing its impacts, so we must rely on the claims made by the authors. Until more progress is made, we should suspend judgment about the utility of the approach both with regard to its effectiveness in handling interpersonal or intergroup conflicts and in transferring the results of the intervention to other segments of societies. We address issues of evaluation of training programs in further detail below.

We now consider approaches to training that deal with the other dimension shown in Figure 6-1: the distinction between the primary-party and

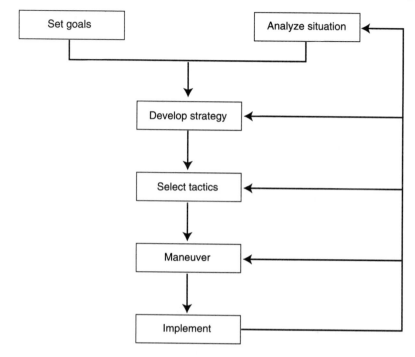

FIGURE 7-2   Strategy development.

third-party roles. In the former role, the soldiers deal directly—somewhat one-on-one—with other individuals or groups. By contrast, in the latter role, the soldiers must orchestrate the interactions between two or more groups and attempt to improve them. Quite different skills are required in each role, and we delineate these in the following sections, relying on a decision-making model (Figure 7-2). Consider first the primary-party role.

Primary-Party Role

Goal Setting

In primary-party missions (e.g., disaster relief, collective enforcement), the soldier must control or modify the other parties' (or group's) behavior in some fashion. A simple example is having individuals line up to receive water allocations; a complex example is having a hostile army withdraw from occupied territory (Abizaid, 1993).

When attempting to control the other parties, the soldier has limited power and   consequently cannot prescribe the behavior of others, ignoring their preferences, goals, ideas, values, etc. Rather, he or she must negotiate and plan to operate from a limited power base. Specifically, the soldier must define his or her aspirations, which are the net outcomes (benefits minus costs) that are expected or sought from the interaction or mission (for example, 200,000 people fed for 3 months with no loss of soldiers' lives at a cost of $10 million, using 1 battalion of troops.)

Such goal setting also consists of developing limits or fallback positions beyond which the soldier will not budge. The soldier could possibly seek to maximize his or her own payoffs without concern for those received by the other parties. Other possibilities exist; for example, the soldier could attempt to maximize the others' payoffs or the joint payoffs. Alternatively, he or she could simply improve the relationship with the parties, rather than raising anyone's outcomes.

Even though goal setting is the first step in a strategy, it must at times be quite fluid. On occasion, the available information is insufficient for establishing a goal. Or the original goal may be incorrect. Or the situation, as well as the behaviors of the various parties, may change radically. Or the mission or demands of superiors may be altered.

It is also possible for these latter determinants—mission and superiors' orders—to require that the goal be very rigid (D. Last, personal interview). In such a case, the soldier has the advantage of a stable goal but the disadvantage of inflexibility—not being able to revise goals as the situation dictates.

Situation Analysis

When choosing a goal and reflecting on the proper strategy, the soldier needs to perform an analysis of the situation, examining (a) his or her own position, (b) the other's (or opponent's) position, (c) the relationship between them, (d) the interaction process, and (e) the broader context within which those interactions occur.

When focusing on his or her own position, the soldier must determine which issues are more or less important: Does an issue have high payoffs or costs? Is it a matter of principle that the soldier feels should be important? Do the constituencies hold the issue to be of importance (Walton and McKersie, 1965)? Which issues can be traded (Pruitt and Rubin, 1986)?

While considering the issues, the soldier judges his or her aspirations as well as the initial offer and limit for each issue. This includes developing a rationale for the choices, possible trade-offs between issues, and the value to be placed on the relationship with the other parties. In weighing trades, a soldier may consider making compromises on issues that result in increasing trust and improved relationships with the other parties.

When making such judgments, the soldier must remember that a settlement is unlikely to occur if he or she fails to consider the others' reactions or the opponents' positions on the issues. Such reflections often require adopting the other's perspective (Neale and Bazerman, 1983); although this has been shown to be a difficult challenge (Johnson, 1967; Summers et al., 1970), it is worth the attempt. It includes deciding which issues are more or less important, getting an idea of the other's aspirations and limits, as well as their evaluation of relationships.[7] For example, if the opponent has attractive alternatives and places a low value on the relationship, he or she is likely to be a tough bargainer; an opponent with limited alternatives and low aspirations will probably be more cooperative (Pinkley, 1995). Gathering information through monitoring the other's statements and proposals is an important part of the bargaining process (Druckman, 1977, 1978). It leads to the kinds of changes in expectations and adjustments of moves that can produce agreements (Coddington, 1968; Snyder and Diesing, 1977).

Strategy

With an initial goal and situation analysis in mind, the soldier develops or selects a strategy. This is the general plan for dealing with the others, whereas the tactics are the specific steps (Wall, 1995). A strategy can range from simple to complex. A simple strategy could be one of consistent force wherein the soldier brings in many troops, places them in strong positions, and then demands that the others withdraw (Abizaid, 1993). A second simple strategy could be one of reciprocity (Esser et al., 1990)—that is, making a concession. If the others reciprocate, the soldier makes another, then awaits a reciprocal concession. If the other party plays tough, making no concessions, then the soldier does likewise. A third strategy is to place the burden of concession making on the other by refusing to compromise. Some implications of these exchanges are demonstrated in experimental studies (e.g., Axelrod, 1984).

A more complex strategy is the bluff-twist (Wall, 1995). Here the soldier begins the bargaining with a bluff that he or she knows the other will call. As the other calls the bluff and overextends himself, the soldier cuts the other's line of retreat, as well as the alternatives, and then exploits the other's vulnerability.

Strategies, simple or complex, can be intended to raise the outcomes for both sides. For example, the soldier can attempt to expand the resources or negotiation scope so that both he or she and the other parties get more of what they want. The soldier can exchange concessions on different issues with the others, having each yield on an issue that has high payoffs for the other but low payoffs for him- or herself (Pruitt and Rubin, 1986). Or the soldier can consider the underlying interests for him- or herself and the other party and develop ways to satisfy those interests (see Fisher and Ury, 1981, for a discussion of this approach).

Tactics

Strategies are developed and attained by piecing together different tactics, that is, the specific steps in the strategies. A large number of tactics are available to the soldier, falling into the broad categories of threatening, coercive, conciliatory, rewarding, posturing, debating, and irrational tactics (Wall, 1995). The negative tactics of threats and coercion are attempts to reduce the other's outcomes. These can be used early in an encounter, to reduce the others' aspirations, or late, somewhat as a last resort (Tedeschi and Bonoma, 1977). The positive tactics of conciliation and reward are attempts to improve the relationship and reinforce desired behavior (e.g., Tedeschi and Bonoma, 1977).

Posturing tactics are used primarily to alter the other's perception of the soldier's role and his or her behavior. Debate consists of problem-solving discussions and exchanges of information (Walcott et al., 1977). For example, the soldier notes the issues and tasks he or she would like to avoid (e.g., to whom God gave the disputed land) or uses logical arguments to convince the other of the merits of the approach. The irrational tactics are those that seem to give the soldier low outcomes or outcomes lower than alternative actions. Yet as the adage "crazy like a fox" suggests, sometimes these tactics can produce fine results.

Maneuvers

Maneuvers are steps to improve the soldier's position. Just as an infantry lieutenant moves his or her platoon to high ground prior to battle, the soldier can take steps to improve his or her position in personal interactions. These include steps to increase his or her own strength, to decrease that of the other, or to leverage the opponent. Efforts to increase one's own strength include stockpiling resources, building adequate hard force, and building alliances. Efforts to decrease the other's strength include closing off the opponent's alternatives, preventing the opponent from forming alliances, and reducing his or her stockpile of resources. The soldier can also leverage the other by attacking his or her weaknesses or by opening a discussion with a more pliant member of the opponent's team whenever one of the others is obdurate.

Implementation

When implementing the strategy, the soldier puts the plan into action with tactics. The keys here are timing and feedback. With regard to timing, some tactics must be used simultaneously and others in selected sequences. With regard to feedback, the soldier must observe the other's responses to his or her tactics and maneuvers. If the other is reacting as expected, the soldier can hold a steady course. If this is not the case, he or she must reconsider and perhaps modify the goals, analysis, strategy, tactics, and maneuvers.

 ## Third-Party Roles

Here we need to reiterate a point made earlier: in some missions, the soldier acts more as a third party than as a primary party. In missions such as traditional peacekeeping, the soldier must, for the most part, control the relationship and interactions between two other groups. The skills required are quite different from those needed in the primary-party role; namely, they are more likened to mediation skills than to negotiation skills.

Goal Setting

When establishing the initial goal in a third-party mission, the soldier must orient him- or herself toward the relationship between the two interacting parties (e.g., the Bosnian Serbs and the Bosnian Muslims) and attempt to forge agreements or interactions between them that maximize their joint outcomes. Admittedly, the soldier must not lose sight of his or her own goals (e.g., safety of troops) and that of constituents (e.g., peace in the area), but the major goal is to improve the interaction between the parties.

Situation Analysis

When analyzing the situation, the third-party soldier must first determine if there is a conflict between the parties. Typically there is, and the soldier must develop skills in analyzing the causes and issues of the conflict.

Causes are often distinct from the issues, and many of the causes lie within the parties themselves (Augsburger, 1992), in their perceptions of each other, their communications, past interactions, and structural relationships (Putnam and Wilson, 1982). A party may have the goal of hurting the other or may simply be angry. Such feelings will generate conflict. With regard to perceptions, conflict is likely to occur whenever one party perceives the other side's interactions to be harmful or unfair. Interpersonal communication leads to conflict (Putnam and Poole, 1987) when it entails insults or intentions to harm the other. Structured interdependence between parties who have opposite goals will quickly engender conflict. Because conflict has so many causes, the soldier must become adept at identifying the genesis of the current conflict and determining which ones can be addressed.

Soldiers must also understand the issues that are generating problems. When parties interact and come into conflict, it is usually over issues that are either large or small, simple or complex, emotional or substantive (Walton, 1987). Certain issue characteristics have been shown to generate conflict and thereby merit the third party's attention. One is complexity. Complex issues are more apt to lead to conflict than simple ones. Multiple (versus a few) issues also more often spawn conflict. The explanation in both cases is rather clear: complex and multiple issues are more likely to generate misunderstanding, tap divergent interests, and unearth dissimilar goals. Issues of principle or nonnegotiable needs also generate conflicts (Fisher, 1994; Rouhana and Kelman, 1994). On these last issues, parties become emotionally bonded to their positions, and once into conflict over them, they find that trades—reciprocal give and take—are quite difficult. Broad or intangible issues also tend to generate conflict and be less amenable to conflict resolution (Vasquez, 1983; Diehl, 1992). Because such issues entail high stakes and are often indivisible, the parties hold strongly to their positions and move toward conflict (Albin, 1993). Once in the conflict, the all-or-nothing characteristic of the issue makes palatable, face-saving, piecemeal trades quite difficult to arrange (Zechmeister and Druckman, 1973).

The soldier should address issues and causes that are of low cost to deal with and about which he or she has some knowledge. He or she should work with the opposing parties to solve complex issues, multiple issues, and issues of principles. Issues and causes that are intractable and minor should be ignored as long as possible. Also, the agenda should be arranged so that early agreement on simple issues and successful elimination of minor causes of conflict produce momentum for improved party relations (Fisher, 1964; Pruitt and Rubin, 1986).

Tactics

Having defined the overall goals for the mission and analyzed the situation, the soldier begins to develop a strategy and to select tactics. The literature on third-party processes reveals that the line between strategy and tactics is blurred (Carnevale and Pruitt, 1992) and that third parties, for the most part, rely on sets of tactics rather than major strategies to improve the parties' interactions.

When acting as a third party, the soldier has three targets for tactical behavior: (1) the parties themselves, (2) the interparty relationship, and (3) the soldier-party relationship (Wall, 1981).

1. *Conflicting Parties.* In general, a soldier can take steps to move the parties off their current positions and to nudge them toward positions that are more agreeable to the other side. Such steps include:

- Help the parties save face when making concessions (Podell and Knapp, 1969; Pruitt and Johnson, 1970; Stevens, 1963);
- Help the sides resolve internal disagreements (Lim and Carnevale, 1990);
- Help them deal with constituents (Wall, 1981);
- Add incentives or payoffs for agreements and concessions (Kissinger, 1979);
- Apply negative sanctions, threats, or arguments (Kissinger, 1979);
- Propose agreement points that were not recognized by either side (Douglas, 1972); and
- Expand the agenda to find a larger arena in which rewards will be higher and costs lower to both sides (Lall, 1966; Pruitt and Rubin, 1986).

2. *Interparty Relationship.* When operating as a third party, the soldier's primary focus is on the interparty relationship and the goal is an agreement that will be implemented. In seeking these goals, the soldier may follow many routes. One is setting up the interaction: often the soldier discovers that the parties are fighting but not talking; there might be a stalemate in which there is neither talking nor fighting; or there could be an absence of interaction because some other third party has separated the parties and prevented their interaction (as in the case of traditional peacekeeping). In such situations, the soldier must often establish a negotiation relationship between the parties and stabilize the process. Doing so may require that the third party identify the membership of the opposing groups or their leaders and then bring the leaders to the bargaining table.

Having established the interaction and identified the disputing parties, the soldier next faces the task of enticing them to negotiate. Often this is a difficult task, because the parties do not like the negotiation format, they feel that negotiating is a sign of weakness, they believe negotiation gives some legitimacy to the opponent, or they believe negotiation puts them at risk in some way (Pruitt and Rubin, 1986). To overcome these and other obstacles, the soldier must discover the parties' objections, then discount or reduce them. Also, the outcomes from negotiating or interacting peacefully may be increased or the costs for refusing to negotiate raised.

After initiating interactions, the soldier can establish the protocol for the negotiation process by suggesting and enforcing mechanisms through which the interaction will be conducted. These can be formal, specific agendas or somewhat more informal ones. In addition, he or she can inform each party as to what behaviors can be expected from the other side and advise each side on its own initial and responsive actions.

When establishing the protocol, the soldier can provide evaluations of the situation. In joint or separate meetings, he or she can enumerate and describe the important issues, interpret their complexity (or simplicity), note how similar problems have been handled, and provide data as to the costs of continued disputing (Lim and Carnevale, 1990).

Once the interaction is under way, the soldier should channel the initial discussion toward an area in which he or she believes the parties can agree (Maggiolo, 1971). As both sides discuss this arena, the soldier needs to expand the agenda to bring in additional issues. When doing so the soldier should set up trades, in which one party gives in on issues that are of low value to it but of high value to the opposing side. As he or she facilitates such trades, the soldier must maintain the integrity of the interaction channel, enforce the protocol rules, and proscribe such behaviors as retracting offers previously made.

At times, the soldier will find it necessary to separate the opponents (Pruitt, 1971). This separation allows him or her to sever, relay, or modify communications for the sake of productive negotiations. He or she might reopen the channels and bring the parties together if this is useful, forbid their interaction if it seems likely to incite antagonism, or create a formal schedule of meetings if such a mechanism proves useful.

As the soldier severs and reconstructs the interactions, he or she can manage the parties' power relationship, a relationship that is of great importance to both the soldier and the parties. Typically, the soldier should strike a balance between the parties' total power positions. Doing so lowers the probability that the stronger side will attempt to exploit the weaker and that the weaker will break off the relationship or seek to undermine the stronger's position (Thibaut, 1968). If he or she cannot balance the power relationship, the soldier must bargain with or use hard force against the stronger side to constrain the exercise of its power.

3. *Soldier-Party Relationship.* To be successful in interactions with the parties, the soldier must gain their trust and confidence. Tactics with these goals are typically labeled "reflexive" (Kressel and Pruitt, 1985, 1989) and include appearing neutral, not taking sides on important issues, letting the parties blow off steam, using humor to lighten the atmosphere, attempting to speak the parties' language, expressing pleasure at progress in the negotiation or conflict resolution, keeping the parties focused on the issues, offering new points of view, bringing in relevant information, and correcting one party's misperceptions.

Using such techniques to develop trust and establish credibility is quite important (see also Harbottle, 1992). Without them, the soldier will have little leverage on the parties.

When utilizing these tactics—as well as many of the preceding ones—the soldier may find that he or she sacrifices the image of neutrality. This is not a major obstacle if the soldier demonstrates trustworthiness and effectiveness or if the parties feel that the intervention provides more benefits than costs.

Maneuvers

When operating as a third party, the soldier's options for maneuvering are the same as in the primary-party role: increasing his or her own strength, reducing that of the parties, or leveraging them. If the soldier attempts to weaken either or both parties, perhaps by closing off some of their options or by preventing them from forming coalitions, he or she risks generating resentment. Possibly one or both parties' retaliation may convert the third-party relationship into an adversarial primary-party affair.

Under some circumstances, the soldier might try leveraging the parties, that is, bringing his or her own strength to bear at a time or place that is to his advantage. (For example, Secretary of State Henry Kissinger in the Yom Kippur war of 1973 delayed munitions shipments to the Israelis until they had only a one-day supply.) Nevertheless, this approach also risks their resentment and encourages retaliation.

Strategy

Currently, the literature does not provide adequate descriptions or prescriptions for third-party strategies. A strategy, in mediation as well as in warfare, football, chess, bridge, and organizational policy, is a broad plan of action for attaining some goal. For example, in a retreat-and-flank battle strategy, an army retreats when the enemy attacks in force. Once the enemy has extended itself, the army flanks the enemy, striking at one or more vulnerable points. Or in a simpler strategy, the football team for one quarter might establish a running attack and then shift to a mix of running and passing.

Note the ingredients in each of these strategies: goals, actions, and timing. Presently, the literature deals adequately with the goals and action components of third-party strategies but ignores the last element.

In this literature, one group of researchers (e.g., Carnevale, 1986; Carnevale and Henry, 1989; Kressel, 1972; Kressel and Pruitt, 1985, 1989; van de Vliert, 1985) describes third-party strategies as techniques (or tactics) that are oriented toward a similar goal. Specifically, Kressel and Pruitt (1985, 1989) hold that a reflexive strategy consists of techniques that orient the third party to the dispute and establish the groundwork for later activities. A substantive strategy includes techniques that deal directly with the issues and actively promote settlement, whereas contextual tactics alter the climate or conditions between the disputants.

A second group of scholars in the literature (e.g., Carnevale and Pruitt, 1992; Kolb, 1987; McLaughlin et al., 1991; Silbey and Merry, 1986; Touval and Zartman, 1985) have taken a different tack, combining techniques that share conceptual or operational similarities (other than goal). For example, Silbey and Merry's (1986) typology contains four principal categories: (1) the third party's presentation of self and program, (2) its control of the mediation process, (3) control over the substantive issues, and (4) activation of commitments and norms. In a similar fashion, Kolb (1987), after in-depth interviews, laid out alternative strategies or postures that the third party assumed. She distinguished between helping and fact-finding corporate ombudsman roles: the helper invents individualized solutions to the problems people present, whereas the fact-finder investigates whether proper procedures were followed and if there are plausible explanations for a complaint.

A third group of researchers (Elangovan, 1995; Lewicki and Sheppard, 1985) classify the third party's techniques into strategies according to the target for control. In the group, Sheppard (1984) maintains that third-party strategic behaviors differ along two principal lines: decision control and process control. A third party's decision control is the management of the outcomes of the dispute. By contrast, process control entails control over the presentation and interpretation of evidence in the dispute. Elangovan (1995), relying heavily on Sheppard's concepts, generates five strategies:

- Means control strategy: the third party influences the process of resolution.
- Ends control strategy: the third party influences the outcomes.
- Full control strategy: the third party influences both.
- Low control strategy: the third party influences neither outcomes nor process.
- Part control strategy: the third party shares both controls with the disputants.

Finally, one group of investigators (e.g., Lim and Carnevale, 1990; Karambayya and Brett, 1989; Kim et al., 1993; Wall and Blum, 1991; Wall and Rude, 1985) have defined (and located) strategies as techniques that are used together by third parties when they deal with disputes. For example Kim et al. (1993), relying on a factor analysis, found techniques used together in four strategic combinations: reconciliation, dependence, analysis, and data gathering. In the "analysis" strategy, third parties were found to rely on the techniques of getting a grasp of the situation, analyzing the parties, and capping the agreement with a handshake, meal, or drink.

The above four approaches deal quite adequately with the goals and action components of third-party strategies. And some of the literature (Elangovan, 1995) deals creatively with the contingencies under which the various strategies are or should be applied.

However, none of the approaches deals with the timing aspect of strategies. This omission is unfortunate, because timing is an essential element in any strategy. In a retreat-and-flank battle strategy, for example, when the army flanks and attacks, timing is essential. If it is either too early or too late, the strategy is a failure. Likewise, when a third party uses various sets of techniques is quite important.

Implementation

We propose a simple contingency strategy for third-party soldiers, based on two observations: (1) The effectiveness of most tactics is contingent on the situation and (2) we know more about what a soldier can do than we do about what is effective, at least given the current state of research findings (see also the discussion below on evaluating effectiveness).

The first observation dictates that the soldier should choose tactics that fit the situation. To date, we know that the following behaviors are likely to be effective in a wide range of situations:

- Separating aggressive opponents (Pruitt, 1971);
- Controlling the agenda and helping the sides to establish priorities among the issues (Lim and Carnevale, 1990);
- Adding control to the process (Prein, 1984); and
- Being friendly to both sides (Ross et al., 1990).

Other behaviors or tactics are more likely to be effective in some situations. Humor might be used when the soldier detects hostility (Harbottle, 1992). If there are many issues, the soldier should simplify the agenda and suggest trade-offs. When the parties lack bargaining experience, the soldier should educate them or note procedures that have been used in the past. And when the parties are able to resolve their own problems, the soldier for the most part should not intrude (Lederach, 1995).

The second observation suggests that soldiers should adopt a pragmatic approach. They should first try techniques that seem reasonable. If none of these works, then they should try a different one or a different set. Again, if there is failure, a new set should be put in place and the failure noted. This approach should be continued until the relationship and the outcomes between the parties improve. Most important, the soldier, in this process, must be diagnostic, remembering what failed and what was successful for each episode; this is consistent with the experiential learning model discussed above. He or she should also use feedback in the process of evaluating and modifying the goals, tactics, and maneuvers.

This trial-with-memory strategy is proposed because currently there is a great deal of uncertainty as to which third-party tactics are successful. In addition, even if we know what was successful in general, techniques have to be fine-tuned to the situation, using an approach like the one just described.

LIMITATIONS OF CONFLICT MANAGEMENT TRAINING

Even if training for operations other than war incorporated all the elements of integrative/distributive processes and primary/third-party roles at all ranks, there still exist several elements that may limit (in absence of countervailing action or training) the utility of that training or affect our ability to judge its effectiveness. Perhaps the most important of these is the influence of culture in conflicts and their management.

Cultural Impacts

While often acknowledging the importance of national cultures, scholars, practitioners, and trainers rarely develop the implications of cultural differences for the role of primary parties and intermediaries in the resolution process. Such deficiencies are unfortunate, because culture has major implications for any operation other than war. In most missions, the soldier is posted to and operates within cultures that are different from his or her own. In turn, these cultures impact on the soldier and determine how the various parties behave as they interact among themselves or with soldiers. In this section, we discuss some possible impacts of national cultures on soldiers, as distinguished from the organizational cultures discussed in Chapter 3.

Culture Shock

One of the major impacts comes from culture shock to the soldier. He or she is thrust into a culture that is often not understood and must work productively with parties whose behaviors, norms, and organizational structures are somewhat perplexing. The soldier may experience culture shock not only from dealing with a new locale and the surrounding population, but also from interacting with soldiers from other countries whenever the mission force or command is multinational. The reverse is also true: soldiers will have to deal with the effects of the culture shock experienced by the local population and multinational soldiers who themselves will be interacting with soldiers of different races, cultures, and approaches.

Grove and Torbiorn (1985) propose a four-stage adjustment cycle for people immersed in new cultures: a period of euphoria, culture shock, recovery, and completion of the adjustment process. For them, the stage at which culture shock is experienced is most interesting; it is the longest and most difficult period, and the one in which the least amount of learning occurs. This is the stage for which predeparture training is likely to be most useful for the soldier, and the programs should be aimed at reducing the severity and duration of this stage. Grove and Torbiorn recommend a training approach that includes a combination of fact-oriented and experiential methods aimed at achieving this goal. (A similar adjustment cycle was proposed earlier by Moskos, 1976, for peacekeeping operations. Although he also identifies a similar Stage II as the most important period, he disagrees with Grove and Torbiorn on the relative value of predeparture training versus field experience for facilitating adjustment.) It may also be necessary to include some soldiers in OOTW units who already have appropriate foreign language capability or a quick capacity for acquiring key phrases and elements of the local language, so as to minimize communication difficulties that exacerbate culture shock (Eyre, 1994).

Military-Civilian Impact

Closely accompanying culture shock is the impact of dealing with civilians. Soldiers, operating for an extensive period within a military culture, are accustomed to taking orders and conforming. They are healthy, well fed, well clothed, and regularly well paid. In short, they exist in a protective, orderly environment that has a great deal of structure. The civilian culture, especially those to which the soldier is likely to be posted, is quite different. It is frequently disorderly, and life for many civilians is very tentative; they are often sick, ill clothed, and paid erratically. Furthermore, civilians, for the most part, do not like being ordered about, especially by military personnel.

The impact of the military civilian divide is multifaceted, with one critical aspect being differences in goals. The soldier's goal of keeping the peace differs from the civilian's goal of staying alive and earning a living, and the simultaneous pursuit of these may generate conflict rather than peace. For example, roadblocks might be set up to keep one militant faction from having access to and attacking the other. The goal from a traditional soldier's perspective is to minimize conflicts, which will result in civilian, as well as military, casualties. This is a legitimate goal, but the farmer's goals might be more pragmatic—to get to his fields without waiting and to gain access to markets on the other side of the dividing line.

Another impact is that civilians often tend to dislike or distrust soldiers; therefore, soldiers in both the primary and third-party roles must vigilantly monitor civilians' reactions to their presence and behavior. Often the most straightforward, nonassertive tactics can be misunderstood and resented.

Cultural differences in the context of a multinational mission may be something of a double-edged sword. The national cultures of some troops may be similar to those of the indigenous civilian population (e.g., Arab troops in another Arab country), and this may serve as a bridge to the rest of the military operation. Nevertheless, additional cultural diversity within the multinational force could complicate relations and coordination among themselves. Diversity within a national force can also affect coordination and cooperation. Recent survey data collected in Somalia by Miller and Moskos (1995) showed that gender, race, and military occupational specialty influenced U.S. soldiers' attitudes toward the conflict and attributions made by them about the plight of the local population. It also affected the choice between adopting a humanitarian or a warrior strategy in dealing with the local population.

Perceptions of Conflict

Another impact of culture is the differential perception of conflict. In most operations other than wars, conflict is likely to exist, and the interacting parties may view it quite differently than does the soldier. Also, across cultures, parties tend to perceive the conflict quite differently (Lederach, 1995). People from many nonindustrialized cultures think of conflict as the normal way of interacting. From childhood, they are taught to settle differences by fighting (Merry, 1989). They tend to accept and even rely on conflict for their social interactions—that is, conflict has a "win-win" appeal. In most Western cultures (i.e., the soldier's culture), conflict is often viewed as one person's opposing or negatively affecting another person's interests (Donohue and Kolt, 1992; Pruitt and Rubin, 1986; Putnam and Poole, 1987; Thomas, 1992)—that is, conflict is perceived as having a "win-lose" effect on the parties.

From a different perspective, Polynesians and several other agriculture-based societies view conflict as a mutual entanglement that is detrimental to both parties (Wall and Callister, 1995)—that is, the situation is "lose-lose." For Koreans and residents of other Asian countries with a strong Confucian underpinning, conflict is viewed as a mutual disruption of society's harmony (Augsburger, 1992; Hahn, 1986). These societies feel that the character and impact of conflict on the disputants is irrelevant, although it is "lose-lose." The major negative impact is the disruption of the larger community and the violation of its norms.

On one hand, the implications of these culturally differentiated perceptions are to some extent rather general and clear-cut. For example, the soldier needs to be informed about how the parties where he or she is posted view conflict and how they are apt to react to his or her mission. Such knowledge, passed along in training, will provide a better operational background for making strategic and tactical decisions in the culture. In many cases, on the other hand, the implications are culture-specific. Consider these examples. In a nonindustrialized society that views conflict as a normal way of interacting, the soldier's attempts to resolve the conflict or control the relationship between the parties will probably fail, because conflict has utility for both sides. Here the soldier can probably be successful in improving his relationship with each side; likewise, he can probably successfully contain the conflict or reduce the negative impact on third parties.

In a Western culture, the soldier can improve the relationship between the parties by pointing out the integrative potential in their positions. Simultaneously, trades can be worked out in which one side loses on one issue but wins on another.

For a society that views conflict as mutual entanglement, the soldier can intervene forcefully, as do mediators in their society (Wall and Callister, 1995). The soldier can forcefully and acceptably point out who is wrong, call for apologies, ask the other side to forgive the offending party, and formalize the disentanglement agreement.

For cultures that view conflict as a disruption of the harmonious status quo, the forceful, hands-on approach will probably not be accepted. Seldom is mediation carried out that way in their society, and whenever it is implemented, the mediation is never undertaken by an outsider (Kim et al., 1993). The soldier, when posted to these cultures, must know to present him- or herself as a resource to the society, which will resolve the disharmony. For example, instead of putting the disputants together, the soldier might offer to transport senior members of the society to the dispute location.

Societal Structure

A fourth cultural factor of concern is the society's structure. Many societies are structured along family, extended-family, and clan lines. Consequently, when conflicts arise between persons, families or clans, these societies traditionally turn to mediation or negotiation by elder members or to ritualistic confrontations for settling the dispute. Given this tradition, the soldier must understand he or she is going to be perceived as an outsider and, when acting as a third party, as an unwanted intervener. In such a culture, the soldier will find it difficult to obtain an agreement between the conflicting parties, let alone one that is fair (by Western standards) or one that maximizes the joint benefits for the parties. In this situation, the standing community powers will determine the agreements and appropriate payoffs.

Norms

As implied above, family/clan structure often brings with it the norm that relationships (including conflicts) among members will be handled within the family or clan. A second norm—of unknown origin—is that of reciprocity (Gouldner, 1960). In Western societies (Homans, 1961) and in Japan (Goldman, 1994), people feel that an outcome given to one individual or group obligates that person, in return, to give an outcome (repayment) in some form to the other person. Similarly, a cost imposed on a person permits, even obligates, him or her to retaliate against the person imposing that cost. Although many cultures abide by this norm, others do not. Rather, they perceive that an outcome given by one party to another is a sign of weakness or deference. Thereby, it does not obligate the recipient to reciprocate; instead, it raises the expectation that the original party should deliver an additional outcome.

Because the reciprocity norm has a strong impact on an individual's behaviors, the soldier needs to know if that norm exists in the culture to which he or she is posted. For example, in cultures with strong hierarchial levels, reciprocity is not a societal norm. There will be some reciprocity within levels, but not between them. Typically, the higher-level person does not initially make a concession to a lower-level person, because that would be incongruous with his or her status. And when receiving a concession from a lower-level person, the higher-level person does not reciprocate, because he or she considers it a gift to which a high-level person is entitled (Augsburger, 1992).

As for the lower-status person (in a high-low status relationship), he or she seldom receives a concession (either initially or reciprocally); one is therefore not expected, nor is reciprocity. In this setting, the soldier will typically not be perceived as having equal status. Consequently, the parties he or she is dealing with will not behave reciprocally toward him or her. Therefore, the soldier as a primary party should not adopt a reciprocity strategy or make undue investments in integrative bargaining tactics when the opponents do not hold to the reciprocity norm. These would probably yield limited benefits.

In addition, the third party should not rely on reciprocity for moving the opponents off their positions and nudging each toward the other. Rather, in the nonreciprocity culture, the soldier should build his or her own strength and rely more on hard force to move the parties.

In sum, soldiers may have to deal with many subcultures in a given operation and thereby use different—seemingly incompatible—tactics. In such situations, the soldier must be observant, responsive, adaptive, and tolerant of his or her own inconsistency. For example, when posted to a developing country, a soldier may find him- or herself negotiating with a group containing a local soldier (who is accustomed to taking orders), an uneducated bandit leader (who handles social relations through conflict), a tribal leader (who expects to be treated as a leader), and a dozen confused, displaced peasants. In such a situation, the soldier might negotiate differently with each party or subgroup. Or he or she might force the group to choose a leader and then negotiate with that leader.

Training

It is evident that soldiers in many operations will have to be aware of cultural differences and trained to deal with them. One approach is elicitive training, in which culture is viewed not simply as an influence on conflict but rather as the essence of the approach. Conflict management is defined through cultural experience, values, and assumptions. The approach contrasts with the idea that techniques can be used in virtually any setting or that they can be adapted to particular settings.

Key features of the elicitive approach to training are elucidated by Lederach (1995):

• Training is intended to build relationships rather than to teach specific skills. Trainees are considered to be resourceful people capable of discovering or creating models of intervention rooted in their own context.

• Training is intended to identify and then coordinate the resources that exist in communities. Rather than transferring concepts and methods used in other settings or teaching everyone to use a common model, the concepts are developed anew within the cultural community.

• The training process moves away from emphasizing trainer expertise and toward emphasizing participant discovery. The interaction process rather than the techniques used is critical.

• Trainer expertise is used together with participants' concepts and methods, taking into account its own cultural origins and biases. The trainer needs to recognize the cultural assumptions implicit in any model and identify explicitly the differences that exist between his or her own and the participants' approaches.

This approach contributes several ideas to the training process. One is that it calls attention to the importance of different cultural experiences in creating and dealing with conflicts. Another is that it increases the motivation of participants to be involved in the training process by placing their views at the center of the experience. It gives them a stake in the process and its outcome. By adopting a more holistic approach than either the distributive or integrative approaches, it encourages a deeper and more long-term involvement in the community and thus perhaps a better chance to develop longer-term solutions to problems. Furthermore, it reduces pressure on trainers to "perform magic"—in the sense that they must prove that their techniques work or at least work better than other techniques.

Counterpoised against these interesting features are several weaknesses of the approach. One is that it may be overly open-ended, providing only vague guidance to the trainer about how to enact his or her role. Another is that it may actually overstate the role played by cultural differences and understate the importance of cultural similarities; cultures are treated as being homogeneous and unique. Its emphasis on "communities of practice" is shared with a more general approach to education referred to as situated learning. In its more extreme versions, proponents of situated learning deny that knowledge learned in one setting can transfer to another. (See the committee's previous report, Druckman and Bjork, 1994:Ch. 3, for a discussion of these issues.) Finally, it leaves issues of evaluation open, relying as it does on a long-term interaction process to demonstrate impacts. To date, applications have been undocumented, a factor that further compounds problems of evaluation.

Despite its shortcomings, the elicitive approach in combination with other prescriptive tools may prove useful. We suggest that soldiers be given precise, timely information about different cultures and the impact such cultures should have on their approaches. The starting point is the accumulation of cultural information on the areas to which the soldier is likely to be posted and presenting it in a lucid form.

Using this information, instructors should describe the culture of an area to which the soldier is likely to be posted, discuss what will probably happen there, and speculate on how he or she will respond. This exercise should be repeated for various countries, allowing the soldier to understand similarities and differences among cultures rather than comparing each to the Western culture. The reasoning is that a soldier can develop insights into cultures by moving from one society to another, using each as a lens to view the other.

Subsequent to the above simple exercise, it seems reasonable to insinuate some of the cultural aspects into the "confidence course" instructions of negotiation and mediation training. Again, we suggest moving from the simple to the difficult. For example, the simulation could advance:

- From mediations between disputants from the same culture to mediations between disputants of different cultures,
- From negotiating with a disputant who speaks English to negotiations with a disputant who speaks no English, and
- From negotiating with a disputant who is affluent to negotiating with a disputant who is very poor.

In addition to these ideas for training, we suggest consideration of some critical issues.[8] How long do officers have to remain in the theater to develop sufficient awareness and build adequate trust to be effective third parties? If training in conflict resolution skills consists of packaging "social know-how," whose knowledge is being packaged and how do we know that it will be useful? What changes in military culture, if any, are needed to allow soldiers to work with civilian agencies toward a conflict resolution goal? Answers to these questions await the results of surveys designed to document the experiences of soldiers in various types of missions. A start along these lines is the Canadian surveys of the Croatian and Bosnian missions described above.

Training Compatibility and Viability

Whenever personnel are asked to perform a variety of tasks, a key issue is how compatible the training is that they receive for the different tasks. Operations other than war encompass a broad range of activities, and soldiers may be placed into any number of different political and cultural contexts. Given this diversity, several aspects may limit the effectiveness of conflict resolution training. Although we are not aware of research that directly addresses these questions, these concerns strike us as potentially important for the way that the military trains and organizes for such missions.

The first concern is whether a given soldier can master all the skills and behaviors outlined above, assuming that present or expanded training regimens could accommodate them. Beyond the sheer number of strategies and techniques, many of the suggestions are situation-specific; what may be effective in one situation or with one type of mission may be counterproductive in another. Will training in one approach (e.g., the primary-party role) undermine the training required in another approach (e.g., the third-party role)? Harris (1994) notes that soldiers sometimes overreacted to situations during the initial deployment of the Multinational Force and Observers operation in the Sinai; in some situations, they reacted more as a traditional military force in a primary-party role rather than as a third-party soldier, their assigned role.

Related to this concern is whether it is advisable to separate missions designated OOTW from those for more traditional military purposes. Can the Army train its soldiers for all these missions? The 10th Mountain Division performed multiple missions in succession during the early 1990s, ranging from fighting in the Persian Gulf to disaster relief after Hurricane Andrew to state building in Haiti (in which the mission changed while airborne from one of a military invasion to peaceful support of democracy) to firefighting. Many of the new missions are less coercive than traditional military operations; will soldiers be able to sort out the necessary skills when faced with a given situation? Most important, traditional war-fighting will continue to be a mission for the U.S. Army, one that will necessarily be top priority. Will soldiers' war-fighting abilities be compromised? For example, traditional peacekeeping operations usually entail rules of engagement that permit a soldier to fire a weapon only in self-defense, something that is counter to conventional military strategy. Although there appears to be some erosion of combat skills for soldiers serving in peacekeeping roles, conventional wisdom in the military is that combat skills can be reacquired quickly with a small amount of additional training (Moskos, 1995).

The U.S. Army at this time appears committed to training soldiers in a general fashion and not training OOTW specialists among its ranks (U.S. Department of the Army, 1994). Even if one supports the idea of training specific units for certain types of operations other than war, can the Army afford this "luxury of specialization"? What if some of these units are never called for action, given the uncertainties of global threats and the changing preferences of national leaders and international organizations? Would such an investment in training be wasted? It may be that certain kinds of units can more easily adapt to specific OOTW missions (e.g., military police units for some pacification and election supervision duties), given the similarity of their traditional duties and those involved in the operation other than war. However, for various reasons that include costs, the Army has not to date introduced the idea of specialized or segmented units for particular types of OOTW missions. Whether specialized units that perform, for example, mediation functions would be more effective than multipurpose task forces that carry out both combat and contact tasks remains an issue to be studied.

Another concern is with the ability of soldiers to shift orientations, and therefore techniques, as the mission evolves. It may be assumed, although not demonstrated empirically, that soldiers can be trained to recognize accurately what types of situations they face. Even if this is true, can soldiers adapt when the shift occurs during the same mission? Many operations other than wars in practice include elements of one or more of the 16 missions outlined above; the UN mission in Somalia began as a purely humanitarian one, but shifted to one that had elements of pacification and state/nation building, to be followed again by a humanitarian effort. Are soldiers, in practice, able to adjust roles, attitudes, and techniques quickly? Or might some problems occur because of the lag time needed for adjustment or the dissonance between the incompatible tasks that soldiers may be asked to perform? These are questions that may only be answered after a series of operational experiences (see Johnson and Layng, 1992, for a framework on how to teach skills that allows adaptation and recombination of skills in the face of novel and complex tasks).

Another consideration is how to train soldiers when it is uncertain which missions are likely in the immediate future. During the cold war, much military planning concerned a conventional and/or tactical nuclear war in Europe against Warsaw Pact forces. Most operations other than war will arise for crises with short lead times that can be easily anticipated by planners. Traditionally, UN peacekeeping operations are organized on an ad hoc basis without significant forewarning. Can the Army provide the necessary training quickly? Will the rapid deployment be compatible with the training and operations that the soldiers were experiencing perhaps only a few days before?

The necessity of cultural training and the immediacy of many of these operations throws open the question of whether soldiers can be properly prepared for all instances. The approach outlined above treats culture as a unique factor for each potential area of deployment. Is it possible for soldiers to become familiar with many different cultures? How will soldiers behave in a multinational force when confronted with many different cultures simultaneously? Currently, U.S. Army personnel are given training about some general characteristics of culture (such as the role of women in society) of which they should be aware in any context, but they do not necessarily receive specialized training on attributes of particular cultures.

Finally, there may be new missions assigned to the U.S. Army that are not covered in the committee's taxonomy and that are not yet even envisioned. The appearance of such a mission, especially on short notice, requires a flexible organization and a recognition that there may be some serious problems (at least until adjustments can be made) if extant training regimens are inappropriate to new duties.

Although training in conflict management is desirable, it is less clear whether such training will be fully useful in practice, given the uncertainties associated with the compatibility of different conflict resolution approaches and the wide variety of missions that fall under OOTW. The difference between specialized and general training is relevant. In a previous book, the committee recognized some limitations of training that is overly specialized and concluded that "varied contexts and general procedures allow (learners) to adapt to new situations not encountered during training" (Druckman and Bjork, 1994:11). Specialized training can lead to inflexible performance to the extent that it fails to anticipate the variability that exists in the performance settings. We offer these concerns as a starting point for consideration, and some or all of them may be allayed by subsequent experience and research.

Some Additional Training Suggestions

In previous sections we have offered suggestions for soldiers' training—specifically, that soldiers participate in increasingly complex role-playing negotiations, that the in-class training equip soldiers with a broad set of contact skills, and that soldiers be trained to deal with cultural differences. To these suggestions we add some additional ones, drawn from the chapter on developing leaders. That chapter emphasized that three factors—training, development, and facilitating conditions—jointly determine the amount of leadership improvement. Those three factors also determine a soldier's OOTW competence.

Operating under this assumption, we suggest that OOTW training programs should have a content that is clear and meaningful and that builds on the soldier's prior knowledge. The training methods should take into account the trainee's/soldier's current skill level and motivation. And trainees/soldiers should receive relevant feedback, from a variety of available sources, that is accurate, timely, and constructive.

Just as useful as training programs are developmental activities, because effective behavior is most often learned from new experiences coupled with feedback engaged within them. As noted in Chapter 4, developmental techniques include (1) special developmental assignments, (2) job rotation, (3) mentoring, (4) after-action reviews, (5) multirater feedback workshops, (6) developmental assessment centers, and (7) action learning. Although some of these techniques will perhaps not be applicable to OOTW skills development, we suggest that they all be considered for implementation.

Finally, competence in OOTW missions, like that of leadership, is based to a large extent on organizational conditions. Such conditions include support for skill development from top leaders, reward systems that encourage the skill development, and cultural values that support learning and development. We encourage readers, including Army officials, to consider the specific aspects of these conditions (which are delineated in Chapter 4) and to extrapolate these from leadership to OOTW skills development.

Unit performance may, however, depend on more than the skills of its members. Team training is also likely to contribute to effectiveness. Such factors as teamwork and coordination, shared mental models, and related forms of team information processing, promotive interactions, and shared identities have been shown to influence performance on group tasks. (See Druckman and Bjork, 1994:Ch. 6 and 7, for a review of the studies.) They may also enable units to move easily from one type of mission to another. A research challenge is to ascertain the extent to which individual versus unit-level skills contribute to effectiveness. An applied challenge is to develop training procedures that contain the desired mix of individual and team-training exercises.

Evaluation

Effective training in contact skills should prepare soldiers to deal with the challenges posed by operations other than war. The extent to which it also contributes to successful missions, however, is not quite so clear. Meaningful performance measures may be difficult to construct, making the committee's suggestions on this point rather problematic in this context. In this section, we discuss problems of evaluation with regard to both the individual soldier and the overall mission.

Effectiveness of Training

The value of predeparture training turns on an answer to the question: Has the training prepared soldiers to deal effectively with the challenges posed by the missions? This question is rarely addressed in discussions of training or preparation; for example, Fetherston (1994) devotes only two pages to these issues; many of the evaluations to date consist of ratings of the course materials and presentations rather than assessments of the skills learned and used. This may be due to the small number of programs initiated to date to train soldiers in contact skills. It may also reflect, however, an early stage in thinking about the tasks and challenges of operations other than war. Before considering evaluation issues, it is necessary to understand the challenges posed by different missions, the skills needed to meet these challenges, and the training needed to acquire and maintain these skills. Evaluation issues will receive more attention as we develop an increased understanding of the missions.

The Canadian survey discussed above addresses the issue of mission challenges. By asking soldiers how often they perform various activities, we can identify the key challenges posed by the mission. Missing, however, from the surveys are questions about the skills needed to perform these tasks. By asking soldiers what was needed in order to perform the tasks, we can identify the key skills corresponding to the mission's challenges (the question of whether the soldiers themselves can accurately identify such skills remains). The idea of matching skills to challenges is the basis for the benchmark approach to leadership development pioneered by the Center for Creative Leadership (McCauley and Hughs-James, 1994; McCauley et al., 1989). Examples of job challenges for executives are unfamiliar responsibilities, developing new directions, high stakes, and influencing without authority. Examples of some corresponding skills are comfort with ambiguity, decisiveness, and acting with flexibility; finding alternatives to solving problems, persevering under adverse conditions, and negotiation with external parties; decisiveness, straightforwardness, composure, and acting with flexibility; and persevering under adverse conditions, getting cooperation, and building and mending relationships. These are also challenges and skills likely to be found in many OOTW missions. We add to this list the skills of gathering and processing information as well as using feedback to perform situation analyses, managing impressions or posturing for tactical maneuvering, and timing of moves for implementing tactics. By highlighting the match between challenges and skills, this approach provides information that addresses the question: What should soldiers be trained to perform?

Another question is how to go about providing the needed training or preparation. With regard to conflict management skills, some guidance is provided by the research completed to date. Trainers can import into their programs research-based knowledge about the conditions and strategies that lead to settlements or resolutions. For example, the research findings discussed above in the section on distributive processes indicate that certain factors influence the extent to which bargainers are likely to be intransigent or flexible in seeking compromise agreements. These factors include the way disputants prepare for bargaining, their orientation toward the interaction, the other's pattern of making concessions, whether there are time pressures, whether the bargainers' interactions are observed by others, and whether their positions are linked to broader values or ideologies. Bargainers are more likely to seek compromise agreements when they do not perform before an audience that creates face-saving pressures, when there are time limits for reaching agreements, when they study the issues prior to bargaining over a large number of issues, and when they are faced with an opponent who conveys a genuinely cooperative attitude toward the interactions. (For a review of these and other findings, see Druckman, 1994.) These are examples of aspects of a situation that can be arranged as part of a tactical approach to negotiating beneficial agreements.

Similarly, recent studies have identified some conditions that contribute to integrative agreements. In our earlier discussion of this approach, we reviewed the findings obtained by Carnevale and Pruitt (1992) and by Kressel and his associates (1994) on the attitudes and procedures that can produce beneficial and durable outcomes. Deutsch and Brickman's (1994) list of skills needed for effective third-party conflict resolution is also relevant. It includes (1) establishing an effective working relationship with the disputants, (2) establishing a cooperative problem-solving attitude, (3) developing a creative group process and group decision making, and (4) acquiring relevant substantive knowledge about the problems. More specifically, the intervening party needs to learn how to obtain and use feedback in competitive situations. Although this approach is promising, more research is needed to discover how best to acquire and maintain the relevant skills over time and in different conflict situations.

Soldiers can learn the necessary attitudes and procedures: showing a high concern for the other's outcomes as well as one's own, engaging in information exchange about priorities and needs, and learning how to obtain and use feedback. These skills can also be practiced in simulation exercises that allow the trainee to apply and adapt them to novel situations. Although research on the elicitive approach has identified skills needed in the facilitator role, there has been little research to date on the effects of these behaviors on conflict-resolving processes or outcomes. The sensitivity to cultural perspectives emphasized by this approach is likely to be relevant to a variety of operations other than wars, and, for this reason, research on impacts is needed. Nevertheless, whether these skills are relevant to most or only some types of missions remains to be determined. This is also a question to be addressed for the skills associated with the other approaches discussed above. (Trainers would benefit from the large amount of research on individual skill acquisition and transfer; for a review, see the committees's earlier volumes, especially Druckman and Bjork, 1991:Ch. 3, and Druckman and Bjork, 1994:Ch. 3).

Confounding the Training-Effectiveness Nexus

Although appropriate training may be an essential component of preparing individual soldiers for an operation other than war, there are some questions as to the impact that this training will have on mission effectiveness vis-à-vis other factors. There is a tendency among peacekeeping veterans and other military personnel to attribute primary or exclusive importance to the operational components of the force in identifying key factors in mission success (Erskine, 1989; Jonah, 1991; Pelcovits, 1991; Murray, 1983). This may largely be the product of a narrow orientation toward the components of an operation over which the military has some control rather than a broader perspective on the contextual factors faced by the operation. It is also a function of whether one defines success at the micro level (the effective performance of certain specific military duties) or whether macro-level concerns are paramount (Was the mission as a whole successful?).

There is some evidence that individual soldier behavior and the organizational performance of a traditional peacekeeping force are not decisive in the overall effectiveness of the mission, at least in the absence of clear incompetence or serious operational mistakes (although the efficiency of the operation may be substantially influenced) (Diehl, 1994). Nevertheless, the neutrality of a military force may be critical in the success of those missions that require a more integrative approach to conflict resolution. Neutrality is the centerpiece of much of traditional peacekeeping theory (Urquhart, 1990; Nelson, 1984-1985), and often violations of that principle are associated with problems in the execution of operations (Diehl, 1994). Of course, training can be an essential component of ensuring that the behavior of individual soldiers or units does not violate principles of engagement (such as those involving neutrality or self-defense). There is some disagreement about the relative importance of training versus actual experience in fostering the desired attitudes and behaviors of soldiers (Moskos, 1976; Grove and Torbiorn, 1985). Yet, even if training is less effective, there is still a void that training can partly fill at the outset of an operation, before some of the military personnel have sufficient experience. Nevertheless, some operations other than war will not even require neutrality, and traditional military training or experience may be sufficient (for example, the coercive missions in the taxonomy).

Other factors will limit mission effectiveness even under the best of training scenarios. Operations other than war will be affected by some contextual constraints imposed on the mission. First is the geographic context for deployment. The different missions will vary among themselves (and in some cases among specific deployments of the same mission) according to whether they separate hostile parties at an adequate distance (Mackinlay, 1990), whether the troops can monitor the situation properly and detect violations of established standards or agreements (Diehl, 1994), and whether the troops themselves are relatively invulnerable to attack from hostile elements (Diehl, 1994). The Army may have limited control over the geographic context of its operations. Second, some types of missions will be more difficult to manage than others because of the situation the troops face. The Army would seem to have the most difficulty when there is considerable violence in the area of deployment, compared with situations following a cease-fire (or, ideally, deployment following a peace agreement among hostile parties or in the absence of any prior hostilities). Of course, problems in the area of deployment may be exacerbated by the presence of "accelerators" (U.S. Army Command and General Staff College, 1994) such as economic crises, elite fragmentation, and the like. These conditions are those largely out of the control of the military force.

Third, beyond the level of violence, the type of conflict present may affect the effectiveness of the mission. Historically, peacekeeping missions, of both the traditional and the post-cold war varieties, have had fewer problems in interstate conflicts than civil ones. Civil conflicts create some inherent difficulties for intervenors, including unfavorable geographic configurations for deployment, a multiplicity of actors, often with irreconcilable preferences, and incentives for some groups to disrupt the operation (Diehl, 1995; Weiss, 1994; Stedman, 1995; James, 1994). Finally, the U.S. Army may find itself involved in operations that include forces of many other states, and U.S. forces may not be solely under the command of U.S. officers. To the extent that other troops' behavior influences the mission's success and command is exercised according to different rules, norms, and protocols, the impact of U.S. military training on outcomes will be mitigated.

Whenever mediation and conflict resolution are a part of training, it must be remembered that such a process is interactive and therefore one must always take into account the other parties involved in the process. Another factor, beyond the contextual ones noted above, that is an intervening variable between training and mission effectiveness is the behavior of other parties in the situation. We noted above that failure to consider this factor was a shortcoming in many distributive bargaining approaches. A key element is the level of host state consent involved in the mission (U.S. Department of the Army, 1994). Whether the host state is supportive (and this assumes that a stable host state even exists) can make the job of the military easier in all of its mission tasks. A related concern is the behavior of third-party states (major powers or neighboring states) who have an interest in the situation; these states may aid or more influentially undermine the operation by direct action or the provision of threats and rewards to those actors that the military mission is trying to influence (Urquhart, 1983; James, 1990; Diehl, 1994); implicitly or explicitly this adds to the number and preference ordering combinations present in the conflict resolution process, thereby complicating the military's effectiveness.

Of particular concern to the military is the possible presence of groups or individuals whose interests may be disadvantaged by the operation; it is often these groups and individuals with whom officers and soldiers will come in contact and will need to apply conflict resolution skills. When the self-interests of these groups or individuals comport well with the mission tasks, the operation is likely to be smooth. But to the extent that interests clash with tasks and large numbers of individuals or powerful groups are involved, the effectiveness of the mission will be in jeopardy and even the best-trained and most well-informed mediators will encounter difficulties. In Bosnia, UN personnel often found it difficult to negotiate safe passage of humanitarian shipments, in part, because of Serbian interest in inhibiting aid to (and indeed attacking) Muslim-populated areas.

Finally, the timing of interventions is often a key element affecting the success of a mission (Fisher, 1990; Kriesberg, 1991; Touval and Zartman, 1985). Unfortunately the military may have little control over when it is deployed in a given area. Too often the deployment occurs after the situation has reached a crisis stage (e.g., a riot has not abated after several days, a war has broken out, significant numbers of refugees have died). It may be too late to have an optimal impact on the problem, and correspondingly there may be inherent limits on how effective the military operation can be.

Evaluating Overall Mission Effectiveness

As difficult as it may be to evaluate the effectiveness of international training programs on soldier behavior, the problems mount when one attempts to extend evaluation to the mission as a whole. Not only is it the case, as noted above, that a multiplicity of factors influence mission effectiveness, but also defining exactly what constitutes effectiveness is often unclear for operations other than war. In studies of peacekeeping missions, analysts and United Nations officials have tended to either ignore a global assessment of mission effectiveness or rely on unspecified face validity criteria (for a general treatment of evaluation problems vis-à-vis the United Nations, see Stiles and MacDonald, 1992). Yet even moving to a more systematic evaluation scheme does not solve all the problems.

An obvious standard for evaluation of success at the macro level would be the extent to which the purpose of the mission, as evidenced in the mandate, was fulfilled (James, 1969; Lefever, 1967). Nevertheless, mandates are often political documents developed in the United Nations or other bodies that are meant to convey broad purposes while maximizing the level of political support behind them. Accordingly, mandates can be vague (Fetherston, 1994), and there is considerable room for disagreement on how purposes are defined and how best to operationalize them; indeed, such ambiguity may be the price of approval in a multilateral coalition. Some operations, such as the multinational force in Beirut, actually had varying mandates across the coalition partners. Finally, a clear mandate is often cited as a factor in the overall success of a peacekeeping mission (Weinberger, 1983; Mackinlay, 1990), thereby begging the question somewhat if mandate fulfillment is used as a standard of success.

A second approach is to consider the specific accomplishments of the operation; these might include the number of people fed, cease-fires achieved, and so on. This type of evaluation allows an analyst to look at tangible items but still leaves open the question about what standard to compare or evaluate the operation against. Did the operation succeed if it accomplished only a few tasks? Obviously, success in this mode is relative and one must specify the basis for comparison. One standard might be comparing the operation's accomplishments to the situation that would have been present in the absence of the operation or that would be the result of traditional military or diplomatic initiatives (Johansen, 1994). Yet there are several flaws in this use of "counterfactuals" (Fearon, 1991).[9] It is most clearly useful when one can point to starving children or damage wreaked by natural disasters. Yet evaluating operations other than war in this way leads one to adopt a "better than nothing" standard that will almost always yield a positive assessment (e.g., Yoder, 1994). Furthermore, we do not know for sure what the absence of military intervention might mean for a given situation. The lack of U.S. or multilateral action may not mean that the status quo is perpetuated, but rather that local actors will manage to work out the difficulties that they face; indeed, there is some suggestion that humanitarian assistance missions, for example, may prolong some conflicts (DeMars, 1995). Evaluating operations against traditional military or diplomatic actions also calls for significant speculation that is hostage to assumptions and scenario constructions; variations on those assumptions and scenarios may yield dramatically different conclusions, and there is often no way to validate such assessments empirically.

A third standard for evaluation is to consider the impact that operations have on the local people affected by the operation (Johansen, 1994); this may be defined as creating a capacity for the host population to help itself (Pelcovits, 1991). One indicator of this might be the level of popularity enjoyed by the force among the local population (Skogmo, 1989; Nelson, 1991). This approach, however, suffers from the same counterfactual standards noted above and ignores the broader impact that the mission may have on aggregate political processes, which themselves have more of an impact in the short and long run on local people's lives.

Other criteria for success focus not so much on what has been accomplished but rather on the manner in which it has been achieved. In these instances, goals specific to the organization carrying out the mission may be valued above those relating to the conflict itself or the local population. Thus, a premium may be put on the efficiency of the operation (Harrell and Howe, 1995; Kemp, 1991), defined in terms of low cost and short deployment times, or on the maintenance of neutrality or impartiality in the conduct of the mission (Berdal, 1995). Success might even be defined in terms of the ability of the OOTW force to avoid casualties, a goal and indicator of success that was used for U.S. troops in Somalia. Although all these criteria may be considered desirable for the organization itself, they may be largely unrelated (or even counterproductive) to the achievement of the mission's purposes or the goals set by the United States government or United Nations for the mission.

Based on these limitations, one might be tempted to consider some overall assessment of the mission performance. For traditional peacekeeping operations, Diehl (1994; see also Wiseman, 1991; Skjelsbaek, 1991) argues that all operations should be judged on their ability to deter or prevent violent conflict in the area of deployment. First, we note that this does generally apply to operations other than war deployed in areas with little prospect of armed conflict (i.e., some domestic missions and disaster relief). Second, measuring the operation on the intended outcome places most of the responsibility for success or failure on that military mission. This may not be reasonable, in that we know that even the best-trained personnel cannot be held responsible for armed conflict between belligerents.

To place that burden on the military operation is probably unreasonable and may obscure positive benefits provided by the operation (Johansen, 1994).

Another possible standard, and one consistent with our emphasis on conflict resolution, is the ability of the operation to facilitate the resolution of disagreements among the local actors (Diehl, 1994; Moskos, 1976). This is often referred to as a "positive peace" standard (Fetherston, 1994), rather than merely the absence of armed conflict. At the macro level, this cannot be done solely or even directly by military personnel but is under the purview of diplomatic forces. Generally the military operation can provide only the environment under which this resolution can occur. This standard is open to the same critiques as above, namely, that the military operation cannot be held responsible for the failure to achieve a lasting peace; too many other intervening factors are at work. Indeed, there is some question whether macro conflict resolution is even an appropriate criterion on which to assess these operations. Only a few of the operations other than war have as their goal imposing a solution on the problems at hand, and even then the duration of such settlements is uncertain and may not be long enough to be considered true examples of conflict resolution.

CONCLUSIONS

The committee draws the following key conclusions from its discussion of the Army's changing missions and conflict management:

1. Traditional peacekeeping is only one of several types of missions that characterize operations other than war. Sixteen types of OOTW missions can be grouped into two dimensions, one reflecting the distinction between primary and third-party roles, the other distinguishing between distributive and integrative processes. Skills needed for particular missions vary along these dimensions.

2. These skills reflect different mixes of combat and contact skills. Currently, training programs devote a small amount of time to the development of contact skills (for example, cross-cultural communication, negotiation, and mediation activities). We suggest that a larger proportion of the training package focus on these skills. Guidance for training approaches is provided by the literatures on interpersonal and intercultural skills training as well as research on approaches to conflict management.

3. Preparation for operations other than war should include dealing with culture shock, interacting with civilians, dealing with people who have different perceptions of the conflict, and dealing with different social structures.

4. A challenge for trainers is the diversity of missions to which soldiers may be assigned. Research is needed on the transfer of skills from one to

another mission and on skill incompatibility. The implications of the choice between training specialists to be sent on specific missions and training generalists who must then adapt to new challenges, sometimes very quickly, need to be investigated. The costs and benefits of the alternative approaches should also be determined.

5. Research is needed to evaluate the extent to which the training of individuals or small groups (compared with other factors) contributes to the overall effectiveness of missions.

6. Research is also needed to ascertain the conditions for effective collaboration in multilateral and joint-service missions. The conditions may vary with the type of mission, the extent of mutual interdependence among the collaborating parties, and the authority structure.

NOTES

[1]Examples of keywords are cross-cultural communication, conflict resolution or management, negotiation, mediation, conciliation, civil affairs, coordination with agencies, language and cultural training, media relations, and the social aspects of operations. It should also be noted that a number of skills do not fit into either the combat or contact categories, for example, personal hygiene, stress awareness, and fact-oriented historical briefings.

[2]The U.S. Institute of Peace emphasizes three skills in their training programs, two of which are contact skills—an international conflict resolution skills training seminar and training in multiparty mediation skills.

[3]Fetherston (1994) distinguishes between situational exercises and simulations. Preferring simulations, she notes that situation exercises typically do not allow for unexpected events that require the sorts of adaptations that are experienced in actual missions (see also Stewman, 1995). Without surprises, it is less likely that trainees will develop the flexibility they need to deal with a variety of unknown situations. (See Druckman and Bjork, 1994:Ch. 3, for a discussion of the issue of fidelity between simulated and work situations.)

[4]Prominent examples are the United Nations Department of Peace-Keeping Operations, the U.S. Army's Peacekeeping Institute at Carlisle Barracks, Pennsylvania, and the Lester B. Pearson Canadian International Peacekeeping Training Center in Nova Scotia.

[5]"Krunching" refers to statements made in order to encourage the other to reexamine or change his or her positions. Examples are "Where do we go from here?," "Is there any flexibility on that?," "Can we talk?," and "What more could you do for us on this?"

[6]We note, however, that in many actual circumstances, settlements are a more realistic goal and may in fact be desired. For example, attempts to negotiate a cease-fire are aimed at an end to the fighting.

[7]One way to do this is through role-playing exercises. A peacekeeper could react to a delegated opponent instructed to perceive and act like the other side. This procedure was used by the U.S. delegation between rounds of talks during the 1970s over mutual and balanced force reductions in central Europe (see Druckman and Hopmann, 1989). A similar procedure is the contrasting-culture adherent pioneered by Danielian (1967). A trainee preparing for overseas service is confronted by a staged contrasting-culture adherent whose script consists of making explicit and challenging the underlying assumptions that characterize the rhetoric of the trainee.

[8]Thanks go to Major David Last of the Canadian Army for suggesting these questions.

[9]By counterfactuals, we refer to claims about events that did not actually occur. With regard to peacekeeping operations, an example of a counterfactual is the statement that if the operation did not occur, then widespread famine would have resulted.

References

SUMMARY

Argyris, C.
1993 *On Organizational Learning*. Cambridge, MA: Blackwell.
Burke, W.W.
1994 *Organization Development: A Process of Learning and Changing*, 2nd ed. Reading, MA: Addison-Wesley.
Dietrich, M.
1994 *Transaction Cost Economics & Beyond: Toward a New Economics of the Firm*. London: Routledge.
Eisenhardt, K.M.
1989 Agency theory: An assessment and review. *Academy of Management Review* 14:57-74.
Powell, W.W., and P.J. DiMaggio, eds.
1991 *The New Institutionalism in Organization Analysis*. Chicago: University of Chicago Press.
Putterman, L., ed.
1986 *The Economic Nature of the Firm: A Reader*. Cambridge, England: Cambridge University Press.

CHAPTER 1
ORGANIZATIONAL CHANGE AND REDESIGN

Abbott, A.
1988 *The System of Professions*. Chicago: University of Chicago Press.
Amburgey, T.L., D. Kelly, and W.P. Barnett
1993 Resetting the clock: The dynamics of organizational change and failure. *Administrative Science Quarterly* 38:51-73.
Bazerman, M.H.
1986 *Judgement in Managerial Decision Making*. New York: John Wiley.

211

Beer, M., and R.E. Walton
1987 Organization change and development. *Annual Review of Psychology* 38:339-367.
Bettis, R.A.
1991 Strategic management and the straightjacket: An editorial essay. *Organization Science* 2(3):315-319.
Brynjolfsson, E.
1993 The productivity paradox of information technology: Review and assessment. *Communications of the ACM* 36:67-77.
Brynjolfsson, E., and S. Yang
1996 Information technology and productivity: A review of the literature. In M. Zelkowitz, ed., *Annals of Computing.*
Brynjolfsson, E., T. Malone, V. Gurbaxani, and A. Kambil
1994 Does information technology lead to smaller firms? *Management Science* 40:12.
Burke, W.W.
1994 *Organization Development: A Process of Learning and Changing.* Reading, MA: Addison-Wesley.
Burke, W.W., and G.H. Litwin
1992 A causal model of organizational performance and change. *Journal of Management* 18(3):523-545.
Burns, L.R., and D.R. Wholey
1993 Adoption and abandonment matrix management programs: Effects of organizational characteristics and interorganizational networks. *Academy of Management Journal* 36:106-138.
Burton, R.M., and B. Obel
1995 *Strategic Organizational Diagnosis and Design: Developing Theory for Application.* Boston: Kluwer Academic Publishers.
Child, John
1972 Organizational structure, environment and performance: The role of strategic choice. *Sociology* 6:1-22.
Cohen, Michael D., and L.S. Sproull
1996 *Organizational Learning.* Thousand Oaks, CA: Sage Publications.
Cox, T.H.
1993 *Cultural Diversity in Organizations.* San Francisco, CA: Berrett-Koehler Publishers.
Cox, T.H., and S. Blake
1991 Managing cultural diversity: Implications for organizational competitiveness. *Academy of Management Executives* 5:45-55.
Cox, T.H., S.A. Lobel, and P.L. McLeod
1991 Effects of ethnic group cultural differences on cooperative and competitive behavior on groups. *Academy of Management Journal* 34(4):827-847.
Daft, R., and A. Lewin
1990 Can organizational studies begin to break out of the normal science straitjacket? An editorial essay. *Organization Science* 1(1):1-9.
De Solla Price, D.
1963 *Little Science, Big Science.* New York: Columbia University Press.
Donaldson, L.
1985 *In Defence of Organization Theory.* New York: Cambridge University Press.
1995 *American Anti-Management Theories of Organization: A Critique of Paradigm Proliferation.* New York: Cambridge University Press.
Doty, H., and W.H. Glick
1994 Topologies as a unique form of theory building: Toward improved understanding and modeling. *Academy of Management Review* 19(2):230-251.

Doty, H., W.H. Glick, and G.P. Huber
  1993   Fit, equifinality and organizational effectiveness: A test of two configurational theo-
         ries. *Academy of Management Journal* 36:1196-1250.
Drazin, R., and A.H. Van de Ven
  1985   Alternative forms of fit in contingency theory. *Administrative Science Quarterly*
         30:514-539.
Drucker, P.F.
  1993   *Post Capitalist Society.* New York: Harper Business.
Eccles, R.G., and D.B. Crane
  1988   *Doing Deals: Investment Banks at Work.* Boston: Harvard Business School Press.
Faucheux, C., G. Amado, and A. Laurent
  1982   Organizational development and change. *Annual Review of Psychology* 33:343-370.
Freidson, E.
  1986   *Professional Powers.* Chicago: University of Chicago Press.
French, W., and C. Bell
  1990   *Organizational Development.* Englewood Cliffs, NJ: Prentice-Hall.
Fulk, J., and G. DeSanctis
  1995   Electronic communication and changing and organizational forms. *Organization Sci-
         ence* 6:337-349.
Galbraith, J.R.
  1977   *Organization Design.* Reading, MA: Addison-Wesley.
Gersick, C.J.G.
  1994   Pacing strategic change: The case of a new venture. *Academy of Management Journal*
         37:9-41.
Golembiewski, R.T.
  1995   *Managing Diversity in Organizations.* Tuscaloosa: University of Alabama Press.
Goodstein, D.
  1995   Peer review after the big crunch. *American Scientist* 83:401-402.
Gould, S.J., and N. Eldredge
  1977   Punctuated equilibria: The tempo and mode of evolution reconsidered. *Paleobiology*
         3:115-151.
Greiner, L.E.
  1972   Evolution and revolution as organizations grow. *Harvard Business Review* July-
         August.
Griggs, L.B., and L.-L. Louw, eds.
  1995   *Valuing Diversity: New Tools for a New Reality.* New York: McGraw-Hill.
Guillen, Mauro F.
  1994   *Models of Management: Work, Authority and Organization in a Comparative Per-
         spective.* Chicago: University of Chicago Press.
Hall, R.H.
  1968   Professionalization and bureaucratization. *American Sociological Review* 33:92-104.
Hannan, Michael T., and John H. Freeman
  1977   The population ecology of organizations. *American Journal of Sociology* 82:929-964.
  1984   Structural inertia and organizational change. *American Sociological Review* 49:149-
         164.
Hannan, Michael T., and Glenn R. Carroll
  1992   *Dynamics of Organizational Populations.* New York: Oxford University Press.
Harris, Douglas H., ed.
  1994   *Organizational Linkages: Understanding the Productivity Paradox.* Panel on Organi-
         zational Linkages, Committee on Human Factors, National Research Council. Wash-
         ington, DC: National Academy Press.

Harrison, Bennett
  1994 *Lean and Mean: The Changing Landscape of Corporate Power in the Age of Flexibil-*
       ity. New York: Basic Books.
Heilbroner, R.
  1995 *Visions of the Future.* New York: Oxford University Press.
Hinings, C.R., and R. Greenwood
  1984 *The Dynamics of Strategic Change.* New York: Blackwell.
Huber, G.P.
  1982 Organizational information processing systems: Determinants of their performance
       and behavior. *Management Science* 28:138-155.
  1984 The nature and design of post-industrial organizations. *Management Science* 30:928-
       951.
  1990 A theory of the effects of advanced information technologies on organizational de-
       sign, intelligence, and decision making. *Academy of Management Review* 15:47-71.
  1991 Organizational learning: The contributing processes and the literatures. *Organiza-*
       tional Science 2(1):88-114.
Huber, G.P., C.C. Miller, and W.W. Glick
  1990 A theory of the effects of advanced information technologies on organizational de-
       sign, intelligence, and decision making. *Academy of Management Review* 15:47-71.
  1993 Understanding and predicting organizational change. Pp. 215-265 in *Organizational*
       Change and Redesign, G.P. Huber, and W.H. Glick, eds. New York: Oxford Univer-
       sity Press.
Huppes, T.
  1987 *The Western Edge: Work and Management in the Information Age.* Boston: Kluwer
       Academic Publishers.
Jackson, S., V. Stone, and E. Alvarez
  1993 Socialization amidst diversity: The impact of demographics on work team oldtimers
       and newcomers. Pp. 45-109 in *Research in Organizational Behavior,* L. Cummings
       and B. Staw, eds. Greenwich, CT: JAI Press.
Kanter, R.M.
  1989 *When Giants Learn to Dance: Mastering the Challenges of Strategy, Management*
       and Careers in the 1990's. New York: Simon and Schuster.
  1994 Collaborative advantage: The art of alliances. *Harvard Business Review* July/Au-
       gust:96-108.
Katz, D., and R.L. Kahn
  1978 *The Social Psychology of Organizations,* 2nd ed. New York: John Wiley and Sons.
Katzenbach, R. Jon, and Douglas K. Smith
  1993 *The Wisdom of Teams.* Boston: Harvard Business School Press.
Kidder, Tracy
  1981 *The Soul of a New Machine.* Boston: Little, Brown.
Kimberly, J., R. Miles, and associates
  1980 *The Organizational Life Cycle.* San Francisco: Jossey-Bass Publishers.
Kornhauser, W.
  1963 *Scientists in Industry.* Berkeley: University of California Press.
Larson, E.W., and D.H. Gobeli
  1987 Matrix management: Contradictions and insights. *California Management Review*
       29:126-138.
Lawrence, P.R.
  1993 The contingency approach to organizational design. Pp. 9-18 in *Handbook of Organi-*
       zational Behavior, R. Golembiewski, ed. New York: Dekker Publishing.

Leidner, D.E., and J.J. Elam
1995 The impact of executive information systems on organizational design, intelligence and decision making. *Organizational Science* 6:645-665.
Levitt, B., and J.G. March
1988 Organizational learning. *Annual Review of Sociology* 14:319-340.
Loveman, G.W.
1994 An assessment of the productivity impact on information technologies. Pp. 84-110 in *Information Technology and the Corporation of the 1990's: Research Studies*, T.J. Allen and M.S. Scott Morton, eds. Cambridge, MA: MIT Press.
Mayer, R.E.
1992 *Thinking, Problem Solving, Cognition.* New York: W.H. Freeman Company.
Meyer, J.W., and B. Rowan
1977 Institutionalized organizations: Formal structure as myth and ceremony. *American Journal of Sociology* 83:340-363.
Meyer, Alan D., Anne S. Tsui, and C.R. Hinings
1993 Configurational approaches to organizational analysis. *Academy of Management Journal* 36(6):1175-1195.
Miles, R.E., and C.C. Snow
1978 *Organizational Strategy, Structure and Process.* New York: McGraw-Hill.
1992 Causes of failure in network organizations. *California Management Review* 34:53-72.
1994 *Fit, Failure and the Hall of Fame.* New York: Free Press.
Miller, D.
1981 Towards a new contingency approach: The search for organizational gestalts. *Journal of Management Studies* 18:1-26.
1987 The genesis of configuration. *Academy of Management Review* 12:686-701.
Miller, D., and P.H. Friesen
1980 Momentum and revolution in organizational adaptation. *Academy of Management Journal* 23:591-614.
1984 A longitudinal study of the corporate life cycle. *Management Science* 30(10):1161-1183.
Miner, John B.
1983 The validity and usefulness of theories in an emerging organizational science. *Academy of Management Review* 9(2):296-306.
Mintzberg, H.
1993 *Structure in Fives: Designing Effective Organizations.* Englewood Cliffs, NJ: Prentice-Hall.
Mohrman, S.A., S.G. Cohen, and A.M. Mohrman, Jr.
1995 *Designing Team-Based Organizations.* San Francisco: Jossey-Bass.
Mokyr, J.
1990 *The Lever of Riches.* New York: Oxford University Press.
Morrison, C.J., and E.R. Berndt
1990 Assessing the Productivity of Information Technology Equipment in the U.S. Manufacturing Industries. Working paper number 3582, National Bureau of Economic Research.
O'Reilly, R., C. Snyder, and J.N. Boothe
1993 Effects of executive team demography on organizational change. Pp. 147-175 in *Organizational Change and Redesign*, G.P. Huber, and W.H. Glick, eds. New York: Oxford University Press.
Peters, T.J., and R.H. Waterman
1982 *In Search of Excellence: Lessons from America's Best-Run Companies.* New York: Harper and Row.

Powell, W.W.
1990 Neither market nor hierarchy: Network forms of organizations. In *Research in Organization Behavior*, vol. 12, B.M. Starr and C.C. Cummings, eds. Greenwich, CT: JAI Press.

Powell, Walter W., and Paul DiMaggio, eds.
1991 *The New Institutionalism in Organizational Analysis*. Chicago: University of Chicago Press.

Quinn, J.B.
1992 *Intelligent Enterprise*. New York: Free Press.

Quinn, Robert E., and K. Cameron
1983 Organizational life cycles and shifting criteria of effectiveness: Some preliminary evidence. *Management Science* 29:333-351.

Roberts, K.H.
1993 *New Challenges to Understanding Organizations*. New York: MacMillan.

Roethlishberger, F.J., and W.J. Dickson
1939 *Management and the Worker*. Cambridge, MA: Harvard University Press.

Sagan, Scott D.
1995 *The Limits of Safety: Organizations, Accidents and Nuclear Weapons*. Princeton, NJ: Princeton University Press.

Schwarzkopf, N.H.
1992 *It Doesn't Take a Hero*. New York: Bantam Books.

Scott, W. Richard
1987 The adolescence of institutional theory. *Administrative Science Quarterly* 32:493-511.
1995 *Institutions and Organizations*. Thousand Oaks, CA: Sage.

Scott Morton, M.S.
1991 *The Corporation of the 1990s: Information Technology Organizational Transformation*. New York: Oxford University Press.

Senge, Peter M.
1990 *The Fifth Discipline*. New York: Doubleday/Currency.

Starbuck, W.H.
1993 Keeping a butterfly and an elephant in a house of cards: The elements of exceptional success. *Journal of Management Studies* 30:885-922.

Suchman, Mark C.
1995 Managing legitimacy: Strategic and institutional approaches. *Academy of Management Review* 20(3):571-610.

Toffler, A.
1990 *Powershift*. Bantam Books.

Tolbert, P.S., and L.G. Zucker
1983 Institutional forces of change in the formal structure of organizations: The diffusion of civil service reform, 1880-1935. *Administrative Science Quarterly* 28:22-39.

Trice, H.M., and J.M. Beyer
1993 *The Cultures of Work Organizations*. Englewood Cliffs, NJ: Prentice-Hall.

Tushman, M.L., and D.A. Nadler
1978 An information processing approach to organizational design. *Academic Management Review* 3(3):613-624.

Tushman, M.L., and E. Romanelli
1985 Organizational evolution: A metamorphosis model of convergence and reorientation. Pp. 171-222 in *Research in Organizational Behavior*, L.L. Cummings and B.M. Staw, eds. Greenwich, CT: JAI Press.

Tushman, M.L., W.H. Newman, and E. Romanelli
 1986 Convergence and upheaval: Managing the unsteady pace of organizational evolution. *California Management Review* 29(1):29-44.
U.S. Army
 1995 Field Manual FM 100-11. *Force Integration.*
Van de Ven, A.H., and R. Drazin
 1985 The concept of fit in contingency theory. *Research in Organizational Behavior* 7:333-365. Greenwich, CT: JAI Press.
Wayne, S., and S. Green
 1993 The effects of leader-member exchange on employee citizenship and impression management behavior. *Human Relations* 46:1431-1440.
Williamson, O., and S.E. Masters, eds.
 1995 *Transaction Cost Economics.* Brookfield, VT: Edward Elgar.
Wurman, R.S.
 1989 *Information Anxiety.* New York: Doubleday.
Zucker, Lynne G.
 1977 The role of institutionalization in cultural persistence. *American Sociological Review* 42:726-743.

CHAPTER 2
TECHNIQUES FOR MAKING ORGANIZATIONS EFFECTIVE

Abbott, L.
 1955 *Quality and Competition.* New York: Columbia University Press.
Anderson, Eugene, and Mary Sullivan
 1993 The antecedents and consequences of customer satisfaction for firms. *Marketing Science* 12:125-143.
Ansari, A.
 1984 An Empirical Investigation of the Implementation of Japanese Just-in-Time Purchasing Practices and Its Impact on Product Quality and Productivity in U.S. Firms. Doctoral dissertation, University of Nebraska.
Behn, R.D.
 1980 Leadership for cutback management. *Public Administration Review* 40:613-620.
Bennett, A.
 1991 Downsizing doesn't necessarily bring an upswing in corporate profitability. *Wall Street Journal* 6 June:B1, B4.
Bolton, W., and K. Oatley
 1987 A longitudinal study of social support and depression in unemployed men. *Psychological Medicine* 17:453-460.
Bowles, J.
 1992 Does the Baldrige Award really work? *Harvard Business Review* 70:127.
Brockner, Joel
 1988 The effects of work layoff on survivors. In *Research in Organizational Behavior,* vol. 10, B.M. Staw and L.L. Cummings, eds. Greenwich, CT: JAI Press.
Brockner, Joel, S. Grover, T. Reed, R. DeWitt, and M. O'Malley
 1987 Survivors' reactions to layoffs. *Administrative Science Quarterly* 32:526-541.
Broderick, Renae F., ed.
 1996 *Issues in Civilian Outplacement Strategies: Proceedings of a Workshop.* Commission on Behavioral and Social Sciences and Education, National Research Council. Washington, DC: National Academy Press.

Buch, K., and J. Aldrich
1991 O.D. under conditions of decline. *Organizational Development Journal* 9:1-5.
Burke, R.J.
1984 The closing at Canadian Admiral: Correlates of individual well-being sixteen months after shutdown. *Psychological Reports* 55:91-98.
1986 Reemployment in a poorer job after plant closing. *Psychological Reports* 58:559-570.
Buss, T.F., and F.S. Redburn
1987 Plant closings: Impacts and responses. *Economic Development Quarterly* 1L:170-177.
Buzzell, R.D., and F.D. Wiersma
1981 Modeling changes in market share. *Strategic Management Journal* 27-42.
Cameron, K.S.
1992 In What Ways Do Organizations Implement Total Quality? Paper delivered at the Academy of Management Meetings, Las Vegas, Nevada.
1995 Downsizing, quality, and performance. In *The Fall and Rise of the American Quality Movement,* Robert E. Cole, ed. New York: Oxford University Press.
Cameron, Kim S., Sarah J. Freeman, and Aneil K. Mishra
1991 Best practices in white-collar downsizing: Managing contradictions. *Academy of Management Executive* 5:57-73.
1993 Downsizing and redesigning organizations. In *Organizational Change and Redesign,* George P. Huber and William H. Glick, eds. New York: Oxford University Press.
Cameron, Kim S., Myung U. Kim, and David A. Whetten
1987 Organizational effects of decline and turbulence. *Administrative Science Quarterly* 32:222-240.
Cameron, K.S., and D.A. Whetten
1996 Organizational effectiveness and quality: The second generation. In *Higher Education: Handbook of Theory and Research*, John R. Smart, ed. New York: Agathon.
Campbell, J.P.
1977 On the nature of organizational effectiveness. In *New Perspectives of Organizational Effectiveness*, P.S. Goodman and J.M. Pennings, eds. San Francisco: Jossey-Bass.
Churchill, Gilbert, and Carol Surprenant
1982 An investigation into the determinants of customer satisfaction. *Journal of Marketing Research* 19:491-504.
Cole, Robert E.
1993 Learning from learning theory: Implications for quality improvements of turnover, use of contingent workers, and job rotation policies. *Quality Management Journal* 1:9-25.
Conrad, C.F., and R.T. Blackburn
1985 Program quality in higher education. Pp. 283-308 in *Higher Education: Handbook of Theory and Research*, J.R. Smart, ed. New York: Agathon.
Crawford-Mason, C.
1992 Does the Baldrige Award really work? *Harvard Business Review* 70:134-136.
Crosby, Philip
1979 *Quality is Free*. New York: New American Library.
1992 Does the Baldrige Award really work? *Harvard Business Review* 70:127-128.
CSC Index
1994 State of reengineering report, 1994. *The Economist* 2 July:6.
D'Aunno, T., and R.I. Sutton
1987 Changes in organizational size: Untangling the effects of people and money. *Academy of Management Journal*.

Davenport, Thomas H., and James E. Short
  1990 The new industrial engineering: Information technology and business process rede-
         sign. *Sloan Management Review.*
Davy, J.A., A.J. Kinicki, and C.L. Schreck
  1991 Developing and testing a model of survivor responses to layoffs. *Journal of Voca-
         tional Behavior* 38:302-317.
Deming, W. Edwards
  1982 *Quality, Productivity, and Competitive Position.* Cambridge, MA: MIT Press.
  1986 *Out of the Crisis.* Cambridge, MA: MIT Press.
Dixon, J. Robb, et al.
  1994 Business process reengineering: Improving in new strategic directions. *California
         Management Review* 36:93-108.
Dooley, D., and R. Catalano
  1988 Recent research on the psychological effects of UE. *Journal of Social Issues* 44:1-12.
Edwards, C.D.
  1968 The meaning of quality. *Quality Progress* October:37.
Feather, N.T.
  1989 The effects of unemployment on work values and motivation. In *Work Motivation,*
         U.W. Klienbeck, H.H. Quast, H. Thierry, and H. Hacker, eds. Hillsdale, NJ: Erlbaum.
Feldman, Daniel, and C.R. Leana
  1995 Better practices in managing layoffs. *Human Resource Management Journal* 33:239-
         260.
Ferdows, Kasra, and Arnoud DeMeyer
  1990 Lasting improvements in manufacturing performance. *Journal of Operations Manage-
         ment* 9:168-184.
Fiegenbaum, Armand V.
  1961 *Total Quality Control.* New York: McGraw-Hill.
Fineman, S.
  1983 *White-Collar Unemployment: Impact and Stress.* Chichester: Wiley.
Flynn, Barbara, Roger Schroeder, and Sadao Sakakibara
  1993 A Framework for Quality Management Research: Definition and Measurement. Work-
         ing paper, University of Iowa.
Fornell, C., and M.D. Johnson
  1993 Differentiation as a basis for explaining customer satisfaction across industries. *Jour-
         nal of Economic Psychology* 14:681-696.
Garvin, David A.
  1988 *Managing Quality: The Strategic and Competitive Edge.* New York: Free Press.
Gilmore, T., and L. Hirschhorn
  1983 Management challenges under conditions of retrenchment. *Human Resource Manage-
         ment* 22:341-357.
Greene, Richard T.
  1993 *Global Quality: A Synthesis of the World's Best Management Methods.* Homewood,
         IL: Business One Irwin.
Greenhalgh, Leonard
  1983 Organizational decline. In *Research in the Sociology of Organizations,* Sam Bacharach,
         ed. Greenwich, CT: JAI Press.
Griffin, Ricky
  1988 Consequences of quality circles in an industrial setting: A longitudinal assessment.
         Academy of Management Journal 31:338-358.
Hackman, Richard, and Edward Lawler
  1971 Employee reactions to job characteristics. *Journal of Applied Psychology* 55:259-
         286.

Hackman, Richard, and Greg Oldham
 1980 *Work Redesign.* Reading, MA: Addison-Wesley.
Hackman, J. Richard, and Ruth Wageman
 1995 Total quality management: Empirical, conceptual, and practical issues. *Administrative Science Quarterly* 40:309-342.
Hall, G., J. Rosenthal, and J. Wade
 1993 How to make reengineering really work. *Harvard Business Review,* November-December:119.
Hamilton, V.L., C.L. Broman, W.S. Hoffman, and D.S. Renner
 1990 Hard times and vulnerable people: Initial effects of plant closing on auto workers' mental health. *Journal of Health and Social Behavior* 31:123-140.
Hammer, Michael
 1990 Reengineering work: Don't automate, obliterate. *Harvard Business Review* 68.
Hammer, Michael, and James Champy
 1993 *Reengineering the Corporation.* New York: Harper Collins.
Hammond, J.
 1992 Does the Baldrige Award really work? *Harvard Business Review* 70:132.
Haworth, J.T., P. Chesworth, and P. Smith
 1990 Research note: Cognitive difficulties in samples on unemployed, middle-aged men. *Leisure Studies* 9:253-257.
Henkoff, Ronald
 1990 Cost cutting: How to do it right. *Fortune* 9 April:17-19.
Imai, Masaaki
 1986 *Kaizen: The Key to Japan's Competitive Success.* New York: Random House.
Ittner, Christopher
 1992 *The Economics and Management of Quality Costs.* Cambridge, MA: Harvard University School of Business Administration.
Iverson, L., and S. Sabroe
 1988 Psychological well-being among unemployed and employed people after a company closedown. *Journal of Social Issues* 44:141-152.
Jacob, Rahul
 1993 TQM: More than a dying fad? *Fortune* 18 October:52-56.
Japanese Industrial Standards Committee
 1981 Industrial Standardization in Japan: 1981. Agency of Industrial Science and Technology, Ministry of International Trade and Industry.
Juran, Joseph M.
 1951 *Quality Control Handbook.* New York: McGraw-Hill.
 1989 *Juran on Leadership for Quality.* New York: Free Press.
 1992 *Juran on Quality by Design.* New York: Free Press.
Kahn, Robert
 1994 M-Quality: A Brief Intellectual History. University of Michigan, Institute for Social Research.
Kasl, S.V., and S. Cobb
 1979 Some mental health consequences of plant closing and job loss. In *Mental Health and the Economy,* L. Ferman and J. Gordus, eds. Kalamazoo, MI: Upjohn Institute for Employment Research.
 1980 The experience of losing a job: Some effects on cardiovascular functioning. *Psychotherapy and Psychosomatics* 34:88-109.
Kessler, R.C., J.S. House, and J.B. Turner
 1987 Unemployment and health in a community sample. *Journal of Health and Social Behavior* 28:51-59.

Khurana, Anil
1994 Managing Complex Processes: Quality in the Global Color Picture Tube Industry. Unpublished doctoral dissertation, University of Michigan.

Kinicki, A.J.
1989 Predicting occupational role choices after involuntary job loss. *Journal of Vocational Behavior* 35:204-218.

Kozlowski, Steven W.J., Georgia T. Chao, Eleanor M. Smith, and Jennifer Hedlund
1993 Organizational downsizing: Strategies, interventions, and research implications. In *International Review of Industrial and Organizational Psychology.* New York: Wiley.

Krafcik, J.F.
1989 Triumph of the lean production system. *Sloan Management Review* Fall:41-52.

Krantz, J.
1985 Group process under conditions of organizational decline. *Journal of Applied Behavioral Science* 21:1-17.

Leana, C.R., and Daniel Feldman
1989 When mergers force layoffs: Some lessons about managing human resource problems. *Human Resource Planning* 12:123-140.

Leana, C.R., and Jack Ivancevich
1987 Involuntary job loss. *Academy of Management Review* 12:301-312.

Leffler, K.B.
1982 Ambiguous changes in product quality. *American Economic Review* December:956.

Liem, R., and J.H. Liem
1988 Psychological effects of unemployment on workers and their families. *Journal of Social Issues* 44:87-105.

Linn, M.W., R. Sandifer, and S. Stein
1985 Effects of unemployment on mental and physical health. *American Journal of Public Health* 75:502-506.

Malcolm Baldrige National Quality Award
1995 *1995 Application Manual.* Washington, DC: U.S. Department of Commerce.

Maynes, E.S.
1976 The concept and measurement of product quality. Pp. 550-554 in *Household Production and Consumption,* Terlecky, ed. New York: National Bureau of Economic Research.

McKinley, William
1992 Decreasing organizational size: To untangle or not to untangle? *Academy of Management Review* 17:112-123.

McKinley, William, A. G. Schick, H.L. Sun, and A.P. Tang
1994 The Financial Environment of Layoffs. Working paper, Southern Illinois University.

McKoewn, K.
1992 Does the Baldrige Award really work? *Harvard Business Review* 70:140.

Noble, I.
1987 Unemployment after redundancy and political attitudes. In *Redundancy, Layoffs, and Plant Closures: Their Character, Causes, and Consequences,* R.M. Lee, ed. London: Croom Helm.

Oliver, Richard, and Wayne DeSarbo
1988 Response determinants in satisfaction judgments. *Journal of Consumer Research* 14.

Pearlin, L.I., M.A. Lieberman, E.G. Meneghan, and J.T. Mullan
1981 The stress process. *Journal of Health and Social Behavior* 22:337-356.

Peterson, Marvin, and Kim Cameron
1995 Total Quality Management in Higher Education: From Assessment to Improvement. Center for the Study of Higher and Postsecondary Education, University of Michigan.

Philips, Lynn, Dae Chang, and Robert Buzzell
    1983   Product quality, cost position, and business performance. *Journal of Marketing* 47:26-43.
Pirsig, R.
    1974   *Zen and the Art of Motorcycle Maintenance.* New York: Bantam.
Pliner, J.
    1990   Staying with or leaving the organization. *Prevention in Human Services* 8:159-177.
Podgursky, M., and P. Swain
    1987   Job displacement and earnings loss. *Industrial and Labor Relations Review* 41:17-29.
Porter, Michael
    1980   *Competitive Strategy.* New York: Free Press.
Price, Richard
    1990   Strategies for managing plant closings and downsizing. In *The Human Side of Corporate Competitiveness*, D. Fishman and C. Cherniss, eds. Beverly Hills, CA: Sage.
Reynolds, R.B.
    1988   An Investigation into the Effectiveness of Quality Circles Applications in the United States. Doctoral dissertation, University of Georgia.
Rowley, K.M., and N.T. Feather
    1987   The impact of unemployment in relation to age and length of unemployment. *Journal of Occupational Psychology* 60:323-332.
Sashkin, M., and K.J. Kiser
    1993   *Putting Total Quality Management to Work.* San Francisco: Barrett-Koehler.
Schonenberger, Richard
    1982   *Japanese Manufacturing Techniques.* New York: Free Press.
Schweiger, D.M., and A.S. DeNisi
    1991   Communication with employees following a merger: A longitudinal field experiment. *Academy of Management Journal* 34:110-135.
Scott, W. Richard, Ann B. Flood, Wayne Ewy, and William H. Forrest
    1978   Organizational effectiveness and the quality of surgical care in hospitals. Pp. 290-305 in *Environments and Organizations,* Marshall Meyer, ed. San Francisco: Jossey-Bass.
Shamir, B.
    1986   Protestant work ethic, work involvement, and the psychological impact of unemployment. *Journal of Occupational Behavior* 7:25-38.
Shewhart, W.A.
    1931   *The Economic Control of Quality of Manufactured Product.* New York: Van Nostrand.
Singhal, Vinod, and Kevin Hendricks
    1993   Quality awards and the value of the firm. *Production and Operations Management Journal.*
Stokes, G., and R. Cochrane
    1984   A study of the psychological effects of redundancy and unemployment. *Journal of Occupational Psychology* 57:309-322.
Sutton, Robert, Kathleen Eisenhart, and John Jucker
    1985   Managing organizational decline: Lessons from Atari. *Organizational Dynamics* 14:17-29.
Swoboda, Frank
    1995   Corporate downsizing goes global. *Washington Post News Service. Ann Arbor News* 11 April:A8.
Taylor, Frederick W.
    1911   *Shop Management.* New York: Harper.
Teboul, James
    1991   *Managing Quality Dynamics.* New York: Prentice-Hall.

Teng, James T.C., Varun Grover, and Kirk D. Fiedler
1994 Business process reengineering: Charting a strategic path for the information age. *California Management Review* 36:9-31.
Tomasko, Robert M.
1987 *Downsizing: Reshaping the Corporation for the Future.* New York: AMACOM.
Tombaugh, J.R., and L.P. White
1990 Downsizing: An empirical assessment of survivors' perceptions of a postlayoff environment. *Organizational Development Journal* 8:32-43.
Tschirhart, M.
1993 The Management of Problems with Stakeholders. Unpublished doctoral dissertation, University of Michigan.
U.S. General Accounting Office
1991 *Management Practices: U.S. Companies Improve Performance Through Quality Efforts.* Washington, DC: U.S. Government Accounting Office.
Webster, D.S.
1981 Methods of assessing quality. *Change* October:20-24.
Weick, K.E.
1984 Small wins: Redefining the scale of social problems. *American Psychologist* 39:40-49.
1993 Small wins in organizational life. *Dividend* Winter:2-6.
Wilhelm, M.S., and C.A. Ridley
1988 Stress and unemployment in rural nonfarm couples. *Family Relations* 37:50-54.
Winn, Bradley
1995 Organizational Quality in Higher Education: An Examination of the Baldrige Framework in the University Work Environment. Doctoral dissertation, University of Michigan.
Zeithaml, Valerie
1988 Consumer perceptions of price, quality, and value: A means-end model and synthesis of evidence. *Journal of Marketing* 52:2-22.

CHAPTER 3
ORGANIZATIONAL CULTURE

Abegglen, James C., and George Stalk, Jr.
1985 *Kaisha, the Japanese Corporation.* New York: Basic Books.
Abrahamson, Eric, and Charles J. Fombrun
1994 Macrocultures: Determinants and consequences. *Academy of Management Review* 19:728-755.
Alvesson, Mats, and Per Olof Berg
1992 *Corporate Culture and Organizational Symbolism.* Berlin and New York: Walter de Gruyter.
Aronson, E., and J. Mills
1959 Effect of severity of initiation on liking for a group. *Journal of Abnormal and Social Psychology* 59:177-181
Barley, Stephen R.
1983 Semiotics and the study of occupational and organizational cultures. *Administrative Science Quarterly* 28:393-413.
1986 Technology as an occasion for structuring: Observations on CT scanners and the social order of radiology departments. *Administrative Science Quarterly* 31:78-108.
Barley, Stephen R., and Meryl R. Louis
1983 Many in One: Organizations as Multicultural Entities. Paper presented at the annual meeting of the Academy of Management, August 14-17, Dallas, TX.

Bellah, Robert N., Richard Masden, William M. Sullivan, Ann Swidler, and Steven M. Tipton
  1985   *Habits of the Heart: Individualism and Commitment in American Life.* New York: Harper and Row.
Bendix, Reinhard
  1956   *Work and Authority in Industry.* New York: Harper and Row.
Berlew, David E., and Douglas T. Hall
  1966   The socialization of managers: Effects of expectations on performance. *Administrative Science Quarterly* 11:207-223.
Biggart, Nicole W.
  1977   The creative-destructive process of organizational change: The case of the Post Office. *Administrative Science Quarterly* 22:410-426.
Brown, L. David
  1983   *Management Conflict at Organizational Interfaces.* Reading, MA: Addison-Wesley.
Browning, Larry D., Janice M. Beyer, and Judy C. Shetler
  1995   Building cooperation in a competitive industry: SEMATECH and the semiconductor industry. *Academy of Management Journal* 38:113-151.
Cameron, K.S.
  1978   Measuring organizational effectiveness in institutions of higher education. *Administrative Science Quarterly* 28:482-495.
Cameron, Kim S., and Deborah R. Ettington
  1988   The conceptual foundations of organizational culture. Pp. 356-396 in *Higher Education: Handbook of Theory and Research.* New York: Agathon.
Cameron, Kim S., and Sarah J. Freeman
  1991   Cultural congruence, strength, and type: Relationships to effectiveness. Pp. 23-58 in *Research in Organizational Change and Development,* vol. 5. Greenwich, CT: JAI Press.
Cameron, K.S., and R.E. Quinn
  1996   *Diagnosing and Changing Organizational Culture.* San Francisco: Jossey-Bass.
Cameron, K.S., and D.O. Ulrich
  1989   Transformational leadership in colleges and universities. In *Higher Education: Handbook of Theory and Research,* vol. 2, J. Smart, ed. New York: Agathon.
Cameron, K.S., and D.A. Whetten
  1983   Models of the organizational life cycle. *Review of Higher Education* 6:269-299.
Cartwright, D.
  1968   The nature of group cohesiveness. In *Group Dynamics,* D. Cartwright and A. Zander, eds. New York: Harper and Row.
Chatov, Robert
  1973   The role of ideology in the American corporation. Pp. 50-75 in *The Corporate Dilemma: Traditional Values Versus Contemporary Problems,* Votaw, Dow, and S. Prakash Sethi, eds. Englewood Cliffs, NJ: Prentice-Hall.
Daft, Richard L., and Karl E. Weick
  1984   Toward a model of organizations as interpretation systems. *Academy of Management Review* 9:284-295.
Deal, T.E., and A.A. Kennedy
  1982   *Corporate Cultures: The Rites and Rituals of Corporate Life.* London: Penguin Books.
Denison, Daniel R.
  1990   *Corporate Culture and Organizational Effectiveness.* New York: John Wiley.
Druckman, D.
  1994   Nationalism, patriotism, and group loyalty: A social-psychological perspective. *Mershon International Studies Review* 38:43-68.

Dutton, J.E., and J.M. Dukerich
  1991 Keeping an eye on the mirror: Image and identity in organizational adaptation. *Academy of Management Journal* 34:517-554.
Dutton, Jane E., and Susan E. Jackson
  1987 Categorizing strategic issues: Links to organizational actions. *Academy of Management Review* 12:76-90.
Enz, Cathy A.
  1988 The role of value congruity in intraorganizational power. *Administrative Science Quarterly* 33:284-304.
Feldman, Martha S., and James G. March
  1981 Information in organizations as signal and symbol. *Administrative Science Quarterly* 26:171-184.
Festinger, L., H. Riecken, and K. Back
  1950 *Social Pressures in Informal Groups.* New York: Harper.
Fitzgerald, Thomas H.
  1988 Can change in organizational culture really be managed? *Organizational Dynamics* 17(Autumn):5-125.
Galbraith, J.R., and E.E. Lawler
  1993 *Organizing for the Future.* San Francisco: Jossey-Bass.
Georges, Robert, and Michael O. Jones
  1980 *People Studying People: The Human Element in Field Work.* Berkeley: University of California Press.
Goffman, E.
  1961 *Asylums: Essays on the Social Situation of Mental Patients and Other Inmates.* Chicago: Aldine.
Gregory, Kathleen L.
  1983 Native-view paradigms: Multiple cultures and culture conflicts in organizations. *Administrative Science Quarterly* 28:359-376.
Harris, Stanley, and Robert I. Sutton
  1986 Functions of parting ceremonies in dying organizations. *Academy of Management Journal* 29(1):5-30.
Hofstede, Geert
  1980 *Culture's Consequences: International Difference in Work-Related Values.* Beverly Hills, CA: Sage.
Hofstede, Geert, Bram Neuijeu, Denise Daval Ahayv, and Geert Sanders
  1990 Measuring organizational cultures: A qualitative and quantitative study across twenty cases. *Administrative Science Quarterly* 35:286-316.
Hoijberg, Robert, and Frank Petrock
  1993 On cultural change: Using the competing values framework to help leaders to a transformational strategy. *Human Resource Management* 32.
Hunt, James G.
  1991 *Leadership: A New Synthesis.* Newbury Park, CA: Sage Publications.
Jablin, Frederic M.
  1987 Organizational entry, assimilation, and exit. Pp. 679-740 in *Handbook of Organizational Communication: An Interdisciplinary Perspective,* Frederic M. Jablin, Linda L. Putman, Karlene H. Roberts, and Lyman W. Porter, eds. Newbury Park, CA: Sage Publications.
Jackall, R.
  1988 *Moral Mazes: The World of Corporate Management.* New York: Oxford University Press.
Janowitz, M.
  1971 *The Professional Soldier: A Social and Political Portrait.* New York: Free Press.

Jones, Gareth R.
1983 Psychological orientation and the process of organizational socialization: An interaction perspective. *Academy of Management Review* 8:464-474.
1986 Socialization tactics, self-efficacy, and newcomer adjustment to the organization. *Academy of Management Journal* 29:262-279.

Kan, Sergei
1989 *Symbolic Immortality*. Washington, DC: Smithsonian Institution Press.

Kopelman, Richard E., Arthur P. Brief, and Richard A. Guzzo
1990 The role of climate and culture in productivity. Pp. 282-318 in *Organizational Climate and Culture*, Benjamin Schneider, ed. San Francisco: Jossey-Bass.

Kunda, Gideon
1991 *Engineering Culture: Control and Commitment in a High Technology Corporation.* Philadelphia: Temple University Press.

Lord, R.G., and R.J. Foti
1986 Schema theories, information processing, and organizational behavior. Pp. 20-48 in *The Thinking Organization*, H.P. Sims, Jr., and D.A. Gioia, eds. San Francisco: Jossey-Bass.

Louis, Meryl R., Barry Z. Posner, and Gary N. Powell
1983 The availability of helpfulness of socialization practices. *Personnel Psychology* 36:857-866.

Lovell, J.P.
1979 *Neither Athens nor Sparta?: The American Service Academies in Transition.* Bloomington: Indiana University Press.

Martin, Joanne
1992 *Cultures in Organizations: Three Perspectives.* New York: Oxford University Press.

Martin, Joanne, Martha S. Feldman, Mary Jo Hatch, and Sim B. Sitkin
1983 The uniqueness paradox in organizational stories. *Administrative Science Quarterly* 28(September):438-452.

Martin, Joanne, Sim B. Sitkin, and Michael Boehm
1985 Founders and the elusiveness of a cultural legacy. Pp. 99-124 in *Organizational Culture*, Peter J. Frost et al., eds. Beverly Hills, CA: Sage Publications.

Martin, Joanne, and Melanie E. Powers
1983 Truth or corporate propaganda: The value of a good war story. Pp. 93-107 in *Managing Ambiguity and Change*, Louis R. Pondy, Richard Boland, Jr., and Howard Thomas, eds. New York: John Wiley.

Mason, Robert O., and Ian I. Mitroff
1973 A program of research management. *Management Science* 19:475-487.

Meyerson, Debra E.
1991 Acknowledging and uncovering ambiguities in cultures. Pp. 254-270 in *Reframing Organizational Culture*, Peter J. Frost et al., eds. Newbury Park, CA: Sage.

Miller, Vernon D., and Frederic M. Jablin
1991 Information seeking during organizational entry: Influences, tactics, and a model of the process. *Academy of Management Review* 16:92-120.

Mitroff, Ian I., and Ralph H. Kilmann
1976 Stories managers tell: A new tool for organizational problem solving. *Management Review* 64:18-28.

Morrison, Robert F.
1977 Career adaptivity: The effective adaptations of managers to changing role demands. *Journal of Applied Psychology* 62:549-558.

Nadler, David A., and Michael L. Tushman
1980 A congruence model for organizational assessment. In *Organizational Assessment: Perspectives on the Measurement of Organizational Behavior and the Quality of Working*

Life, Edward E. Lawler, David A. Nadler, and Cortland Camman, eds. New York: Wiley.

Oliver, Nick, and Barry Wilkinson
1988 *The Japanization of British Industry.* Oxford: Basil Blackwell.

O'Reilly, Charles
1983 Corporations, Cults, and Organizational Culture: Lessons from Silicon Valley Firms. Paper presented in the Academy of Management meetings, Dallas.
1989 Corporations, culture, and commitment: Motivation and social control in organizations. *California Management Review* 31(Summer):9-25.

Ott, J.S.
1989 *The Organizational Culture Perspective.* Pacific Grove, CA: Brooks/Cole.

Ouchi, William
1981 *Theory Z: How American Business Can Meet the Japanese Challenge.* Reading, MA: Addison-Wesley.

Ouchi, W.G., and J. Johnson
1978 Types of organizational control and their relationship to emotional well-being. *Administrative Science Quarterly* 23:293-317.

Pascale, R.T.
1990 *Managing on the Edge.* New York: Simon and Schuster.

Pascale, Richard T., and Anthony G. Athos
1981 *The Art of Japanese Management.* New York: Simon and Schuster.

Peters, Thomas J., and Robert H. Waterman
1982 *In Search of Excellence: Lessons from America's Best Run Companies.* New York: Harper and Row.

Quinn, R.E., and J. Rohrbaugh
1983 A spatial model of effectiveness criteria: Towards a competing values approach to organizational analysis. *Management Science* 29:363-377.

Quinn, Robert E., and Gretchen M. Spreitzer
1991 The psychometrics of the competing values culture instrument and an analysis of the impact of organizational culture on quality of life. Pp. 115-142 in *Research in Organizational Change and Development,* vol. 5. Greenwich, CT: JAI Press.

Rohlen, Thomas P.
1974 *For Harmony and Strength.* Berkeley: University of California Press.

Rousseau, Denise M.
1990 Assessing organizational culture: The case for multiple methods. Pp. 153-192 in *Organizational Climate and Culture,* Benjamin Schneider, ed. San Francisco: Jossey-Bass.

Roy, Donald
1960 Banana time: Job satisfaction and informal interaction. *Human Organization* 18:158-161.

Sathe, V.
1985 *Culture and Related Corporate Realities: Text, Cases, and Readings on Organizational Entry, Establishment and Change.* Homewood, IL: Irwin.

Schall, Maryan S.
1983 A communication-rules approach to organizational culture. *Administrative Science Quarterly* 28:557-581.

Schein, Edgar H.
1991 What is culture? Pp. 243-254 in *Reframing Organizational Cultures,* Peter J. Frost, Larry Moore, Meryl R. Louis, Craig C. Lundburg, and Joanne Martin, eds. Newbury Park, CA: Sage.
1992 *Organizational Culture and Leadership,* 2nd ed. San Francisco: Jossey-Bass.

Schneider, Benjamin, ed.
1990 *Organizational Climate and Culture.* San Francisco: Jossey-Bass.

Siehl, Caren, and Joanne Martin
1990 Organizational culture: A key to financial performance? Pp. 241-281 in *Organizational Climate and Culture,* Benjamin Schneider, ed. San Francisco: Jossey-Bass.

Smircich, Linda
1983 Concepts of culture and organizational analysis. *Administrative Science Quarterly* 18:339-358.

Smith, M. Brewster
1968 Toward a conception of the competent self. Pp. 271-320 in *Socialization and Society,* John A. Clausen, ed. Boston: Little, Brown.

Snyder, R.C.
1988 New for old: Changing the managerial culture of an aircraft factory. Pp. 191-208 in *Inside Organizations: Understanding the Human Dimension,* M.O. Jones, M.D. Moore, and R.C. Snyder, eds. Newbury Park, CA: Sage.

Sutton, Robert I., Seymour E. Harris, Carl Kaysen, and James Tobin
1956 *The American Business Creed.* Cambridge, MA: Harvard University Press.

Swidler, Ann
1986 Culture in action: Symbols and strategies. *American Sociological Review* 51:273-286.

Trice, Harrison M.
1991 Comments and discussion. Pp. 298-308 in *Reframing Organizational Culture,* Peter J. Frost et al., eds. Newbury Park, CA: Sage.
1993 *Occupational Subculture in the Workplace.* Ithaca, New York: ILR Press.

Trice, Harrison M., and Janice M. Beyer
1984 Studying organizational cultures through rites and ceremonials. *Academy of Management Review* 9(4):653-669.
1993 *The Cultures of Work Organizations.* Englewood Cliffs, NJ: Prentice-Hall.

Trice, Harrison M., and William Sonnenstuhl
1988 Drinking behavior and risk factors related to the workplace: Implications for research and prevention. *Journal of Applied Behavioral Science* 14(4):327-346.

Turner, Barry A.
1990 The rise of organizational symbolism. Pp. 83-96 in *The Theory and Philosophy of Organizations: Critical Issues and New Perspectives,* John Hassard and Pym Denies, eds. London: Routledge & Kegan Paul.

United States Military Academy
1993 *West Point 2002 and Beyond. Strategic Guidance for the United States Military Academy.* West Point, NY: United States Military Academy.

Van Maanen, John
1973 Observations on the making of policemen. *Human Organization* 32(Winter):407-417.
1975 Police socialization: A longitudinal examination of job attitudes in an urban police department. *Administrative Science Quarterly* 20:207-228.

Van Maanen, John, and Edgar H. Schein
1979 Toward a theory of organizational socialization. Pp. 209-264 in *Research in Organizational Behavior,* vol 1. Barry M. Staw, ed. Greenwich, CT: JAI.

Wanous, John P.
1980 *Organizational Entry: Recruitment, Selection, and Socialization of Newcomers.* Reading, MA: Addison-Wesley.

Weiss, Howard M.
1978 Social learning of work values in organizations. *Journal of Applied Psychology* 63:711-18.

Wilkins, Alan L.
1984 The creation of company cultures: The role of stories and human resources systems. *Human Resources Management* 23(Spring):41-60.
1990 *Developing Corporate Character: How to Successfully Change an Organization Without Destroying It.* San Francisco: Jossey-Bass.
Wilkins, Alan L., and William G. Ouchi
1983 Efficient cultures: Exploring the relationship between culture and organizational performance. *Administrative Science Quarterly* 28:468-481.
Williams, Robin M., Jr.
1970 *American Society*, 3rd ed. New York: Knopf.
Wilmer, W.W., A.J. Hardcastle, and D.M. Zell
1994 Cultural transportation at NUMMI. *Sloan Management Review* Fall:99-113.
Yeung, Arthur K.O., J. Wayne Brockbank, and David O. Ulrich
1991 Organizational culture and human resources practices: An empirical assessment. Pp. 59-81 in *Research in Organizational Change and Development*, vol. 5. Greenwich, CT: JAI Press.
Zald, Mayer N., and Michael A. Berger
1978 Social movements in organizations. *American Journal of Sociology* 83:823-861.
Zammuto, Raymond F., and Jack Y. Krakower
1991 Quantitative and qualitative studies of organizational culture. Pp. 83-114 in *Research in Organizational Change and Development*, vol. 5. Greenwich, CT: JAI Press.

CHAPTER 4
DEVELOPING LEADERS

Argyris, C.
1991 Teaching smart people how to learn. *Harvard Business Review* 69(3):99-109.
Avolio, B.J., and J.M. Howell
1992 The impact of leadership behavior and leader-follower personality match on satisfaction and unit performance. Pp. 225-235 in *Impact of Leadership,* K. Clark, M.B. Clark, and D.P. Campbell, eds. Greensboro, NC: Center for Creative Leadership.
Baldwin, T.T., and J.K. Ford
1988 Transfer of training: A review and directions for future research. *Personnel Psychology* 41:63-105.
Baldwin, T.T., R.J. Magjuka, and B.T. Loher
1991 The perils of participation: Effects of choice of training on trainee motivation and learning. *Personnel Psychology* 44:51-66.
Baldwin, T.T., and M.Y. Padgett
1993 Management development: A review and commentary. Pp. 35-85 in *International Review of Industrial-Organizational Psychology*, vol. 8, C.L. Cooper and I.T. Robertson, eds. New York: Wiley.
Bass, B.M.
1985 *Leadership and Performance Beyond Expectations.* New York: Free Press.
1990 *Handbook of Leadership: A Survey of Theory and Research.* New York: Free Press.
Bennis, W.G., and B. Nanus
1985 *Leaders: The Strategies for Taking Charge.* New York: Harper and Row.
Bernard, C.I.
1938 *The Functions of the Executive.* Cambridge, MA: Harvard University Press.
Blake, R.R., and J.S. Mouton
1982 Management by grid principles or situationalism: Which? *Group and Organization Studies* 7:207-210.

Boehm, V.R.
1985   Using assessment centers for management development—Five applications. *Journal of Management Development* 4(4):40-51.

Boyatzis, R.E.
1982   *The Competent Manager.* New York: John Wiley.

Bradford, D.L., and A.R. Cohen
1984   *Managing for Excellence: The Guide to Developing High Performance Organizations.* New York: John Wiley.

Bray, D.W., R.J. Campbell, and D.L. Grant
1974   *Formative Years in Business: A Long Term AT&T Study of Managerial Lives.* New York: John Wiley.

Bunker, K.W., and A.D. Webb
1992   *Learning How to Learn from Experience: Impact of Stress and Coping.* Technical Report #154. Greensboro, NC: Center for Creative Leadership.

Burke, M.J., and R.R. Day
1986   A cumulative study of the effectiveness of managerial training. *Journal of Applied Psychology* 71:232-246.

Burns, J.M.
1978   *Leadership.* New York: Harper and Row.

Campbell, J.P.
1988   Training design for performance improvement. Pp. 177-216 in *Productivity in Organizations*, J. P. Campbell, R. J. Campbell, and associates, eds. San Francisco: Jossey-Bass.

Campion, M.A., L.Cheraskin, and M.J. Stevens
1994   Career-related antecedents and outcomes of job rotation. *Academy of Management Journal* 37:1518-1542.

Carroll, S.J., Jr., and D.J. Gillen
1987   Are the classical management functions useful in describing managerial work? *Academy of Management Review* 12:38-51.

Chao, G.T., P.M. Walz, and P.D. Gardner
1992   Formal and informal mentorships: A comparison on mentoring functions contrasted with nonmentored counterparts. *Personnel Psychology* 45:619-636.

Conger, J.A.
1989   *The Charismatic Leader: Behind the Mystique of Exceptional Leadership.* San Francisco: Jossey-Bass.
1993   The brave new world of leadership training. *Organizational Dynamics* Winter:46-58.

Cotton, J.L., D.A. Vollrath, K.L. Froggatt, M.L. Lengneck-Hall, and K.R. Jennings
1988   Employee participation: Diverse forms and different outcomes. *Academy of Management Review* 13:8-22.

Daft, R.L., J. Sormunen, and D. Parks
1988   Chief executive scanning, environmental characteristics, and company performance: An empirical study. *Strategic Management Journal* 9:123-139.

Davies, J., and M. Easterby-Smith
1984   Learning and developing from managerial work experiences. *Journal of Management Studies* 2:169-183.

Dechant, K.
1990   Knowing how to learn: The neglected management ability. *Journal of Management Development* 9(4):40-49.
1994   Making the most of job assignments: An exercise in planning for learning. *Journal of Management Education* 18:198-211.

Dreher, G. F., and R.A. Ash
  1990   A comparative study of mentoring among men and women in managerial, professional, and technical positions. *Journal of Applied Psychology* 75:539-546.
Druckman, D., and R.A. Bjork, eds.
  1991   *In the Mind's Eye: Enhancing Human Performance.* Committee on Techniques for the Enhancement of Human Performance, National Research Council. Washington, DC: National Academy Press.
  1994   *Learning, Remembering, and Believing: Enhancing Human Performance.* Committee on Techniques for the Enhancement of Human Performance, National Research Council. Washington, DC: National Academy Press.
Engelbracht, A.S., and A.H. Fischer
  1995   The managerial performance implications of a developmental assessment center process. *Human Relations* 48:1-18.
Facteau, J.D., G.H. Dobbins, J.E.A. Russell, R.T. Ladd, and J.D. Kudisch
  1995   The influence of general perceptions of the training environment on pretraining motivation and perceived training transfer. *Journal of Management* 21:1-25.
Field, H., and S.G. Harris
  1991   Entry-level, fast-track management development programs: Developmental tactics and perceived program effectiveness. *Human Resource Planning* 14:261-273.
Fisher, B.M., and J.E. Edwards
  1988   Consideration and initiating structure and their relationships with leader effectiveness: A meta-analysis. *Proceedings of the Academy of Management* August:201-205.
Fleishman, E.A.
  1953   The description of supervisory behavior. *Personnel Psychology* 37:1-6.
Fleishman, E.A., E.F. Harris, and H.E. Burtt
  1955   *Leadership and Supervision in Industry.* Technical Report #33. Columbus: Bureau of Educational Research, Ohio State University.
Fletcher, C.
  1990   Candidates' reactions to assessment centres and their outcomes: A longitudinal study. *Journal of Occupational Psychology* 63:117-127.
Ford, J. K., M.A. Quinones, D.J. Sego, and J.S. Sorra
  1992   Factors affecting the opportunity to perform trained tasks on the job. *Personnel Psychology* 45:511-527.
Goodge, P.
  1991   Development centres: Guidelines for decision makers. *Journal of Management Development* 10(3):4-12.
Grinyer, P.H., D. Mayes, and P. McKiernan
  1990   The sharpbenders: Achieving a sustained improvement in performance. *Long Range Planning* 23:116-125.
Hall, D.T., and F.K. Foulkes
  1991   Senior executive development as a competitive advantage. *Advances in Applied Business Strategy* 2:183-203.
Hall, D.T., and K.W. Seibert
  1992   Strategic management development: Linking organizational strategy, succession planning, and managerial learning. Pp. 255-275 in *Career Development: Theory and Practice,* D. H. Montross and C. J. Shinkman, eds. Springfield, IL: Charles C. Thomas.
Halpin, A.W., and B.J. Winer
  1957   A factorial study of the leader behavior descriptions. Pp. 39-51 in *Leader Behavior: Its Description and Measurement,* R.M. Stogdill and A.E. Coons, eds. Columbus: Bureau of Business Research, Ohio State University.

Hand, H.H., M.D. Richards, and J.W. Slocum, Jr.
1973 Organizational climate and the effectiveness of a human relations program. *Academy of Management Journal* 16:185-195.

Hand, H., and J.W. Slocum
1972 A longitudinal study of the effect of a human relations training program on managerial effectiveness. *Journal of Applied Psychology* 56:412-418.

Hater, J.J., and B.M. Bass
1988 Superiors' evaluations and subordinates' perceptions of transformational and transactional leadership. *Journal of Applied Psychology* 73:695-702.

Hazucha, J.F., S.A. Hezlett, and R.J. Schneider
1993 The impact of 360-degree feedback on management skills development. *Human Resource Management* 32:325-351.

Hicks, W.D., and R.J. Klimoski
1987 Entry into training programs and its effects on training outcomes: A field experiment. *Academy of Management Journal* 30:542-552.

Hillman, L.W., D.R. Schwandt, and D.E. Bartz
1990 Enhancing staff member's performance through feedback and coaching. *Journal of Management Development* 9:20-27.

House, R.J., and T.R. Mitchell
1974 Path-goal theory of leadership. *Contemporary Business* 3(Fall):81-98.

House, R.J., W.D. Spangler, and J. Woycke
1991 Personality and charisma in the U.S. presidency: A psychological theory of leadership effectiveness. *Administrative Science Quarterly* 36:364-396.

Howard, A., and D.W. Bray
1988 *Managerial Lives in Transition: Advancing Age and Changing Times.* New York: Guilford Press.

Howell, J.M., and P. Frost
1989 A laboratory study of charismatic leadership. *Organizational Behavior and Human Decision Processes* 43:243-269.

Howell, J.M., and C.A. Higgins
1990 Leadership behaviors, influence tactics, and career experiences of champions of technological innovation. *Leadership Quarterly* 1:249-264.

Howell, W.C., and N.J. Cooke
1989 Training the human information processor: A review of cognitive models. Pp. 121-182 in *Training and Development in Organizations,* I.L. Goldstein, ed. San Francisco: Jossey-Bass.

Huczynski, A.A., and J.W. Lewis
1980 An empirical study into the learning transfer process in management training. *Journal of Management Studies* 17:227-240.

Hunt, D.M., and C. Michael
1983 Mentorship: A career training and development tool. *Academy of Management Review* 8:475-485.

Hunt, J.G.
1991 *Leadership: A New Synthesis.* Newbury Park, CA: Sage.

Iles, P., I. Robertson, and U. Rout
1989 Assessment-based development centers. *Journal of Managerial Psychology* 4(3):11-16.

Ilgen, D.R., and M.S. Youtz
1986 Factors influencing the evaluation and development of minorities. Pp. 307-337 in *Research in Personnel and Human Resource Management,* vol. 4, K. Rowland and G. Ferris, eds. Greenwich, CT: JAI Press.

Indvik, J.
1986 Path-goal theory of leadership: A meta-analysis. Pp. 189-192 in *Proceedings of the Academy of Management Meetings.*

Jacobs, T.O., and E. Jaques
1987 Leadership in complex systems. Pp. 7-65 in *Human Productivity Enhancement: Organizations, Personnel, and Decision Making,* vol. 2. J. Zeidner, ed. New York: Praeger.
1990 Military executive leadership. Pp. 281-295 in *Measures of Leadership,* K.E. Clark and M.B. Clark, eds. West Orange, NJ: Leadership Library of America.

Jaques, E.
1989 *Requisite Organization.* Arlington, VA: Cason Hall.

Jones, R.G., and M.D. Whitmore
1992 When Will Developmental Feedback from an Assessment Center Make a Difference in People's Careers? Paper presented at the Annual Meeting of the Society for Industrial and Organizational Psychology, Montreal.

Kanter, R.M.
1983 *The Change Masters.* New York: Simon and Schuster.

Kaplan, R.E.
1984 Trade routes: The manager's network of relationships. *Organizational Dynamics* Spring:37-52.
1990 Character change in executives as reform in the pursuit of self-worth. *Journal of Applied Behavioral Science* 26(4):461-481.
1993 360-degree feedback PLUS: Boosting the power of co-worker ratings for executives. *Human Resource Management* 32(2/3):299-314.

Kaplan, R.E., M.M. Lombardo, and M.S. Mazique
1985 A mirror for managers: Using simulation to develop management teams. *Journal of Applied Behavioral Science* 21:241-253.

Katz, D., and R.L. Kahn
1978 *The Social Psychology of Organizations,* 2nd ed. New York: John Wiley.

Katz, R.L.
1955 Skills of an effective administrator. *Harvard Business Review* January-February:33-42.

Kelleher, D., P. Finestone, and A. Lowy
1986 Managerial learning: First notes from an unstudied frontier. *Group and Organization Studies* 11:169-202.

Kerr, S., and J.M. Jermier
1978 Substitutes for leadership: Their meaning and measurement. *Organizational Behavior and Human Performance* 22:375-403.

Keys, B., and J. Wolfe
1990 The role of management games and simulation in education and research. *Journal of Management* 16:307-336.

Kim, H., and G. Yukl
1995 Relationships of self-reported and subordinate-reported leadership behaviors to managerial effectiveness and advancement. *Leadership Quarterly* 6:361-377.

Komaki, J.
1986 Toward effective supervision: An operant analysis and comparison of managers at work. *Journal of Applied Psychology* 71:270-278.

Kotter, J.P.
1982 *The General Managers.* New York: Free Press.

Kouzes, J.M., and B.Z. Posner
1987 *The Leadership Challenge: How to Get Extraordinary Things Done in Organizations.* San Francisco: Jossey-Bass.

Kozlowski, S.W.J., and B.M. Hults
   1987   An exploration of climates for technical updating and performance. *Personnel Psychology* 40:539-564.
Kram, K.E.
   1985   *Mentoring at Work: Developmental Relationships in Organizational Life.* Glenview, IL: Scott Foresman.
Kram, K.E., and D.T. Hall
   1989   Mentoring as an antidote to stress during corporate trauma. *Human Resource Management* 28:493-510.
Kram, K.E., and L.A. Isabella
   1985   Mentoring alternatives: The role of peer relationships in career development. *Academy of Management Journal* 28:110-132.
Kraut, A.I., P.R. Pedigo, D.D. McKenna, and M.D. Dunnette
   1989   The role of the manager: What's really important in different management jobs. *Academy of Management Executive* 3(4):286-293.
Larson, J.R., and C. Callahan
   1990   Performance monitoring: how it affects productivity. *Journal of Applied Psychology* 75:530-538.
Latham, G.P.
   1988   Human resource training and development. *Annual Review of Psychology* 39:545-582.
   1989   Behavior approaches to the training and learning process. Pp. 256-295 in *Training and Development in Organizations,* I.L. Goldstein, ed. San Francisco: Jossey-Bass.
Latham, G.P., and L. Saari
   1979   The application of social learning theory to training supervisors through behavioral modeling. *Journal of Applied Psychology* 64:239-246.
Leana, C.R.
   1986   Predictors and consequences of delegation. *Academy of Management Journal* 29:754-774.
Leana, C.R., E.A. Locke, and D.M. Schweiger
   1990   Fact and fiction in analyzing research on participative decision making: A critique of Cotton, Vollrath, Froggatt, Legnick-Hall, and Jennings. *Academy of Management Review* 15:137-146.
Lindsey, E., V. Homes, and M.W. McCall, Jr.
   1987   *Key Events in Executive Lives.* Technical Report #32. Greensboro, NC: Center For Creative Leadership.
London, M.
   1989   *Managing the Training Enterprise.* San Francisco: Jossey-Bass.
London, M., and E.M. Mone
   1987   *Career Management and Survival in the Workplace.* San Francisco: Jossey-Bass.
London, M., A.J. Wohler, and P. Gallagher
   1990   A feedback approach to management development. *Journal of Management Development* 9(6):17-31.
Luthans, F., S.A. Rosenkrantz, and H.W. Hennessey
   1985   What do successful managers really do? An observational study of managerial activities. *Journal of Applied Behavioral Science* 21:255-270.
Mann, F.C.
   1965   Toward an understanding of the leadership role in formal organization. In *Leadership and Productivity,* R. Dubin, G.C. Homans, F.C. Mann, and D.C. Miller, eds. San Francisco: Chandler.

Margerison, C.J.
1988 Action learning and excellence in management development. *Journal of Management Development* 7:43-54.
Marson, P.P., and C.D. Bruff
1992 The impact of classroom leadership training on managerial/supervisory job performance. In *Impact of Leadership,* K.E. Clark, M.B. Clark, and D.P. Campbell, eds. Greensboro, NC: Center for Creative Leadership.
Mayer, S.J., and J.S. Russell
1987 Behavior modeling training in organizations: Concerns and conclusions. *Journal of Management* 13:21-40.
McCall, M.
1992 Executive development as a business strategy. *The Journal of Business Strategy* 3 (Jan./Feb.):25-31.
1994 Identifying leadership potential in future international executives: Developing a concept. *Consulting Psychology Journal* 46(1):49-63.
McCall, M.W., Jr., and M.M. Lombardo
1983 *Off the Track: Why and How Successful Executives Get Derailed.* Technical Report #21. Greensboro, NC: Center for Creative Leadership.
McCall, M.W., Jr., M.M. Lombardo, and A. Morrison
1988 *The Lessons of Experience.* Lexington, MA: Lexington Books.
McCall, M.W., Jr., A.M. Morrison, and R.L. Hannan
1978 *Studies of Managerial Work: Results and Methods.* Technical Report #9. Greensboro, NC: Center for Creative Leadership.
McCauley, C.D.
1986 *Developmental Experiences in Managerial Work* Technical Report #26. Greensboro, NC: Center for Creative Leadership.
McCauley, C.D., L.J. Eastman, and P.J. Ohlott
1995 Linking management selection and development through stretch assignments. *Human Resource Management* 34(1):93-115.
McCauley, C.D., and M.W. Hughes-James
1994 *An Evaluation of the Outcomes of a Leadership Development Program.* Greensboro, NC: Center for Creative Leadership.
McLennan, K.
1967 The manager and his job skills. *Academy of Management Journal* 3:235-245.
Meindl, J.R.
1990 On leadership: An alternative to the conventional wisdom. In *Research in Organizational Behavior,* B.M. Staw and L.L. Cummings, eds. Greenwich, CT: JAI Press.
Michael, J., and G. Yukl
1993 Managerial level and subunit function as determinants of networking behavior in organizations. *Group and Organizational Management* 18:328-351.
Miller, D., and J. Toulouse
1986 Chief executive personality and corporate strategy and structure in small firms. *Management Science* 32:1389-1409.
Miller, K.I., and P.R. Monge
1986 Participation, satisfaction, and productivity: A meta-analytic review. *Academy of Management Journal* 29:727-753.
Morse, J.J., and F.R. Wagner
1978 Measuring the process of managerial effectiveness. *Academy of Management Journal* 21:23-35.
Mulder, M., J.R. Ritsema van Eck, and R.D. de Jong
1970 An organization in crisis and noncrisis conditions. *Human Relations* 24:19-41.

Munchus, G., III, and B. McArthur
  1991 Revisiting the historical use of the assessment center in management selection and development. *Journal of Management Development* 10(1):5-13.
Nemeroff, W., and J. Cosentino
  1979 Utilizing feedback and goal setting to increase performance appraisal interviewer skills of managers. *Academy of Management Journal* 22:566-576.
Noe, R.A.
  1988 An investigation of the determinants of successful assigned mentoring relationships. *Personnel Psychology* 41:457-479.
  1991 Mentoring relationships for employee development. Pp. 475-482 in *Applying Psychology in Business: The Manager's Handbook*, J.W. Jones, B.D. Steffy, and D.W. Bray, eds. Lexington, MA: Lexington Press.
Noe, R.A., and J.K. Ford
  1992 Emerging issues and new directions for training research. In *Research in Personnel and Human Resource Management*, K. Rowland and G. Ferris, eds. Greenwich, CT: JAI Press.
Noe, R.A., and N. Schmitt
  1986 The influence of trainee attitudes on training effectiveness: Test of a model. *Personnel Psychology* 39:497-523.
Ohlott, P.J., M.N. Ruderman, and C.D. McCauley
  1994 Gender differences in manager's developmental job experience. *Academy of Management Journal* 37:46-67.
Papa, M.J., and E.E. Graham
  1991 The impact of diagnosing skill deficiencies and assessment-based communication training on managerial performance. *Communication Education* 40:368-384.
Pavett, C., and A. Lau
  1983 Managerial work: The influence of hierarchical level and functional specialty. *Academy of Management Journal* 26:170-177.
Peters, T.J., and N. Austin
  1985 *A Passion for Excellence: The Leadership Difference.* New York: Random House.
Podsakoff, P.M., S.B. MacKenzie, R.H. Morrman, and R. Fetter
  1990 Transformational leaders behaviors and their effects on follower's trust in leader satisfaction and organizational citizenship behaviors. *Leadership Quarterly* 1:107-142.
Podsakoff, P.M., and W.D. Todor
  1985 Relationships between leader reward and punishment behavior and group processes and productivity. *Journal of Management* 11:55-73.
Podsakoff, P.M., W.D. Todor, R.A. Grover, and V.L. Huber
  1984 Situational moderators of leader reward and punishment behavior: Fact or fiction? *Organizational Behavior and Human Performance* 34:21-63.
Porras, J.I., and B. Anderson
  1981 Improving managerial effectiveness through modeling-based training. *Organizational Dynamics* Spring:60-77.
Prideaux, G., and J.E. Ford
  1988 Management development: Competencies, teams, learning contracts, and work experience based learning. *Journal of Management Development* 7:13-21.
Ragins, B.R., and J.L. Cotton
  1991 Easier said than done: Gender differences in perceived barriers to gaining a mentor. *Academy of Management Journal* 34:939-951.
  1993 Gender and willingness to mentor in organizations. *Journal of Management* 19:97-111.

Ragins, B.R., and D.B. McFarlin
  1990 Perceptions of mentoring roles in cross-gender mentoring relationships. *Journal of Vocational Behavior* 37:321-339.
Rayner, T., and P. Goodge
  1988 New techniques in assessment centres: LRT's experience. *Journal of Management Development* 7(4):21-30.
Revans, R.W.
  1982 *The Origin and Growth of Action Learning.* Hunt, England: Chatwell-Bratt.
Robertson, I.T.
  1990 Behavioral modeling: Its record and potential in training and development. *British Journal of Management* 1:117-125.
Rouiller, J.S., and I.L. Goldstein
  1993 The relationship between organizational transfer climate and positive transfer of training. *Human Resource Development Quarterly* 4:377-390.
Scandura, T.A.
  1992 Mentorship and career mobility: An empirical investigation. *Journal of Organizational Behavior* 13:169-174.
Schein, E.H.
  1992 *Organizational Culture and Leadership,* 2nd ed. San Francisco: Jossey-Bass.
Segal, D.
  1992 Environmental challenges for strategic managers. Pp. 29-44 in *Strategic Leadership: A Multiorganizational-Level Perspective,* R.L. Phillips and J.G. Hunt, eds. Westport, CT: Quorum Books.
Seltzer, J., and B.M. Bass
  1990 Transformational leadership: Beyond initiation and consideration. *Journal of Management* 16:693-703.
Selznick, P.
  1957 *Leadership in Administration: A Sociological Interpretation.* Evanston, IL: Row, Peterson.
Shamir, B., R.J. House, and M.B. Arthur
  1993 The motivational effects of charismatic leadership: A self-concept based theory. *Organization Science* 4:1-17.
Shipper, F., and C.L. Wilson
  1992 The impact of managerial behaviors on group performance, stress and commitment. In *Impact of Leadership,* M.B. Clark and D.P. Campbell, eds. Greensboro, NC: Center for Creative Leadership.
Stewart, R.
  1982 *Choices for the Manager: A Guide to Understanding Managerial Work.* Englewood Cliffs, NJ: Prentice-Hall.
Tannenbaum, S.I., and G. Yukl
  1992 Training and development in work organizations. *Annual Review of Psychology* 43:399-441.
Tetrault, L.A., C.A. Schriesheim, and L.L. Neider
  1988 Leadership training interventions: A review. *Organizational Development Journal* 6(3):77-83.
Thomas, D.A.
  1990 The impact of race on manager's experiences of developmental relationships (mentoring and sponsorship): An intraorganizational study. *Journal of Organizational Behavior* 11:479-492.
Thornton, G.C., and J.N. Cleveland
  1990 Developing managerial talent through simulation. *American Psychologist* 45:190-199.

Tichy, N.M., and M.A. Devanna
1986   *The Transformational Leader.* New York: John Wiley.
Tracey, B., S.I. Tannenbaum, and M.J. Kavanagh
1995   Applying trained skills on the job: The importance of the work environment. *Journal of Applied Psychology* 80:239-252.
Turban, D.B., and T.W. Dougherty
1994   Role of protégé personality in receipt of mentoring and career success. *Academy of Management Journal* 37:688-702.
Valerio, A.M.
1990   A study of the developmental experiences of managers. Pp. 521-534 in *Measures of Leadership,* K. E. Clark and M. B. Clark, eds. West Orange, NJ: Leadership Library of America.
Van Velsor, E., E. Ruderman, and A.D. Phillips
1989   The lessons of the looking glass. *Leadership and Organizational Development Journal* 10:27-31.
Vroom, V.H., and A.G. Jago
1988   *The New Leadership: Managing Participation in Organizations.* Englewood Cliffs, NJ: Prentice-Hall.
Vroom, V.H., and P.W. Yetton
1973   *Leadership and Decision Making.* Pittsburgh: University of Pittsburgh Press.
Wagner, J.A., and R.Z. Gooding
1987   Shared influence and organizational behavior: A meta-analysis of situational variables expected to moderate participation-outcome relationships. *Academy of Management Journal* 30:524-541.
Waldman, D.A., B.M. Bass, and W.O. Einstein
1987   Effort, performance, and transformational leadership in industrial and military service. *Journal of Occupational Psychology* 60:1-10.
White, R.P.
1992   Job as classroom: Using assignments to leverage development. Pp. 190-206 in D.H. Montross and J. Christopher, eds., *Career Development: Theory and Practice.* Springfield, IL: Charles C. Thomas.
Whitely, W.T., and P. Coetsier
1993   The relationship of career mentoring to early career outcomes. *Organization Studies* 14(3):419-441.
Wikoff, M., D.C. Anderson, and C.R. Crowell
1983   Behavior management in a factory setting: Increasing work efficiency. *Journal of Organizational Behavior Management* 4:97-128.
Wilson, C.L., D. O'Hare, and F. Shipper
1990   Task cycle theory: The processes of influence. Pp. 185-204 in K.E. Clark and M.B. Clark, eds., *Measures of Leadership.* West Orange, NJ: Leadership Library of America.
Winter, D.G.
1979   *Navy Leadership and Management Competencies: Convergence Among Tests, Interviews, and Performance Ratings.* Boston: McBer.
Wofford, J.C., and V.L. Goodwin
1994   A cognitive interpretation of transactional and transformational leadership theories. *Leadership Quarterly* 5:162-186.
Wofford, J.C., and L.Z. Liska
1993   Path-goal theories of leadership: A meta-analysis. *Journal of Management* 19:857-876.
Wolfe, J., and C.R. Roberts
1993   A further study of the external validity of business games: Five-year peer group indicators. *Simulation and Gaming* 24(1):21-33.

Yammarino, F.J., and B.M. Bass
1990   Long-term forecasting of transformational leadership and its effects among naval officers. Pp. 151-170 in *Measures of Leadership,* K.E. Clark and M.B. Clark, eds. West Orange, NJ: Leadership Library of America.

Yukl, G.
1981   *Leadership in Organizations.* Englewood Cliffs, NJ: Prentice-Hall.
1994   *Leadership in Organizations,* 2nd ed. Englewood Cliffs, NJ: Prentice-Hall.

Yukl, G., and D. Van Fleet
1982   Cross-situational, multi-method research on military leader effectiveness. *Organizational Behavior and Human Performance* 30:87-108.

Zey, M.G.
1988   A mentor for all reasons. *Personnel Journal* January:46-51.

CHAPTER 5
INTERORGANIZATIONAL RELATIONS

Adams, J.S.
1976   The structure and dynamics of behavior in organizational boundary roles. In *Handbook of Industrial and Organizational Psychology.* M.D. Dunnette, ed. Chicago: Rand McNally.

Alderfer, C.P.
1977   Group and intergroup relations. In *Improving Life at Work,* J.R. Hackman and J.L. Suttle, eds. Santa Monica, CA: Goodyear.

Aldrich, H., and D. Whetten
1981   Organization sets, action sets, and networks: Making the most of simplicity. In *Handbook of Organizational Design,* P.C. Nystrom and W. Starbuck, eds. New York: Oxford University Press.

Auster, E.R.
1994   Macro and strategic perspectives on interorganizational linkages: A comparative analysis and review with suggestions for reorientation. *Advances in Strategic Management* 10B:3-40.

Barley, S.R., J. Freeman, and R.C. Hybel
1992   Strategic alliances in commercial biotechnology. In *Networks and Organizations: Structure, Form and Action,* N. Nohria and R. Eccles, eds. Boston: Harvard Business School Press.

Biggart, Nicole Woolsey, and Gary Hamilton
1992   On the limits of a firm-based theory to explain business networks: The western bias of neoclassical economics. Pp. 471-490 in *Networks and Organization: Structure, Form and Action,* Nitin Nohria and Robert G. Eccles, eds. Boston MA: Harvard Business School Press.

Blau, P., and R.W. Scott
1962   *Formal Organizations.* San Francisco: Chandler.

Bleeke, J., and D. Ernst
1995   Is your strategic alliance really a sale? *Harvard Business Review* 73(1):97-105.

Bleeke, J., and D. Ernst, eds.
1993   *Collaborating to Compete: Using Strategic Alliances and Acquisitions in the Global Marketplace.* New York: Wiley.

Bontempo, R.
1991   Behavioral Decision Theory and the Negotiation Process: Effects of Agenda and Frame. Doctoral dissertation, University of Illinois.

Boulding, K.E.
1956 General systems theory: The skeleton of science. *Management Science* 1:197-208
Brewer, M.B.
1968 Determinants of social distance among East African tribal groups. *Journal of Personality and Social Psychology* 10:279-289.
Burke, W.W., and P. Jackson
1991 Making the SmithKline Beecham merger work. *Human Resource Management* 30:69-87.
Burke, W.W., and G. Litwin
1992 A causal model of organization performance and change. *Journal of Management* 18(3):532-545.
Caves, R.
1982 *American Industry: The Social Structure of Competition.* Cambridge, MA: Harvard University Press.
Druckman, D.
1968 Ethnocentrism in the inter-nation simulation. *Journal of Conflict Resolution* 12:45-68.
1977 Boundary role conflict: Negotiation as dual responsiveness. *Journal of Conflict Resolution* 21:639-662.
1994 Nationalism, patriotism, and group loyalty: A social psychological perspective. *Mershon International Studies Review* 38:43-68.
Druckman, D., and P.T. Hopmann
1989 Behavioral aspects of mutual security negotiations. In *Behavior, Society, and Nuclear War,* Volume I, P. Tetloch et al., eds. New York: Oxford University Press.
Fedor, K.J., and W.B. Werther
1995 Making sense of cultural factors in international alliances. *Organizational Dynamics* 23(4):33-48.
Fishbein, M.
1963 The perception of non-members: A test of Merton's reference group theory. *Sociometry* 26:271-286.
Fligstein, N.
1990 *The Transformation of Corporate Culture.* Cambridge, MA: Harvard University Press.
Flippen, A.R., H.A. Hornstein, W.E. Siegal, and E.A. Weitzman
1995 A Comparison of Similarity and Interdependence as Triggers for Ingroup Formation. Unpublished paper, Teacher's College, Columbia University.
Galasckiewicz, J.
1979 *Exchange Networks and Community Politics.* Beverly Hills, CA: Sage.
Gerybadze, A.
1994 *Strategic Alliances and Process Redesign: Effective Management and Restructuring of Cooperative Projects and Networks.* Berlin: Walter de Gruyter.
Gomes-Casseres, B.
1988 Joint venture cycles: The evolution of ownership strategies of US MNEs, 1945-1975. In F.J. Contractor and P. Lorange, eds., *Strategies in International Business.* Lexington, MA: D.C. Heath.
Haas, Ernst
1980 Why collaborate?: Issue linkage and International regimes. *World Politics* 32:357-405.
Harrigan, K.R.
1985 *Strategies for Joint Ventures.* Lexington, MA: D.C. Heath.
1986 *Managing for Joint Venture Success.* Lexington, MA: Lexington Books.
Haspeslgh, P.C., and D.B. Jemison
1991 *Managing Acquisitions.* New York: Free Press.

Haunschild, P.R., R.L. Moreland, and A.J. Murrell
1994   Sources of resistance to mergers between groups. *Journal of Applied Social Psychology* 24(13):1150-1178.
Hirsch, P.
1972   Processing fashions and fads: An organization-set analysis of cultural industry systems. *American Journal of Sociology* 77:639-659.
1975   Organizational effectiveness and the institutional environment. *Administrative Science Quarterly* 20:327-344.
Kahn, R.L.
1990   Organizational theory and international relations: Mutually informing paradigms. In *Organizations and Nation-States: New Perspectives on Cooperation,* R.L. Kahn and M.N. Zald, eds. San Francisco: Jossey-Bass.
Kahn, Robert L., and Mayer N. Zald
1990   *Organizations and Nation-States: New Perspectives on Conflicts and Cooperation.* San Francisco: Jossey-Bass.
Kanter, R.M.
1989   Becoming PALS: Pooling, allying, and linking across companies. *The Academy of Management Executive* 3:183-193.
1994   Collaborative advantage: The art of alliances. *Harvard Business Review* 72(4):96-108.
Knoke, D., and D.L. Rogers
1979   A block-model analysis of interorganizational networks. *Sociology and Social Research* 64:28-52.
Kotter, J.P., and J.L. Heskett
1992   *Corporate Culture and Performance.* New York: Free Press.
Krasner, S., ed.
1982   *International Regimes.* Ithaca, NY: Cornell University Press.
Kratochwil, Friedrich, and John Ruggie
1989   International organization: The state of the art. Pp. 17-27 in *The Politics of International Organizations: Patterns and Insights,* Paul F. Diehl, ed. Pacific Grove, CA: Brooks/Cole.
Kuman, S., and H. Rosovsky, eds.
1992   *Cultural and Social Dynamics,* vol. 3. Stanford, CA: Stanford University Press.
Laumann, E.O., and F.U. Papi
1976   *Networks of Collective Action.* New York: Academic Press.
Levine, R.A., and D.T. Campbell
1972   *Ethnocentrism.* New York: Wiley.
Mayer, Peter, Volker Rittberger, and Michael Zurn
1993   Regime theory: State of the art and perspectives. Pp. 391-430 in *Regime Theory and International Relations,* Volcker Rittberger, ed. Oxford: Clarendon Press.
Miles, R., and K.S. Cameron
1982   *Coffin Nails and Corporate Strategies.* Englewood Cliffs, NJ: Prentice-Hall.
Mizruchi, M., and M. Schwartz, eds.
1986   *The Structural Analysis of Business.* Cambridge, England: Cambridge University Press.
Nisbett, R., and L. Ross
1980   *Human Inference: Strategies and Shortcomings of Social Adjustment.* Englewood Cliffs, NJ: Prentice-Hall.
Nohria, N., and R. Eccles, eds.
1992   *Networks and Organizations: Structure, Form and Action.* Boston: Harvard Business School Press.

Oliver, C.
1990 Determinants of interorganizational relationships: Integration and future directions. *Academy of Management Review* 15(2):241-265.

Ouchi, W.G., and M.K. Bolton
1988 The logic of joint research and development. *California Management Review* 30:9-33.

Palmer, D.R.
1983 Broken ties: Interlocking directorates and intercorporate coordination. *Administrative Science Quarterly* 28:40-55.

Paré, T.P.
1994 The new merger boom. *Fortune* 130(11):95-106.

Perrow, C.
1992 *Complex Organizations: A Critical Essay.* Glenview, IL: Scott Foresman.

Pfeffer, J., and P. Nowak
1976 Joint ventures and interorganizational interdependence. *Administrative Science Quarterly* 11:398-418.

Pfeffer, J., and G.R. Salancik
1978 *The External Control of Organizations.* New York: Harper and Row.

Porter, M.E.
1980 *Competitive Strategy.* New York: Free Press.
1990 *The Competitive Advantage of Nations.* New York: Free Press.

Porter, M.E., and M. Fuller
1986 Coalitions and global strategy. In M.E. Porter, ed., *Competition in Global Industries.* Boston: Harvard Business School Press.

Rice, A.K.
1969 Individual, group and intergroup processes. *Human Relations* 22:565-584.

Sankar, C.S., W.R. Boulton, N.W. Davidson, and C.A. Snyder, with R.W. Usery
1995 Building a world-class alliance: The universal card—TSYS case. *Academy of Management Executive* 9:20-29.

Scherer, F.M.
1980 *Industrial Market Structure and Economic Performance.* Chicago: Rand McNally.

Schwenk, C.R.
1994 Commentary: Macro and strategic perspectives on interorganizational linkages. *Advances in Strategic Management* 10B:41-46.

Scott, W.R.
1987 *Organizations: Rational, Natural, and Open Systems.* Englewood Cliffs, NJ: Prentice-Hall.

Singer, J.E., L.S. Radloff, and D.M. Wark
1963 Renegades, heretics, and changes in sentiment. *Sociometry* 26:178-189.

Smith, K.K., and D.N. Berg
1987 *Paradoxes of Group Life.* San Francisco: Jossey-Bass.

Strange, S.
1989 Cave Hic Dragones: A critique of regime analysis. Pp. 51-65 in *The Politics of International Organizations: Patterns and Insights*, Paul F. Diehl, ed. Pacific Grove, CA: Brooks/Cole.

Tajfel, H.
1981 *Human Groups and Social Categories: Studies in Social Psychology.* Cambridge, England: Cambridge University Press.
1982 Social psychology of intergroup relations. *Annual Review of Psychology* 33:1-39.

Wallis, A.D.
1994 Value barriers to coordination of human services networks. In *Proceedings of the Annual Meeting of the Association of Researchers in Non-Profit Organizations and Voluntary Action* (ARNOVA).

Walton, R.E., and R.B. McKersie
1965 *A Behavioral Theory of Labor Negotiations.* New York: McGraw-Hill.
Warren, R.L.
1967 The interorganizational field as a focus for investigation. *Administrative Science Quarterly* 12:396-419.
Wilder, D.A.
1986 Social categorization: Implications for creation and reduction of intergroup bias. In L. Berkowitz, ed., *Advances in Experimental Social Psychology* 19:291-355.
Williamson, O.
1992 Markets, hierarchies, and the modern corporation: An unfolding perspective. *Journal of Economic Behavior and Organization* 17:335-352.
Yoshino, M.Y., and U.S. Rangan
1995 *Strategic Alliances: An Entrepreneurial Approach to Globalization.* Boston: Harvard Business School Press.
Young, Oran
1989 The politics of international regime formation: Managing natural resources and the environment. *International Organization* 43:349-375.

CHAPTER 6
NEW MILITARY MISSIONS

Beigbeder, Y.
1994 *International Monitoring of Plebiscites, Referenda, and National Elections.* Dordrecht: Martinus Nijhoff.
Boutros-Ghali, B.
1992 *An Agenda for Peace.* New York: United Nations.
Cox, D.
1993 *"An Agenda for Peace" and the Future of Peacekeeping.* Report of the Mobonk Mountain House Workshop. Ottawa: Canadian Center for Global Security.
Cuny, Frederick
1991 Dilemmas of military involvement in humanitarian relief. Pp. 52-81 in *Soldiers, Peacekeepers, and Disasters,* L. Gordenker and T. Weiss, eds. New York: St. Martin's Press.
Diehl, P.
1994 *International Peacekeeping.* Baltimore, MD: Johns Hopkins University Press.
Diehl, P., and C. Kumar
1991 Mutual benefits from international intervention: New roles for UN peacekeeping forces. *Bulletin of Peace Proposals* 22:369-375.
Downs, G., ed.
1994 *Collective Security Beyond the Cold War.* Ann Arbor: University of Michigan Press.
Goodman, L.A., and W.H. Kruskal
1954 Measures of association for cross classification. *Journal of the American Statistical Association* 49:732-764.
Gordenker, L., and T. Weiss, eds.
1991 *Soldiers, Peacekeepers, and Disasters.* New York: St. Martin's Press.
Jurado, S., and P. Diehl
1994 United Nations peacekeeping and arms control verification. *Contemporary Security Policy* 15:38-54.
Krepon, M., and J. Tracey
1990 Open skies and UN peace-keeping. *Survival* 32:251-263.

Kruskal, J.B., and M. Wish
    1990 *Multidimensional Scaling.* University paper series on Quantitative Applications in the
          Social Sciences, 07-011. Beverly Hills: Sage.
Kumar, C.
    1995 When Atlas Did Not Shrug: Reconstructing Failed States in an Era of Retrenchment.
          Unpublished paper, International Peace Academy, New York.
Mackinlay, J.
    1990 Powerful peace-keepers. *Survival* 32:241-250.
Mackinlay, J., and J. Chopra
    1992 Second generation multinational operations. *Washington Quarterly* 15:113-134.
Mandell, B.
    1987 *The Sinai Experience: Lessons in Multimethod Arms Control Verification and Risk
          Management.* Ottawa: Department of External Affairs.
McCalla, R.
    1994 Collective Conflict Management, the US Armed Forces, and the Post-Cold War World.
          Unpublished paper, University of Wisconsin-Madison.
Minear, L., and T. Weiss
    1993 *Humanitarian Action in Times of War: A Handbook for Practitioners.* Boulder, CO:
          Lynne Rienner Publications.
Natsios, A.
    1994 Food through force: Humanitarian intervention and US policy. *Washington Quarterly*
          17:129-144.
Nunn, S.
    1993 *Domestic Missions for the Armed Forces.* Fourth Annual Conference of Strategy, U.S.
          Army War College. Carlisle Barracks, PA: Strategic Studies Institute.
Rikhye, I.J.
    1991 The future of peacekeeping. Pp. 171-199 in I.J. Rikhye and K. Skjaelsbaek, eds., *The
          United Nations and Peacekeeping: Results, Limitations, and Prospects—The Lessons
          of 40 Years Experience.* New York: St. Martin's Press.
Thurman, E.
    1992 Shaping an Army for peace, crisis, and war. *Military Review* April:27-35.
Urquhart, B.
    1990 Beyond the sheriff's posse. *Survival* 32:196-205.
U.S. Department of the Army
    1994 *FM 100-23: Peace Operations.* Washington, DC: U.S. Department of the Army.
U.S. President, The White House
    1992 *National Drug Control Strategy: A Nation Responds to Drug Use.* Washington, DC:
          U.S. Government Printing Office.
Wainhouse, D.
    1966 *International Peace Observation.* Baltimore, MD: Johns Hopkins University Press.
Walton, R.E., and R.B. McKersie
    1965 *A Behavioral Theory of Labor Negotiations: An Analysis of a Social Interaction Sys-
          tem.* New York: McGraw-Hill.

CHAPTER 7
CONFLICT MANAGEMENT TRAINING FOR
CHANGING MISSIONS

Abizaid, J.P.
    1993 Lessons for peackeepers. *Military Review* March:11-19.

Albin, C.
  1993   The role of fairness in negotiation. *Negotiation Journal* 9:223-244.
Augsburger, D.W.
  1992   *Conflict Mediation Across Cultures: Pathways and Patterns.* Louisville, KY: Westminster, John Knox.
Axelrod, R.
  1984   *The Evolution of Cooperation.* New York: Basic Books.
Berdal, M.
  1995   United Nations peacekeeping in the former Yugoslavia. Pp. 228-247 in *Beyond Traditional Peacekeeping,* D. Daniel and B. Hayes, eds. New York: St. Martin's Press.
Brislin, R.W.
  1986   A cultural general assimilator: Preparation for various types of sojourns. *International Journal of Intercultural Relations* 10:215-234.
Brown, B.R.
  1977   Face-saving and face-restoration in negotiation. In *Negotiations: Social-Psychological Perspectives,* D. Druckman, ed. Beverly Hills, CA: Sage.
Burton, J.W.
  1969   *Conflict and Communication.* New York: Free Press.
Carnevale, P.J.D.
  1986   Mediating disputes and decisions in organizations. *Research on Negotiation in Organizations* 1:251-269.
Carnevale, P., and R. Henry
  1989   Determinants of mediation tactics in public sector disputes: A contingency analysis. *Journal of Applied Social Psychology* 19:469-488.
Carnevale, P.J., and E.J. Lawler
  1986   Time pressure and the development of integrative agreements in bilateral negotiation. *Journal of Conflict Resolution* 30:636-659.
Carnevale, P.J.D., and D.G. Pruitt
  1992   Negotiation and mediation. *Annual Review of Psychology* 43:531-582.
Coddington, A.
  1968   *Theories of the Bargaining Process.* Chicago: Aldine.
Cohen, H.
  1980   *You Can Negotiate Anything.* Secaucus, NJ: Lyle Stewart.
Cooper Management Institute
  1993   *Negotiate to Win: The Win-Win Negotiating Program.* McLean, VA: Cooper Management Institute, Inc.
Danielian, J.
  1967   Live simulation of affect-laden cultural cognitions. *Journal of Conflict Resolution* 11:312-324.
DeMars, W.
  1995   Does International Humanitarian Action Prolong or Resolve Civil Wars? Paper presented at the Annual Meeting of the International Studies Association, Chicago.
Deutsch, M., D. Canavan, and J. Rubin
  1971   The effects of size of conflict and sex of experimenter upon interpersonal bargaining. *Journal of Experimental Social Psychology* 7:258-267.
Deutsch, M., and E. Brickman
  1994   Conflict resolution. *Pediatrics in Review* 15:16-23.
Diehl, P.
  1992   What are they fighting for? The importance of issues in international conflict research. *Journal of Peace Research* 29: 333-344.
  1994   *International Peacekeeping.* Baltimore, MD: Johns Hopkins University Press.

1995 Peacekeeping in civil wars. Pp. 223-236 in *A Crisis of Expectations: UN Peacekeeping in the 1990s*, R. Thakur and C. Thayer, eds. Boulder, CO: Westview Press.

Donohue, W.A., and R. Kolt
1992 *Managing Interpersonal Conflict.* Newbury Park, CA: Sage.

Doob, L.W.
1970 *Resolving Conflict in Africa: The Fermeda Workshop.* New Haven: Yale University Press.

Douglas, A.
1972 *Industrial Peacekeeping.* New York: Columbia University Press.

Druckman, D.
1977 Boundary role conflict: Negotiation as dual responsiveness. *Journal of Conflict Resolution* 21:639-662.
1978 The monitoring function in negotiation: Two models of responsiveness. In *Contributions to Experimental Economics: Bargaining Behavior,* H. Sauermann, ed. Tubingen, Germany: J.C.B. Mohr.
1986 Stages, turning points, and crises: Negotiating military base rights, Spain and the United States. *Journal of Conflict Resolution* 30:327-360.
1994 Determinants of compromising behavior in negotiation: A meta-analysis. *Journal of Conflict Resolution* 38:507-556.

Druckman, D., and R.A. Bjork, eds.
1991 *In the Mind's Eye: Enhancing Human Performance.* Committee on Techniques for the Enhancement of Human Performance, National Research Council. Washington, DC: National Academy Press.
1994 *Learning, Remembering, Believing: Enhancing Human Performance.* Committee on Techniques for the Enhancement of Human Performance, National Research Council. Washington, DC: National Academy Press.

Druckman, D., and T.V. Bonoma
1976 Determinants of bargaining behavior in a bilateral monopoly situation II: Opponent's concession rate and similarity. *Behavioral Science* 21:252-262.

Druckman, D., and P.T. Hopmann
1989 Behavioral aspects of negotiations on mutual security. In *Behavior, Society, and Nuclear War,* vol. I, P.E. Tetlock et al., eds. New York: Oxford University Press.

Druckman, D., and C.R. Mitchell, eds.
1995 Flexibility in international negotiation and mediation. *Annals of the American Academy of Social and Political Science* 542.

Elangovan, A.R.
1995 Managerial third-party dispute intervention: A prescriptive model of strategy selection. *Academy of Management Review* 20:800-830.

Erskine, Emmanuel
1989 *Mission with UNIFIL: An African Soldier's Reflections.* London: Hurst and Co.

Esser, J.K., M.J. Calvillo, M.R. Scheel, and J.L. Walker
1990 Oligopoly bargaining: Effects of agreement pressure and opponent strategies. *Journal of Applied Social Psychology* 20:1256-1271.

Eyre, D.
1994 Cultural awareness and negotiation skills in peace operations. Pp. 101-114 in *Peace Operations: Workshop Proceedings,* D. Segal, ed. Research Report 1670. Washington, DC: U.S. Army Research Institute for the Behavioral and Social Sciences.

Fearon, J.
1991 Counterfactuals and hypothesis testing in political science. *World Politics* 43:169-195.

Fetherston, A.B.
1994 *Toward a Theory of United Nations Peacekeeping.* New York: St. Martin's Press.

Fisher, R.
1964 Fractionating conflict. In *International Conflict and Behavioral Science: The Craigville Papers*, R. Fisher, ed. New York: Basic Books.
1990 *The Social Psychology of Intergroup and International Conflict Resolution.* New York: Springer-Verlag.
1994 Generic principles for resolving intergroup conflict. *Journal of Social Issues* 50:47-66.
Fisher, R., and S. Brown
1988 *Getting Together.* Boston: Houghton Mifflin.
Fisher, R.J., and L. Keashly
1991 The potential complementarity of mediation and consultation within a contingency model of third party intervention. *Journal of Peace Research* 28:29-42.
Fisher, R., and W. Ury
1981 *Getting to Yes: Negotiating Agreement Without Giving In.* Boston: Houghton Mifflin.
Fisher, R., W. Ury, and B. Patton
1991 *Getting to Yes: Negotiating Agreement Without Giving In*, 2nd ed. New York: Penguin Books.
Goldman, A.
1994 The centrality of Ningensei to Japanese negotiating and interpersonal relationships: Implications for U.S.-Japanese communication. *International Journal of Intercultural Relations* 18:29-54.
Gouldner, A.W.
1960 The norm of reciprocity: A preliminary statement. *American Sociological Review* 25:161-178.
Grove, C.L., and I. Torbiorn
1985 A new conceptualization of intercultural adjustment and the goals of training. *International Journal of Intercultural Relations* 9:205-233.
Hahn, P.-C.
1986 *Korean Jurisprudence, Politics and Culture.* Seoul, Korea: Yonsei University Press.
Hamner, W.C., and G.A. Yukl
1977 The effectiveness of different offer strategies in bargaining. In *Negotiations: Social-Psychological Perspectives*, D. Druckman, ed. Beverly Hills, CA: Sage.
Hannigan, T.P.
1990 Traits, attitudes, and skills that are related to intercultural effectiveness and their implications for cross-cultural training: A review of literature. *International Journal of Intercultural Relations* 14:89-111.
Harbottle, M.
1992 What is Proper Soldiering? Report from the Centre for International Peacebuilding, Oxon, England.
Harrell, M.C., and R. Howe
1995 Military issues in multinational operations. Pp. 189-204 in *Beyond Traditional Peacekeeping*, D. Daniel and B. Hayes, eds. New York: St. Martin's Press.
Harris, J.
1994 Human dimensions of peacekeeping: Sinai observations—The first iteration. Pp. 37-46 in *Peace Operations: Working Proceedings*, D. Segal, ed. Research Report 1670. Washington, DC: U.S. Army Research Institute for the Behavioral and Social Sciences
Homans, G.C.
1961 *Social Behavior: Its Elementary Forms.* New York: Harcourt, Brace and World.
James, A.
1969 *The Politics of Peacekeeping.* New York: Praeger.
1990 International Peacekeeping: The Disputants View. *Political Studies* 8:215-230.

1994 Internal Peacekeeping. Pp. 3-24 in *Peacekeeping and the Challenge of Civil Conflict Resolution*, D. Charters, ed. New Brunswick, N.S.: Centre for Conflict Studies.

Johansen, R.
1994 U.N. peacekeeping: How should we measure success. *Mershon International Studies Review* 38:307-310.

Johnson, D.W.
1967 The use of role reversal in intergroup competition. *Journal of Personality and Social Psychology* 7:135-142.

Johnson, K.R., and T.V. Layng
1992 Breaking the structuralist barrier: Literacy and numeracy with fluency. *American Psychologist* 47:1475-1490.

Jonah, James
1991 The Management of UN Peacekeeping. Pp. 75-90 in *The United Nations and Peacekeeping: Results, Limitations and Prospects — The Lessons of 40 Years of Experience*, I. J. Rikhye and K. Skjelsbaek, eds. New York: St. Martin's Press.

Karambayya, R., and J.M. Brett
1989 Managers handling disputes: Third-party roles and perceptions of fairness. *Academy of Management Journal* 32:687-704.

Karrass, C.L.
1974 *Give and Take: The Complete Guide to Negotiating Tactics and Strategies*. New York: Thomas Y. Crowell.

Karrass, G.
1985 *Negotiate to Close*. New York: Simon & Schuster.

Kelley, H.H., and D.P. Schenitzki
1972 Bargaining. In *Experimental Social Psychology*, C.G. McClintock, ed. New York: Holt.

Kelman, H.C.
1972 The problem-solving workshop in conflict resolution. In *Communication in International Politics*, R.L. Merritt, ed. Urbana: University of Illinois Press.

Kemp, G.
1991 The American peacekeeping role in Lebanon. Pp. 131-142 in A. McDermott and I.C. Skjelsbaek, eds., *The Multinational Force in Beirut, 1982-1984*. Miami: Florida International University Press.

Kim, N.H., J.A. Wall, D.-W. Solm, and J.S. Kim
1993 Community and industrial mediation in South Korea. *Journal of Conflict Resolution* 37:361-381.

Kissinger, H.
1979 *White House Years*. Boston: Little, Brown.

Kolb, D.M.
1987 Corporate ombudsman and organizational conflict. *Journal of Conflict Resolution* 31:673-692.

Kressel, K.
1972 Labor mediation: An exploratory survey. Albany, NY: Association of Labor Mediation Agencies.

Kressel, K., and D. Pruitt
1985 Themes in the mediation of social conflict. *Journal of Social Issues* 41:179-196.
1989 Conclusion: A research perspective on the mediation of social conflict. Pp. 394-436 in K. Kressell and D.G. Pruitt, eds., *Mediation Research*. San Francisco: Jossey-Bass.

Kressel, K., et al.
1994 The settlement orientation vs. the problem-solving style in custody mediation. *Journal of Social Issues* 50:67-84.

Kriesberg, L.
1991 Formal and quasi-mediators in international disputes. *Journal of Peace Research* 28:19-28.

Lall, A.
1966 *Modern International Negotiation: Principles and Practice.* New York: Columbia University Press.

Last, D., and K.C. Eyre
1995 Combat and Contact Skill in Peacekeeping: Surveying Recent Canadian Experience in UNPROFOR. Unpublished manuscript, The Lester B. Pearson Canadian International Peacekeeping Training Centre.

Lederach, J.P.
1995 *Beyond Prescription: Perspectives on Conflict, Culture, and Training.* Syracuse, NY: Syracuse University Press.

Lefever, E.
1967 *Uncertain Mandate: Politics of the U.N. Congo Operation.* Baltimore, MD: Johns Hopkins University Press.

Lewicki, R., and B. Sheppard
1985 Choosing how to intervene: Factors affecting the use of process and outcome control in third party dispute resolution. *Journal of Occupational Behavior* 6:49-64.

Lim, R., and P. Carnevale
1990 Contingencies in the mediation of disputes. *Journal of Personality and Social Psychology* 58:259-272.

Mackinlay, J.
1990 Powerful peace-keepers. *Survival* 32:241-250.

Maggiolo, W.A.
1971 *Techniques of Mediation in Labor Disputes.* Dobbs Ferry, NY: Oceana.

McCauley, C.D., and M.W. Hughs-James
1994 *An Evaluation of the Outcomes of a Leadership Development Program.* Greensboro, NC: Center for Creative Leadership.

McCauley, C.D., M.M. Lombardo, and C.J. Usher
1989 Diagnosing management development needs: An instrument based on how managers develop. *Journal of Management* 15:389-403.

McLaughlin, M.E., P. Carnevale, and R.G. Lim
1991 Professional mediators' judgements of mediation tactics: Multidimensional scaling and cluster analysis. *Journal of Applied Psychology* 76:465-472.

Merry, S.
1989 Mediation in nonindustrial societies. Pp. 68-90 in *Mediation Research,* K. Kressel and D.G. Pruitt, eds. San Francisco: Jossey-Boss.

Miller, L.L., and C. Moskos
1995 Humanitarians or warriors? Race, gender, and combat status in Operation Restore Hope. *Armed Forces and Society* 21:615-637.

Moskos, C.
1976 *Peace Soldiers: The Sociology of a United Nations Military Force.* Chicago: University of Chicago Press.
1995 Able Sentry: GIs on the Serb Border. U.S. Army Institute in the Behavioral and Social Sciences report.

Murray, J.D.
1983 Military aspects of peacekeeping: Problems and recommendations. Pp. 175-202 in *Peacekeeping: Appraisals and Proposals,* H. Wiseman, ed. New York: Pergamon.

Neale, M.A., and M.H. Bazerman
1983 The role of perspective-taking in negotiating under different forms of arbitration. *Industrial and Labor Relations Review* 36:378-388.

Nelson, R.
1991   The multinational force in Beirut. Pp. 95-100 in A. McDermott and K. Skjelsbaek, eds., *The Multinational Force in Beirut, 1982-1984*. Miami: Florida International University Press.
1984-
1985   Multinational peacekeeping in the Middle East and the United Nations model. *International Affairs* 61:67-89.
Nierenberg, G.I.
1968   *The Art of Negotiating*. New York: Cornerstone Library.
Pelcovits, N.
1991   What went wrong. Pp. 37-79 in A. McDermott and K. Skjelsbaek, eds., *The Multinational Force in Beirut, 1982-1984*. Miami: Florida International University Press.
Pinkley, R.L.
1995   Impact of knowledge regarding alternatives to settlement in dyadic negotiations: Whose knowledge counts? *Journal of Applied Psychology* 80:403-417.
Podell, J.E., and W.M. Knopp
1969   The effect of mediation on the perceived firmness of the opponent. *Journal of Conflict Resolution* 13:511-520.
Prein, H.
1984   A contingency approach to conflict resolution. *Group and Organizational Studies* 9:81-102.
Pruitt, D.G.
1971   Indirect communication and the search for agreement in negotiations. *Journal of Applied Social Psychology* 1:205-239.
1981   *Negotiating Behavior*. New York: Academic Press.
Pruitt, D.G., and J.Z. Rubin
1986   *Social Conflict: Escalation, Stalemate, and Settlement*. New York: Random House.
Pruitt, D., and D. Johnson
1970   Mediation as an aid to face saving in negotiation. *Journal of Personality and Social Phsychology* 14:239-246.
Pruitt, D.G., and M.J. Kimmel
1977   Twenty years of experimental gaming: Critique, synthesis, and suggestions for the future. *Annual Review of Psychology* 28:363-392.
Putnam, L.L., and M.S. Poole
1987   Conflict and negotiation. Pp. 549-599 in *Handbook of Organizational Communication Yearbook*, F.M. Jablin, L.L. Putnam, K.H. Roberts, and L.W. Porter, eds. Newbury Park, CA: Sage.
Putnam, L.L., and S.R. Wilson
1982   Communication strategies in organizational conflicts: Reliability and validity of a measurement scale. Pp. 629-652 in *Communication Yearbook*, M. Burgood, ed. Beverly Hills, CA: Sage.
Ross, W.H., D.E. Conlon, and A. Lind
1990   The mediator as a leader: Effects of behavioral style and deadline certainty on negotiation. *Group and Organizational Studies*.
Rouhana, N.N., and H.C. Kelman
1994   Promoting joint thinking in international conflicts: An Israeli-Palestinian continuing workshop. *Journal of Social Issues* 50:157-178.
Rubin, J.Z., and B.R. Brown
1975   *The Social Psychology of Bargaining and Negotiation*. New York: Academic Press.
Saunders, H.H.
1991   Officials and citizens in international relationships: The Dartmouth Conference. In *The Psychodynamics of International Relationships*, vol. 2, V.D. Volkan, J.V. Montville, and D.A. Julius, eds. Lexington, MA: Lexington Books.

Schelling, T.C.
1960 *The Strategy of Conflict.* Cambridge, MA: Harvard University Press.
Sheppard, B.H.
1984 Third party conflict intervention: A procedural framework. *Research in Organizational Behavior* 6:141-190.
Siegel, S., and L.E. Fouraker
1960 *Bargaining and Group Decision Making: Experiments in Bilateral Monopoly.* New York: McGraw-Hill.
Silbey, S., and S. Merry
1986 Mediator settlement strategies. *Law and Policy* 8:7-32.
Skjelsbaek, Kjell
1991 UN peacekeeping: Expectation, limitations, and results. Pp. 52-67 in *The United Nations and Peacekeeping: Results, Limitations, and Prospects — The Lessons of 40 Years of Experience,* I.J. Rikhye and K. Skjelsbaek, eds. New York: St. Martin's Press.
Skogmo, B.
1989 *UNIFIL: International Peacekeeping in Lebanon, 1978-1988.* Boulder, CO: Lynne Rienner.
Snyder, G.H., and P. Diesing
1977 *Conflict Among Nations: Bargaining, Decision-Making, and System Structure in International Crisis.* Princeton, NJ: Princeton University Press.
Snyder, M.
1974 Self-monitoring of expressive behavior. *Journal of Personality and Social Psychology* 30:526-537.
Stedman, S.
1995 UN intervention in civil wars: imperatives of choice and strategy. Pp. 40-63 in *Beyond Traditional Peacekeeping,* D. Daniel and B. Hayes, eds. New York: St. Martin's Press.
Stern, P.C., and D. Druckman
1995 Has the "earthquake" of 1989 toppled international relations theory? *Peace Psychology Review* 1:109-122.
Stevens, C.M.
1963 *Strategy and Collective Bargaining Negotiations.* New York: McGraw-Hill.
Stewman, S.
1995 Wargaming Peace. Paper presented at the International Studies Association, Chicago.
Stiles, K., and M. MacDonald
1992 After consensus what? Performance criterion for the UN in the post-cold war era. *Journal of Peace Research* 29(3):299-312.
Summers, D.A., J.D. Taliaferro, and D.J. Fletcher
1970 Judgment policy and interpersonal learning. *Behavioral Science* 15:514-521.
Tedeschi, J.T., and T.V. Bonoma
1977 Measures of last resort: Coercion and aggression in bargaining. In *Negotiations: Social-Psychological Perspectives,* D. Druckman, ed. Beverly Hills, CA: Sage.
Thibaut, J.
1968 The development of contractual norms in bargaining: Reliction and refinement. *Journal of Conflict Resolution* 12:102-112.
Thomas, K.W.
1992 Conflict and negotiation processes in organizations. Pp. 651-717 in *Handbook of Industrial and Organizational Psychology,* M.D. Dunnette and L.M. Hough, eds. Palo Alto, CA: Consulting Psychologists Press.
Touval, S., and I.W. Zartman, eds.
1985 *The Man in the Middle: International Mediation in Theory and Practice.* Boulder, CO: Westview.

Urquhart, B.
  1983 Peacekeeping: A view from the operational center. Pp. 161-174 in *Peacekeeping: Appraisals and Proposals*, H. Wiseman, ed. New York: Pergamon.
  1990 Beyond the sheriff's posse. *Survival* 32:196-205.
U.S. Army Command and General Staff College
  1994 *Operations Other Than War: The Challenge of the Future*. Ft. Leavenworth, KS: U.S. Army Command and General Staff College.
U.S. Department of the Army
  1994 *FM 100-23: Peace Operations*. Washington, DC: U.S. Department of the Army.
Van de Vliert, E.
  1985 Conflict and conflict management. Pp. 51-63 in *A New Handbook of Work and Organizational Psychology*, H. Thierry, P.J.D. Drenth, and C.J. de Wolff, eds. Have, England: Erlbaum.
Vasquez, J.
  1983 The tangibility of issues and global conflict: A test of Rosenau's issue area typology. *Journal of Peace Research* 20:179-192.
Walcott, C., P.T. Hopmann, and T.D. King
  1977 The role of debate in negotiation. In *Negotiations: Social-Psychological Perspectives*, D. Druckman, ed. Beverly Hills, CA: Sage.
Wall, J.A.
  1981 Mediation: An analysis, review and proposed research. *Journal of Conflict Resolution* 25:157-180.
  1995 *Negotiation: Theory and Practice*. Glenview, IL: Scott, Foresman.
Wall, J.A., and M. Blum
  1991 Community mediation in the People's Republic of China. *Journal of Conflict Resolution* 35:3-20.
Wall, J.A., and R.R. Callister
  1995 Conflict and its management. *Journal of Management* 21:515-558.
Wall, J., and D. Rude
  1985 Judicial mediation: Techniques, strategies, and situational effects. *Journal of Social Issues* 41:47-64.
Walton, R.E.
  1987 *Managing Conflict*. Reading, MA: Addison-Wesley.
Walton, R.E., and R.B. McKersie
  1965 *A Behavioral Theory of Labor Negotiations: An Analysis of a Social Interaction System*. New York: McGraw-Hill.
Weinberger, N.
  1983 Peacekeeping options in Lebanon. *Middle East Journal* 37:341-369.
Weiss, T.
  1994 United Nations and civil wars. *Washington Quarterly* 17:139-159.
Wiseman, H.
  1991 Peacekeeping in the international political context: Historical analysis and future directions. Pp. 32-51 in *The United Nations and Peacekeeping: Results, Limitations, and Prospects — The Lessons of 40 Years of Experience*, I.J. Rikhye and K. Skjelsbaek, eds. New York: St. Martin's Press.
Yoder, A.
  1994 *UN Military Operations Before and After the New Era*. Columbus, OH: Mershon Center.
Zechmeister, K., and D. Druckman
  1973 Determinants of resolving a conflict of interest: A simulation of political decision making. *Journal of Conflict Resolution* 17:63-88.

Appendices

A

Military Organizational Characteristics

Organizations are studied in general terms because they share regularities and common features. Were they truly unique, only case studies would be possible. The success and utility of organizational studies is a demonstration that organizations have enough similar features, structures, and purposes to make comparative studies feasible.

Conversely, all organizations are different in some respects. And these differences often have an effect on the organization's structure and function, so that similar changes in different organizations have different impacts. Either a classification scheme that groups organizations by relevant characteristics is necessary, or the particular features that modify a change must be specified in order for the effects of the change to be understood. There must be a comparable base of organizational characteristics in order to assess the regularities in their operations. There is no general scheme that enables an organization to know in advance which differences are cogent for which changes.

That there is variability in the purposes, structures, and functions of organizations is hardly a radical or novel observation. Organizational scholars are well aware of this and consider it in their discussions. Sometimes, however, because of the focus of their studies, scholars may concentrate on one or another type of organization and neglect to delimit the generalizations of their findings to those actually examined. For example, studies attempting to relate organizational culture to productivity are most often conducted by researchers located in schools of business or management. Their general discussions expound on a wide range of possible cases but, when empirical evaluations are made, the focus of the studies narrows to only corporate organizations (see, e.g., Ouichi, 1981; Kotter and Heskitt, 1992).

Generalizations from corporate to noncorporate organizations may of course be valid. That is a matter of fact to be ascertained on a case-by-case basis. But there is no reason not to articulate the differences between corporate organizations and noncorporate ones so that they may become salient and brought into consideration more appropriately and clearly.

The United States military is a large and complex organization that is *not* corporate in nature. There are differences between the military and corporate organizations (this is not to say that all corporate organizations are alike) that may relate to structure, downsizing, leadership, interorganizational cooperation, and a host of other topics. Not all of these features are unique to the military, nor are all of them stark in contrast to corporate features. They do give reason to consider carefully these issues before positively affirming the applicability to the military of relationships developed in nonmilitary milieus.

The remainder of this appendix is a list of features within military organizations that are not likely to appear in similar form in nonmilitary organizations. The list is not exhaustive, nor is it in any particular order. Some of the differences may be pertinent, others not. Not all of the differences are unique to the military. Some are common to government agencies in general; others are specific to the U.S. federal system; others are shared by nonprofit organizations; still others are characteristic of organizations dealing with matters of public safety. Nevertheless, as a cluster of characteristics, they serve to characterize the current United States military and also as a set of markers or constraints against the blanket application of techniques developed for corporate organizations.

Two points should be noted. First, these differences are well known to those in the military, who live with them and their consequences. They are not usually articulated, so that these different feature may routinely pass unnoticed by those not familiar with the military organization on a day-to-day basis. Second, the point is not merely that the military is subject to congressional rules. All organizations (in the United States) are subject to such strictures. Fair labor practices, requirements of the Occupational Safety and Health Administration, rules of the Securities and Exchange Commission, civil and criminal law, the Internal Revenue Code, and antitrust legislation, to name just a few, represent some of the legal regulations that define and constrain all organizations. It is the particular nature of the rules governing the military that makes its organizational operations so different.

- First and foremost is the military's distinct mission. The military is the only organization with the mission to destroy and kill enemies of the nation. No one, neither police nor police-like organizations, is authorized to kill in this manner. Although the military may be charged with a host of other missions, the use of deadly force in aggressive and defensive actions against the nation's enemies is its defining characteristic. No other organization has a similar mission.

• The budget for the military is approved by Congress on a year-by-year basis (with the exception of special categories, such as major equipment, that may be obligated over several years). This poses limitations on the military's ability to make organizational plans beyond the current fiscal year and means that funds unspent in a given fiscal year cannot be carried over to the next. The annual budget also drives end-of-the-year spending, which in turn creates disincentives for the implementation of various improvements in efficiency and undercuts the rationale for prudent spending. The budget also has an impact on authorized number of personnel for each year. For instance, Congress may mandate a decrease in personnel, an increase in the procurement of materiel, and a decrease in budget unrelated to either.

• There are several separate but related sets of personnel in the military, such as active-duty service members, civilian employees, reserves, and the national guard. Both the military and civilian sets cover the breadth and depth of the organization, from clerk to secretary of defense on the civilian side and from recruit to chairman of the joint chiefs on the active-duty side. The President, a civilian, is designated commander in chief by the Constitution. The active-duty component can be further divided in a number of ways: officer versus enlisted, flag, field, and company grade, and so forth.

These several sets of personnel are recruited differently, managed differently, evaluated differently, often held to different performance standards, serve different terms of office, and differ from each other in a number of other ways. The implications of having several distinct workforces are complex and cannot be specified completely. Unless explicitly noted, the rest of the points made here refer to the active-duty component of the military organization, with the civilian comparison left implicit. Congress can direct trade-offs among these groups by such means as privatizing, transferring responsibility to a reserve component, and using civilians to replace military personnel.

• The military has a fixed rank structure. There are at least 15 standard levels of rank (9 enlisted and 6 officer); others, such as warrant officers and flag rank officers (generals and admirals), add additional ones. The rank structure is determined by federal law, and the number of incumbents at each rank is fixed. This requirement has as one of its consequences, for example, that the military has no ability on a short-term basis to change its organizational management strategy by flattening or expanding its rank structure to better accommodate its mission-based needs. The military may make a case or a request for such a change, but it cannot be implemented without legislative and executive approval. There is a differential impact of rank structure on operational force units on one hand, and various headquarters and staffs on the other. Headquarters and staffs can be transformed in many ways; units must be systematically restructured—command billets must be filled or abolished.

• Military personnel cannot organize for the purposes of collective bargaining, or for the negotiation of working conditions, pay, or benefits. Service members can join voluntary organizations, but they cannot advocate for such changes either. Even civilians employed by the military are limited compared with their private-sector counterparts. They are executive branch employees and are prohibited by law from trying to influence pending legislation—the major pathway to modifying their conditions of employment—because such legislation is in the purview of the legislative branch of government, and the separation of powers principle keeps the executive branch at arm's length. Needless to say, strikes or other work actions are out of the question for the military. As a counterbalance to these restrictions, there is a sizable number of other nongovernmental organizations that testify on behalf of the military budget and about various conditions of employment. Among such groups are veterans' organizations, retired officers' associations, retired enlisted associations, and variations of these for each of the separate services.

• Military enlisted personnel serve fixed terms of enlistment. They cannot resign or quit unilaterally, unless they are at the end of their terms. Even then, resignation is with the permission of the service and can be refused. If the military is engaged in an operational procedure, such as a military action, departure at the end of a term may have to be postponed for those engaged in the operation. Officers have different rules for resignation and retirement, but they are also limited in their options by the current state of operations and by the payback owed for previous military-supplied educational opportunities. Employee dissatisfaction cannot always be translated into immediate resignation or separation from duty. There are even limits on the ability of personnel to voice their dissatisfactions publicly.

• The pay structure of the military is fixed. It is entirely determined by rank and time in service. In some cases, there may be supplementary special pay, as in the case of extra salary awarded to physicians whose medical specialties are in short supply. A key issue is that bonuses or merit pay are not and cannot be used in individual cases for either rewards or incentives. Merit is recognized through the issuance of (nonmonetary) awards and medals. In the long run, superior performance is recognized in a number of ways, such as special honors, earlier than usual promotion, and selection for a higher position on the rank pyramid. However, the short-term use of salary and bonuses to motivate and encourage achievement cannot be utilized, nor can failure to award a bonus be used as a sign of disapproval.

The use of salary-based incentives and rewards occurs through the promotion system, but, for many officer ranks, that system is not under the control of the immediate commander but rather goes through a complex Promotion Board review procedure. In addition, there are some special pay and promotion attributes of the military. Prisoners of war, although away from their jobs, still accumulate pay, length of service, and promotions. Under some circumstances even military members serving jail time in military stockades still amass some pay and retirement credits.

• Unlike most other organizations, the military's rules of conduct have the force of law. In most organizations, a violation of company policy may result in being fired; in the military, violation of company policy may result in formal charges, trial, and imprisonment. In addition to the U.S. criminal and civil codes, the Uniform Code of Military Justice also governs the conduct of military personnel. And to enforce its standards of conduct, the military maintains its own judicial and penal systems. The mechanisms of control of military members stands in sharp contrast to the treatment of civilians employed by the organization. They have the employee protections of the Civil Service Code, have a number of avenues of appeal, and are not subject to the procedures of the Uniform Code of Military Justice. In the civilian world, certain conduct may result in loss of employment but is not criminal, such as unbecoming conduct and certain forms of disrespect to one's superiors. In the military, these are crimes and one is under threat of imprisonment for such lapses.

The military regulates not only the conditions of employment and conduct of its members but also aspects of their personal life. Mandatory drug screening and a prohibition on abortions at military hospitals represent a type of involvement in members' personal lives to an extent that is not usual in the civilian world.

• All active-duty military personnel are on permanent 24-hour call. Except for times when they are on official authorized leave status, all active-duty military may be called in to a duty station at any time. Even their leave is subject to cancellation. Equally pertinent is that they may be deployed—that is, assigned to duty at a station remote from home and family—at any time as required by government policy. As noted above, personnel do not have the option of resigning rather than reporting or being deployed. Nor do they receive any special compensation, unless combat or hazardous duty pay is officially authorized for the period of the assignment.

• The military operate under a distinctive retirement scheme. Personnel must serve a threshold amount of time in the service to qualify for a retirement pay. The minimum time requirement is 20 years. Separation from the military before this length of service, either voluntary or involuntary, means no retirement pay. Some benefits, such as health care up to age 65, are bundled with the retirement status. The military medical system cares for both retirees and their dependent family members; former military personnel who are preretirees are cared for by the Veterans Administration medical system; their family members are not covered. A retired active-duty service member can accept employment in the private sector. If he or she serves as an active-duty officer and then accepts a postretirement job with the federal government in a nonmilitary capacity, the retirement pay will be reduced during the tenure of this second job; in some circumstances, this reduction can be waived. An officer in retirement pay status is eligible and liable for recall to active duty.

• Major decisions in the military are often confounded with civilian political issues that are not necessarily related to the military's plans or effectiveness. The acquisition of major weapon systems and the continued operation of bases are determined by many factors, not the least of which are political and economic considerations. A base that employs hundreds or thousands of civilians and houses many active-duty military is a large economic engine. The closure of one or another base may be proposed on grounds of purely military efficiency; the decision of which base to close is made by a process that is politicized, with states and communities competing for bases on, at best, quasi-military grounds. Almost all aspects of higher levels of mission, structure, and function of the military, including discretionary acquisition of weapons and other equipment, are controlled by elements in the larger political system rather than determined solely by the organization itself. Although consultation with senior military officers is routine, major and strategic decisions are determined by the political process and are often responsive to extraorganizational priorities and pressures. Civilian appointed leadership in each military department and at the Department of Defense, not active-duty military personnel, control budget decisions.

• The budget of the military is imposed from outside, even to the point of subcategory specification. The budget is not directly linked to organizational performance, and it may contain mandates for specific programs or operations that have absolute priority: they can be neither cancelled nor deferred. The provision of resources for these externally established programs cannot be offset by adding personnel; staffing must be provided by diverting personnel from other programs or operations.

• Almost all of the military's regular management functions are governed by large sets of externally imposed, complex sets of regulations. These rules may have been designed for other purposes and other organizations. The domains of civilian personnel, nonoperational travel, and procurement are particularly constrained. It is cumbersome and time-consuming to hire a low-level clerk, and the process is not completely orderly. At any point a recruitment action may require the hiring of an employee whose job in another part of the organization or government has been terminated.

If the person whose hiring is compulsory earns a higher salary than what has been budgeted for the position, the hiring unit must absorb the increased cost from other parts of its operating budget for up to two years. It requires difficult and heavily bureaucratic procedures to discharge a poorly performing or nonfunctional civilian employee. Similar complexities and difficulties exist in almost all areas of routine management operations.

• It is customary for corporate organizations to distinguish among customers, employees, and stockholders, especially when assessing productivity or effectiveness of performance. These distinctions are not clear for the military. The employees are distinctive enough, but it is unclear whether the general citizenry are customers or stockholders, or how exactly to characterize the role of Congress and the secretary of defense. In operations other than war, these distinctions are even fuzzier. The organizational responsibility for a military operation, such as a peacekeeping mission in conjunction with the United Nations, leaves many issues of management and control ambiguous. For clarity of mission these issues should be resolved prior to commitment of U.S. forces.

• The military organization makes a distinction between line and specialized staff functions. In many ways the specialized staff is favored by being able to move more quickly through the officer rank structure. Physicians, dentists, and clinical psychologists, for example, are recruited as O-3 officers, Navy lieutenants, and Army and Air Force captains, reflecting the military service credit they are given for their specialized training and education. Line officers in all service branches start their careers as O-1 officers, Navy ensigns, or Army, Marine, and Air Force second lieutenants. Yet at the higher ranks, particularly at the general officer level, the line officers have a large role in the promotions of the higher levels of staff. Indeed, as specialized staff officers move up the rank ladder to serve in command positions within their specialties, they are judged more and more on whether they have acquired skills and experience in command and control; in some ways their line-like experience outweighs their professional achievements in determining whether they are promoted.

• The relationship between the internal and external control of the organization is fixed by law. The military chiefs of staff work for their civilian counterparts, the politically appointed service secretaries. At the highest level, this is paralleled by the joint stewardship of the secretary of defense and the chairman of the joint chiefs of staff. At lower levels there are various civilian assistant secretaries, as well as military deputy chiefs. Although in theory the responsibilities of these two groups differ, there is some partial overlap in how they actually function. Many issues of management and service policy are vetted by both groups, and the formal lines of demarcation between their responsibilities and authority are sometimes shaded in practice. Civilian authority, however, is paramount. The chiefs of staff/

commander of naval operations have no authority similar to that exercised by the commander in chief, the secretary of defense, the deputy secretary, the undersecretaries, the service secretaries, etc.

• The organization assumes a responsibility for the entire military community, including family members and retirees. In part to serve that obligation, the military maintains a pastoral corps, a social work capability, a family housing stock, schools for dependent family members, and a large medical system. In some cases in which the military is not able to provide these services with its own resources, it will contract for them to ensure access to them by the entire military community. The Exceptional Family Member Act makes the services responsible for the care and education of exceptional children from birth up to the age when that responsibility devolves to the community or the military school system.

• The military often engages in sudden and unexpected transitions from regular operations to what are often dangerous and life-threatening operations. The movements of personnel are not voluntary, involve the separation of families, and are impervious to the demands of unfinished business and personal crises. One of the distinguishing features of military operations, in contrast to those of fire departments or police forces, is the length of time involved—from months to years—and the distances—up to thousands of miles—to be covered. There is no easy way to bring a service member home routinely from such a mission. The stresses imposed on both the service members and their families by these separations are very different from those of dangerous occupations in the civilian sector. Even on a daily basis there are differences: Police and fire departments, for example, are organized by shifts, with the day shift replacing the night shift, and so forth. On military deployments, there are no formal shifts.

• The structure of the officer force in the military is pyramidal in nature: the higher the rank, the fewer the incumbents. Some of the thinning out is accomplished by the attrition of officers voluntarily separating from the force, but most of it comes from their forced exit from the military through a process of selective retention. Officers and noncommissioned officers are reviewed for promotion at all levels. At the field grade level, after a certain time in rank, the situation for a candidate officer is up or out—and it is repeated for each new rank. Those not selected for a higher rank must leave (under some circumstances, those not selected may be retained at the old rank). Although it does not usually happen, nonselected field grade officers may not have served long enough to qualify for retirement. If this occurs, they lose their pension rights, and they and their family members lose other benefits, such as access to the military medical system. In the Army in the early 1990s, of a given cohort of captains, 80 percent would be promoted to major. Of the cohort of majors, 70 percent would be promoted to lieutenant colonel; of the cohort of lieutenant colonels, only 50 percent would be promoted to colonel. Thus only 28 percent of the original captains, about 1 in 4, will make colonel. Approximately 5 percent of colonels will be promoted to general. The finality and inexorableness of the system promotes both excellence and competition, but it also produces anxiety and disappointment.

In past years, an officer who attained the rank of O-6 (Navy captain or Army, Air Force, and Marine colonel) could expect to serve up to 20 years, the minimum service to qualify for retirement, or longer, up to 30 years. With the end of the cold war and the subsequent downsizing of the military, that is no longer the universal case. In some instances, the services have temporarily lowered the requisite years of service to qualify for retirement, an action that has consequences for a longevity-based retirement pay plan. They have also established Selective Early Retirement Boards that may select eligible senior officers for involuntary retirement before the 30-year limit.

• The military has an internal system of organizational culture that lends support to its personnel. In some instances, this culture also creates resistance to organizational change. This cultural system extends into groups that are related but marginal to it. They include other governmental entities, such as the Veterans Administration, and voluntary civilian groups, such as the American Legion, Veterans of Foreign Wars, and service alumni organizations. All these groups share in the culture of the military and to varying extents participate in the public political process of testifying before Congress and the administration and lobbying on military matters. Sometimes these efforts are concordant with the command management of the military; sometimes they are at cross-purposes. Other groups tied to but not part of the military also influence the organization's wherewithal and allocation decisions. The industrial part of the military-industrial complex pursues its own goals within the political system, goals that partially establish the parameters of the military's operations.

• The military has detailed uniform requirements that are quite complex. These vary from service to service from four to six levels of formality, each requiring a different uniform. They range from the informality of battle dress uniforms (camouflage print work clothes worn with boots in the Army, called "cami" in the Navy and Marine Corps and fatigues in the Air Force) to the formality of mess dress uniforms—the military equivalent of the civilian's white tie and tails. In addition, all uniforms have a public display of the wearer's rank that clearly identifies the wearer's place in a hierarchical structure. Some uniforms contain medal ribbons, length of service indicators, unit patches, and special achievement insignia. At times it is almost possible to read a service member's military history and level of accomplishment from the attachments to his or her sleeves, collar, and chest. Military uniforms are established and serve several important functions, such as identification of friends and enemies, pride, and tradition. They inhibit the adoption of organizational changes based on informality of dress codes and the minimization of status differences.

• The military organization is made up of several suborganizations, the most prominent of which are the component services: Army, Navy, Air Force, and Marines. These subunits both cooperate and compete. Each is supported by a large public constituency, and each strives to maximize its own role in the larger organization. Their successes in this competition result in seeming redundancy. Currently, the military has four air forces, two infantries, three medical corps, and lots of other units that seem to be duplicative across the services. The ability to analyze critically and to evaluate which of these duplications are functionally useful and cost-effective and which are vestiges of a dysfunctional competition is complicated by the heavily political nature of both the analysis and the decision elements, as well as the heavy influence of tradition that is a counterpoise to optimization.

• The military operate under a series of mission-driven constraints about the assignment of personnel to various operational roles and even about the suitability of individuals for military service. There exists a highly debated and still controversial policy about the role of homosexual men and lesbian women in the military. The current policy was established after discussion during the 1992 presidential election campaign and was one of the first initiatives put forward by the Clinton administration. The present "Don't ask, don't tell" policy is politically as well as militarily derived. Similarly, there is a debate about a national policy concerning the role of women in combat. That policy is the topic of much discussion and involves various political agendas that are not strictly concerned with the optimal use of human resources and military efficiency.

• The organizational boundaries of the military are somewhat unclear. It conducts a set of shared activities with other organizations that have affiliations with it. These include various reserve components (federal units), the national guard (state units that may be federalized when needed), and the reserve officer training corps, control of which is shared by the military and the colleges, universities, and schools in which they are located. These other organizations may share some of the same duties as the military. They may serve as front-line units; they may serve as supplementary units when emerging tasks require additional or specialized personnel; and they may backfill rear-echelon positions when regular armed services are deployed. The reserve components are in competition with the regular forces for current allocations of money and equipment, as well jockeying for position in long-range and strategic planning. Congress decides the funding and force structure for the reserve components; the national guard is handled on a state-by-state basis.

• The military does not have final control of the location of its operations. There are statutory limits, for example, on how many personnel can be assigned to the Washington, D.C., area. These limits are set independently of the organization's own judgments about efficient placement of personnel. On a more general level, decisions about the placement of military bases are heavily interwoven with local economies and jobs. As mentioned above, base closures and decisions about size and staffing are often based on civilian economic concerns and heavily brokered in a political arena that often ignores the functional and strategic requirements of the organization.

The other major factor is that operations in the future will be manned following today's predictions of likely missions. These predictions are often made by expert panels to meet a preconceived goal of either cutting or expanding the military, regardless of the desirable force mix. When the experts are incorrect in their estimates, the active-duty military leaders are often called to explain to Congress why they had the wrong troop mix, weapons systems, or inadequate training.

• The military does not determine all of its own standards for its personnel. Such rules as age requirements and limits, physical standards, and other aspects of policy regarding the attributes of the officer component are partially determined by legislation. In particular, the Defense Officer Personnel Management Act sets some of the standards for service. The organization has difficulty in arranging exceptions to statutory standards for specific operational purposes. The services may impose their own supplemental standards regarding height, weight, physical fitness, disqualifying disabilities, and so forth, as they find appropriate. All are potentially subject to congressional review.

As noted above, this list is not complete, nor are all the items of equal importance. They do give a start to suggesting differences between the United States military as an organization and some of the other organizations more frequently examined by corporately oriented organizational theorists.

REFERENCES

Kotter, J.P., and Heskett, J.L.
  1992 *Corporate Culture and Performance.* New York: Free Press.
Ouchi, W.G.
  1981 *Theory Z: How American Business Can Meet the Japanese Challenge.* Reading, MA: Addison-Wesley.

B

Committee Activities

In order to cover the topics of our charge, the committee undertook a number of activities—including site visits to relevant field settings and briefings by experts—in addition to full committee meetings, evaluation of reports provided by research and operational centers, and reviews of available research literature. The committee met four times during 1994-1995 at the National Research Council facilities in Washington, D.C., and Irvine, California. These meetings included presentations by the following Army experts to acquaint us with both specific Army interest in particular topics and Army experience and practice:

Dr. Michael Drillings, Army Research Institute
Dr. Edgar M. Johnson, Army Research Institute
Lt. General Theodore G. Stroup, Jr., Deputy Chief of Staff for Personnel, U.S. Army
Colonel Michael Shaler (retired), Steamboat Leadership Institute
Dr. Zita Simutos, Army Research Institute
Dr. Alma Steinberg, Army Research Institute
Dr. Steven Zaccaro, George Mason University

Most of the rest of the committee's work was carried out by subcommittees on specific topics. Our subcommittee organization tracks directly to the chapter organization of this report, and members wrote the drafts of chapters.

ORGANIZATIONAL DESIGN

George P. Huber, Robert L. Kahn, and Harold Van Cott constituted this subcommittee. It convened a roundtable discussion with organizational consultants held at the National Research Council on August 31, 1994. In addition to the subcommittee, participants included Larry Bailey from Coopers & Lybrand, Richard Burton from Duke University, Joyce Doria from Booz, Allen & Hamilton, and Ira Goldstein from Arthur Anderson. It also held a conference call meeting on October 10, 1994, with Robert Keller from Fort Leavenworth on issues of organizational design in the Army.

TECHNIQUES FOR CHANGING ORGANIZATIONS

Kim S. Cameron and George P. Huber constituted this subcommittee. In addition to reviews of evaluation studies on popular techniques, the members participated in the consultants' roundtable at the National Research Council referred to above.

ORGANIZATIONAL CULTURE

Janice M. Beyer, Kim S. Cameron, John M. Wattendorf, and Jerome E. Singer constituted this subcommittee. Mary E. Zellmer of the University of Wisconsin prepared a paper reviewing the practitioner literature on organizational cultures. The subcommittee also participated in a conference call discussion on socialization issues coordinated by E.F. Baskin and conducted with the training staff at Anderson Consulting in St. Charles Illinois.

LEADERSHIP

Gary Yukl, David L. DeVries, Myrna H. Williamson, and John Wattendorf constituted this subcommittee. It was briefed by Lt. General (ret.) Thomas Carney on July 28, 1994, at the National Research Council on issues of leadership in the Army. It was briefed on how Army leaders at the lieutenant and captain ranks are trained at the Center for Army Leadership (hosted by Sue Metlan), Fort Leavenworth, Kansas, on September 29-30, 1994. The subcommittee was also briefed on training issues by Bart Michelson at the Industrial College of the Armed Forces (ICAF) in Washington, D.C., on October 25, 1994. This briefing was followed by an interview by Jerome Singer with Dean John Johns at ICAF. A visit to the Army War College at Carlisle Barracks, Pennsylvania, on October 28, 1994, hosted by Herbert Barber and attended by Daniel Druckman, Jerome E. Singer, and Harold Van Cott, also provided information on leadership training at the colonel rank. Members were also briefed on the research being conducted by the staff at the Center for Creative Leadership in Greensboro, North Carolina, on March 21-23, 1995. The subcommittee was joined by Jerome Singer, Harold Van Cott, and Daniel Druckman at this site visit.

INTERORGANIZATIONAL RELATIONS

W. Warner Burke and Nicole W. Biggart constituted this subcommittee. William E. Siegal of Columbia University assisted in the preparation of the draft chapter on interorganizational relations. Subcommittee members attended the annual meeting of the Association of Researchers in Nonprofit Organizations and Voluntary Action at Berkeley Marina, California, on October 21-22, 1994, and held a conference call discussion about joint service and multilateral operations with Colonel Joseph Tyo of the Army War College at Carlisle Barracks, Pennsylvania. In addition, Jerome Singer and Daniel Druckman were briefed on interorganizational coordination issues by Michael Austin at the Federal Emergency Management Agency (FEMA) on December 22, 1995. This meeting was the basis for a conference call discussion between the subcommittee and Michael Austin's staff at FEMA on March 24, 1995.

CONFLICT MANAGEMENT

Paul F. Diehl, Daniel Druckman, and James A. Wall constituted this subcommittee. It was briefed on international peacekeeping issues on a visit to the International Peace Academy hosted by Lt. Colonel Stephen Moffat and at the United Nations arranged by Juergen Dedring and Chris Coleman on August 29, 1994. Briefings on peacekeeping missions were also arranged for the subcommittee by Lt. Colonel Murray Swan and Major David Last at Fort Leavenworth, Kansas, on October 12, 1994. In addition, the subcommittee held conference call discussions on December 21, 1994, with Jim Thomas of Cooper Management, Inc., of McLean, Virginia, on negotiation training and on January 23, 1995, with Professor Morton Deutsch of Columbia University on approaches to conflict management training.

MILITARY ORGANIZATION CHARACTERISTICS

Jerome E. Singer and Myrna H. Williamson constituted this subcommittee. It received valuable information in interviews with Robert J.T. Joy, Craig H. Llewellyn, and Michael Drillings.

C

Biographical Sketches

JEROME E. SINGER (*chair*) is professor and chair of the Department of Medical and Clinical Psychology at the Uniformed Services University of the Health Sciences. He has taught at the Pennsylvania State University and the State University of New York at Stony Brook. He has been a visiting scholar at the University of New York at Stony Brook and at the Educational Testing Service, a guest researcher at the University of Stockholm, a staff associate at the Social Science Research Council, and study director at the National Research Council. He has been the recipient of the American Association for the Advancement of Science's sociopsychological prize and the outstanding contributor award of the Division of Health Psychology of the American Psychological Association. He was founding editor of the *Journal of Basic and Applied Social Psychology* and co-editor of the two-monograph series, *Advances in Environmental Psychology* and *Handbook of Psychology and Health*. He has a B.A. in social anthropology from the University of Michigan and a Ph.D. in psychology from the University of Minnesota.

JANICE M. BEYER is Rebecca L. Gale centennial professor in business and professor of sociology at the University of Texas in Austin. She was the 1996 recipient of the university's award for outstanding research contributions from the Graduate School of Business and has been named to the Harkins and Company Centennial Chair in Business Administration effective September 1, 1996. She earlier served as professor of organizational behavior at the State University of New York at Buffalo and professor of management at New York University. Her current research interests focus on the cultures of work organizations and organizational change. She has served as editor of the *Academy of Management Journal* and is currently a member of the editorial boards of the *Administrative Science Quarterly* and the *Journal of Quality Management*. She also has been president of the Academy of Management and of the International Federation of Scholarly Associations in Management. She is a fellow of the Academy of Management and holds a Ph.D. in organizational behavior from Cornell University.

NICOLE WOOLSEY BIGGART is professor of management and sociology at the University of California, Davis. Her research has been concerned largely with the social structure bases of economic organization. Her book *Charismatic Capitalism: Direct Selling Organizations in America* examined the ways in which the direct selling industry makes economic use of the social relations of distributors. She has written about the network relations of the Japanese, South Korean, and Taiwanese economies and is the author, with Gary Hamilton and Marco Orru, of *Economic Organization of East Asia*. Her publications have appeared in the *American Journal of Sociology*, *Administrative Science Quarterly*, *Social Problems*, and elsewhere. In 1996 she was Arthur Andersen distinguished visitor at the Judge Institute of Management Studies, Cambridge University, England. She holds a Ph.D. from the University of California, Berkeley.

W. WARNER BURKE is professor of psychology and education and chair of the Department of Organization and Leadership at Teachers College, Columbia University (since 1979). He earlier served as professor and chair of the Department of Management at Clark University, executive director of the Organization Development Network, and an executive for eight years at the NTL Institute for Applied Behavioral Science. He was editor of *Organizational Dynamics* (1978-1985) and of *The Academy of Management Executive* (1986-1989). He is a fellow of the Society for Industrial/Organizational Psychology, the American Psychological Society, and the Academy of Management. He was awarded NASA's public service medal and the American Society for Training and Development's distinguished contribution to human resource development award. He is a diplomat in industrial/ organizational psychology, American Board of Professional Psychology, and has published over 90 articles and 13 books. His research interests include leadership, organization change, and interorganizational relations. He holds a Ph.D. in social psychology from the University of Texas, Austin.

KIM S. CAMERON is professor of organizational behavior and associate dean in the Marriott School of Management at Brigham Young University. Previously, he was professor of organizational behavior and human resource management at the University of Michigan. He is currently conducting research on downsizing and redesign in several manufacturing organizations, and he is investigating organizational quality and performance in higher education and business organizations. He has been a past department chair and director of the University of Michigan's Management of Managers Program and Managing Critical Issues Programs. He actively consults with a variety of business, government, and educational organizations in North America, South America, and Europe. He has been a Fulbright distinguished scholar and a recipient of the outstanding educator award presented by the Organizational Behavior Teaching Society. He has M.A. and Ph.D. degrees from Yale University.

DAVID L. DeVRIES is co-president of Kaplan DeVries Inc., where he is focused on the issues of selection and development with senior-level executives. He served from 1975 to 1990 in various management roles at the Center for Creative Leadership in Greensboro, North Carolina. At the center, he led teams in tackling issues of executive development, creativity in organizations, managerial feedback, and the creation of innovative executive educational tools (e.g., behavioral simulations). Since 1990 he has retained a role at the center as a senior fellow. He taught at Johns Hopkins University from 1970 to 1975, where he conducted research on self-managing teams. He has published widely on selected topics in the psychological and management literatures, and has consulted with such organizations as IBM, Ford, EPA, Westinghouse Electric, Johnson & Johnson, Goodyear, General Electric, Bellcore, and the World Bank. He has also conducted workshops on selected topics—such as performance appraisal for human resource managers from over 400 organizations in the United States and Europe. He has a Ph.D. in social psychology from the University of Illinois.

PAUL F. DIEHL is professor of political science and was the 1993 Alan M. Hallene university scholar at the University of Illinois at Urbana-Champaign. He has held faculty positions at the University of Georgia and SUNY-Albany. His recent books include *The Dynamics of Enduring Rivalries*, *International Peacekeeping*, and *Territorial Changes and International Conflict*. He is the editor of 5 other books and the author of more than 60 articles on international security matters. He is the recipient of numerous grants and awards, including those from the National Science Foundation, the U.S. Institute of Peace, and the Lilly Foundation. His areas of expertise include the causes of war, United Nations peacekeeping, international law, and arms control. He has a Ph.D. in political science from the University of Michigan.

DANIEL DRUCKMAN is study director at the National Research Council and professor of conflict management at George Mason University. Previously he held senior positions at Mathematica, Inc., and Booz, Allen, and Hamilton and was a research scholar at the International Institute of Applied Systems Analysis in Laxenburg, Austria. He has also been a consultant to the U.S. Foreign Service Institute, the U.S. Arms Control and Disarmament Agency, and the U.S. Institute of Peace. His primary research interests are in the areas of conflict resolution and negotiation, nationalism, group process, nonverbal communication, and modeling methodologies, including simulation. He has published more than 100 articles on these topics and received the 1995 Otto Klineberg intercultural and international relations award from the Society for the Psychological Study of Social Issues. He currently serves on the editorial boards of the *Journal of Conflict Resolution, International Negotiation*, the *Negotiation Journal*, and the *Journal of Applied Social Psychology* and is an associate editor of *Simulation & Gaming*. He holds a Ph.D. in social psychology from Northwestern University.

GEORGE P. HUBER is the Charles and Elizabeth Prothro regents chair in business administration and the associate dean for research of the Graduate School of Business at the University of Texas at Austin. His current research focuses on organizational change, organizational design, and organizational decision making. His pioneering article, "The Nature and Design of Post-Industrial Organizations," was awarded first prize in an international prize competition sponsored by The Institute of Management Sciences in 1983. His coauthored article, "Fit, Equifinality, and Organizational Effectiveness," was selected as the best article of the year in the *Academy of Management Journal* for 1993. He is co-editor of *Organizational Change and Redesign: Ideas and Insights for Improving Performance* and *Longitudinal Field Research Methods: Studying Processes of Organizational Change*. He has held positions with the Emerson Electric Manufacturing Company, the Procter and Gamble Manufacturing Company, the U.S. Department of Labor, Execom Systems Corporation, and the Universities of California, Texas, and Wisconsin. He has served as a consultant to many corporations and public agencies and is a fellow of the Academy of Management and of the Decision Sciences Institute. He has a Ph.D. in administrative science from Purdue University.

ROBERT L. KAHN is a social psychologist at the University of Michigan, where he is now professor emeritus of psychology and of public health, as well as research scientist emeritus in the Institute for Social Research. His research has concentrated for many years on large-scale organizations, both their overall effectiveness and their effects on their members. His more recent work links organizational theory to international relations by treating organizations as models for nation states. He has been a fellow at the

Center for Advanced Study in the Behavioral Sciences (Stanford) and at the American Academy of Arts and Sciences and the American Association for the Advancement of Science. He holds a Ph.D. degree from the University of Michigan and an honorary degree from the University of Amsterdam.

JAMES A. WALL Jr. is professor of management in the College of Business and Public Administration at the University of Missouri, Columbia. Before assuming his position at Missouri, he was associate professor at Indiana University and has been a visiting professor at Nanjing University in China. He is president of the International Association of Conflict Management and has served as the chair of the Conflict Management Division of the Academy of Management and as the executive officer of the International Association of Conflict Management. He is the author of *Negotiation: Theory and Practice* (1986) and *Bosses* (1987). His research includes articles on negotiation and mediation in journals such as the *American Journal of Trial Advocacy,* the *Journal of Applied Psychology,* the *Journal of Conflict Resolution,* the *Journal of Dispute Resolution,* the *Journal of Experimental Social Psychology,* and others. Currently, he is studying mediation in the People's Republic of China, South Korea, Japan, and Hong Kong. He holds a Ph.D. in business administration from the University of North Carolina, Chapel Hill.

JOHN M. WATTENDORF is a leadership and management development consultant with IBM Leadership Development, IBM HR USA. He retired from the U.S. Army in summer 1995 as a brigadier general and was awarded the distinguished service medal, the nation's highest award given to a member of the United States Army during peacetime. His military career included specialization in combat engineering, petroleum logistics, and leadership education. His service included combat in Vietnam as well as assignments in three foreign countries and in a variety of leadership, teaching, and staff positions. He served on the faculty of the United States Military Academy, West Point, for 16 years, culminating in his appointment as professor and head of the Department of Behavioral Sciences and Leadership. During his tenure at the Academy he served as director of West Point's first and only graduate program, the Eisenhower Program of Graduate Studies in Leadership Development. He also served as chairman of West Point's Human Resources Council and as a member of the Academic Board. He served as a human resources consultant to the highest levels of the U.S. Army and to other public service agencies, including the Los Angeles Police Department and the Association of Chiefs of Police for the state of New Jersey. He is a member of Phi Kappa Phi national honor society, the Beta Gamma Sigma national business honor society, and the Academy of Management. He holds a Ph.D. in sociology from Stanford University.

MYRNA WILLIAMSON is a professional speaker, business consultant, and director of human relations for A & E Electronics of Alexandria, Virginia. She retired from the U.S. Army in 1989 following a 28-year career, during which she rose from second lieutenant to brigadier general. Her varied assignments included recruiting, staff assignments, training of officers and enlisted soldiers, personnel policy development, and command of soldiers around the world. She conducted Army basic training for Eskimos in Ground Self-Defense Forces in Tokyo and serving four years as U.S. delegate to a committee of the North Atlantic Treaty Organization. General Williamson serves as a member and past president of a college foundation and on several non-profit boards. She is a summa cum laude graduate of South Dakota State University, from which she has been named "distinguished alumna for professional achievement," and is included in *Who's Who in America.* She has an M.A. in human relations from the University of Oklahoma.

GARY YUKL is professor of management at the State University of New York at Albany. His research is primarily in the areas of leadership, power and influence, management development, and motivation. He is the author of a widely used textbook on leadership and has designed management development programs for many corporations and public sector organizations. Honors include two best paper awards at professional conferences, two best article awards, and the president's award for excellence in research from SUNY-Albany in 1992. He is a fellow of the American Psychological Association and the American Psychological Society. He has served on the editorial board of the *Academy of Management Journal,* the *Academy of Management Review,* the *Journal of Applied Psychology* and the *Leadership Quarterly.* He holds a Ph.D. in industrial-organizational psychology from the University of California, Berkeley.

Index

Index